DEVELOPMENT IN CRISIS

This cutting-edge collection expands the domain of the sociology of development to the Global North as well as the Global South, illustrating the explanatory power of Sociology's analytical tools. A must-read for all those interested in development, globalization, gender, and theory.
Dr. Valentine M. Moghadam, *Director, International Affairs Program,*
Professor of Sociology, Northeastern University, USA

Development in Crisis: Threats to human well-being in the Global South and Global North, is a provocative, engaging and interesting collection of real-world case studies in development and globalization focusing on under-emphasized threats to growth and human welfare worldwide. Created by two of America's top development sociologists, it targets undergraduates, graduates, academics and development professionals. Crises such as falling state capacity, declining technological innovation, increasing class inequality and persisting gender inequality are considered, along with their economic and social consequences.

Rae Lesser Blumberg is William R. Kenan, Jr. Professor of Sociology at the University of Virginia.

Samuel Cohn is Professor of Sociology at Texas A&M University.

DEVELOPMENT IN CRISIS

Threats to human well-being in the Global South and Global North

Edited by Rae Lesser Blumberg and Samuel Cohn

LONDON AND NEW YORK

First published 2016
by Routledge
2 Park Square, Milton Park, Abingdon, Oxon OX14 4RN

and by Routledge
711 Third Avenue, New York, NY 10017

Routledge is an imprint of the Taylor & Francis Group, an informa business

© 2016 Rae Lesser Blumberg and Samuel Cohn

The right of the editors to be identified as the authors of the editorial material, and of the authors for their individual chapters, has been asserted in accordance with sections 77 and 78 of the Copyright, Designs and Patents Act 1988.

All rights reserved. No part of this book may be reprinted or reproduced or utilised in any form or by any electronic, mechanical, or other means, now known or hereafter invented, including photocopying and recording, or in any information storage or retrieval system, without permission in writing from the publishers.

Trademark notice: Product or corporate names may be trademarks or registered trademarks, and are used only for identification and explanation without intent to infringe.

British Library Cataloguing in Publication Data
A catalogue record for this book is available from the British Library

Library of Congress Cataloging in Publication Data
Development in crisis : threats to human well-being in the global south and global north / edited by Rae Lesser Blumberg and Samuel Cohn. — 1 Edition.
pages cm
1. Economic development—Developed countries. 2. Economic development—Developing countries. 3. Social policy. 4. Economic policy.
I. Blumberg, Rae Lesser, editor. II. Cohn, Samuel, 1954- editor.
HD82.D389484 2015
338.9009172'4—dc23
2015012316

ISBN: 978-1-138-77835-1 (hbk)
ISBN: 978-1-138-77836-8 (pbk)
ISBN: 978-1-315-77204-2 (ebk)

Typeset in Bembo
by Fish Books Ltd.

To Valerie and David Blumberg with love
To Alexander and Lynn Wallisch for tolerating this book's writing

CONTENTS

List of tables ix
Notes on contributors xi
Acknowledgements xiii

1 Introduction: crisis in development – how development
   lives and dies   1
   Samuel Cohn and Rae Lesser Blumberg

2 The crisis of international development and the case of Haiti:
   the making of an outer-periphery   33
   Robert Fatton Jr.

3 Why cutting taxes does not increase employment: or why
   shrinking the state does not provide compensating
   economic development   51
   Samuel Cohn

4 The state and economic development in East and
   Southeast Asia: the advantage of an ancient civilization   66
   Harold R. Kerbo

5 Does a post-scarcity world mean an end to development?   84
   Herman Mark Schwartz

6   (Pro)Creating a crisis? Gender discrimination, sex ratios
    and their implications for the developing world   100
    Abigail Weitzman

7   Gender, development and the environment: female
    empowerment and the creation of sustainable societies   115
    Stephen J. Scanlan

8   A walk on the wild side of gender, war and development
    in Afghanistan and Northern Uganda   134
    Rae Lesser Blumberg

9   Zimbabwe: a case study in bipolar development   155
    Lorna Lueker Zukas

10 Advancing while losing: indigenous land claims and
    development in Argentina   173
    Matthias vom Hau

11 What we don't talk about when we talk about the global
    in North American higher education   191
    Richard Handler

12 Landmines and sustainability: remaking the world through
    global citizenship, activism, research and collaborative mine
    action   204
    P. Preston Reynolds

    Index   *223*

TABLES

1.1 World GDP per capita in 1990 US dollars 3
1.2 World vs. sub-Saharan African GDP per capita for selected dates 3
1.3 The five great Kondratieff Cycles 10
4.1 Origins and sustainability of the development state in late-late developing nations 69
7.1 Variable descriptions and sources 119
7.2 Components of sustainable societies as indicated by the Environmental Performance Index, 2014 121
7.3 Regression of sustainability index on gender and development indicators controlling for economic development, population pressure, democratization, war and oil economies 123
12.1 Mine-affected states and other areas with mined areas as of October 2014 219

CONTRIBUTORS

Rae Lesser Blumberg is William R. Kenan Jr. Professor of Sociology, University of Virginia. Her theories of gender stratification and gender and development illuminate much of her work; she's authored approximately 90 publications since *Stratification: Socioeconomic and Sexual Inequality* (1978). She's worked in development in 45 countries since the Peace Corps in Venezuela.

Samuel Cohn is Professor of Sociology at Texas A&M University, and the founder and first president of the American Sociological Association Section on Development. His books *Process of Occupational Sex-typing* and *Employment and Development Under Globalization* have won prizes from the ASA.

Robert Fatton Jr. is Julia A. Cooper Professor of Politics at the University of Virginia. His publications include *The Making of a Liberal Democracy*; *Predatory Rule: State and Civil Society in Africa*; *Haiti's Predatory Republic*; *The Roots of Haitian Despotism* and *Haiti: Trapped in the Outer Periphery*.

Richard Handler is a cultural anthropologist who has written on nationalism and the politics of culture, museums and the representation of history, anthropology and literature, and the history of Boasian anthropology. He is currently Professor of Anthropology and Director of the Program in Global Studies at the University of Virginia.

Harold R. Kerbo is Professor Emeritus at California Polytechnic State University and author of *Social Stratification and Inequality* (now in its 8th edition). A recipient of an Abe Fellowship to conduct fieldwork on poverty and poverty programs in Thailand, Vietnam, Laos and Cambodia, his first book from this fieldwork is titled *The Persistence of Cambodian Poverty*.

P. Preston Reynolds is a physician, scholar, educator and leader. She teaches and conducts research on professionalism, medical history, global health and human rights. She served on the Board of Physicians for Human Rights from 1986–2002, which was awarded the 1997 Nobel Peace Prize. A professor of medicine at the University of Virginia, in 2014 she became Master of the American College of Physicians.

Stephen J. Scanlan is an Associate Professor of Sociology at Ohio University. His interests include poverty, development and social change, environmental sociology and food insecurity. He has published in *Contexts*; *International Journal of Comparative Sociology*; *International Journal of Agriculture and Food*; *Journal of Conflict Resolution* and *World Development* among others.

Herman Mark Schwartz is a Professor of Politics at the University of Virginia. He has written books on economic development, globalization, and most recently, geo-economics in *Subprime Nation: American Power, Global Capital and the Housing Bubble*. He has also co-edited four books and written over 50 articles and chapters.

Matthias vom Hau is an Assistant Professor of Comparative Politics at the Institut Barcelona d'Estudis Internacionals (IBEI). A political sociologist by training, he explores the relationship between identity politics, state power and development, with a regional focus on Latin America.

Abigail Weitzman received her PhD in Sociology at New York University. Her research has been funded by the National Science Foundation, the William and Flora Hewlett Foundation and the International Institute for Education. Prior to receiving her doctorate, she served in the Peace Corps in Peru and Belize.

Lorna Lueker Zukas is Professor of Sociology and BA Global Studies faculty advisor at National University, San Diego, California. She teaches courses in Sociology, Global Studies and African Studies. Her publications focus on human rights, political transformations in Southern Africa and gender and information technology in sub-Saharan Africa.

ACKNOWLEDGEMENTS

This book is the result of an extensive and constructive collaboration between the Sociology of Development Section of the American Sociological Association and the University of Virginia. It is the brainchild of Majida Bargach, who was acting as Director of the University of Virginia's Center for International Studies. In the interest of producing a book on crisis in development, Majida offered to host a conference at the University of Virginia that would combine the annual conference of the ASA Sociology of Development Section with presentations by the substantial number of non-sociological development scholars at Virginia. The result would be an interdisciplinary dialogue that would combine the best insights from both traditions. Majida saw to it that the plan would be supported by generous resources from the University of Virginia. Thus it was possible for the talents of both organizations to come together – providing a great deal of insight into the profound challenges that development faces today.

Since the point of the exercise was to produce a coherent book on development crises, substantial intellectual engagement and effort occurred after the conference itself. Scholars and articles were brought in on critical topics that had not been discussed in Virginia. The most dazzling and innovative presentations in the Virginia conference found their way into the emerging volume, with other items added to round out what became an exciting book. The dazzlers came equally from the development sociologists (located nationally and internationally) and the interdisciplinary scholars based at Virginia. The results exceeded even our most optimistic initial projections.

Primary credit for all this goes to Majida Bargach. But building a book this way is an administratively intensive proposition. Here, Majida and the editors of this volume received impressive support from many wonderful people at the University of Virginia and the American Sociological Association. We would like to thank the university's Vice Provost for Global Affairs, Jeffrey Legro, for supporting and attending the conference. Two key administrators whose imagination, as well as organizational skills, made the conference not only well-planned but also highly enjoyable were Mary Jo Bateman and Clifford Maxwell. Two undergraduate students played critical roles as well (how often do undergraduates make a contribution to a book over and above clerical work or simple research tasks?). Amelie Sahar D'Urso recruited a large and enthusiastic corps of student volunteers that made everything work at the conference. Anna Cai handled the communications and designed the striking poster. What made these contributions remarkable and over the top is not the normal course of duties involved in an academic meeting. The week of the conference, Hurricane Sandy hit the entire East Coast of the United States, devastating the New York metropolitan area – and paralyzing transportation systems virtually nationwide. The storm wiped out nearly every previously made administrative arrangement. The Bargach-Bateman-Maxwell-D'Urso-Cai team rescued the conference with a million diving saves and a million desperate improvisations at the last minute. Somehow – torrential rains, cancelled transportation and all – the whole thing came off.

On the American Sociological Association side, Gregory Hooks, then Chair of the Sociology of Development Section, and his Council, organized vast efforts so that superlative development sociologists from around the world would participate in the grand endeavor. The pool of talent that was recruited to come to Virginia was formidable.

All of this would have only produced great talk but not a realized scholarly product without a publishing house willing to make Magida Bargach's vision a reality. Routledge editors Gerhard Boomgaarden and Alyson Claffey provided not only extraordinary support but wise advice on the substantive aspects of the project as well.

We also have to thank the infinite patience of our authors. To keep the volume integrated into a larger scheme of crisis in development, we asked for revision after revision. We have no doubt that some of the authors – after receiving yet another request for further changes – were researching whether homicide is legal in the Commonwealth of Virginia. Yet their final essays are wonderful and we are grateful for all their work.

This was a huge collective effort and we are thankful to everyone who participated in the process.

Rae Lesser Blumberg, *Chair, Sociology of Development Section of the ASA*
Sam Cohn, *Founding Chair, Sociology of Development Section of the ASA*

1
INTRODUCTION

Crisis in development – how development lives and dies

Samuel Cohn and Rae Lesser Blumberg

This is a book about Crisis in Development.
  Consider the following two statements:

1. Development is the process by which the world raises its rate of economic growth and with it the standard of living of the world population. Crisis in development is a non-issue, since development is powerful and robust and difficult to stop.
2. Development is the process by which the world raises the rate of economic growth for a small specialized subset of the world population. It creates a substantial proportion of the human misery on the planet. Crisis in development is perpetual since the development process itself is fragile.

The two statements are both true. The two statements do not contradict each other.

Development is good for human welfare but it leaves victims

Economic development has increased the standard of living of the people of the world. Greater production of goods and services has increased the number of jobs and increased the wages for those jobs. In a famous study of 62 less-developed nations, Firebaugh and Beck (1994) found that GNP was the most important determinant of levels of hunger (measured by average caloric intake) and of health (measured by three different measures of life expectancy). Even if local elites seize a disproportionate share of the financial returns from economic growth, enough trickles down to the masses to make people better fed and to give them longer, more comfortable lives. Another way to promote economic growth and facilitate greater well-being is to economically empower women: Women who not only earn but also *control* income and economic resources contribute directly to national income growth, while also tending to spend their income in ways that increase the health and human capital of both their own children and the population as a whole.

However, all economic processes have their dark sides. New productive industries drive out old traditional craftworkers who have no place to go. Efficient businesses keep prices low through production in sweatshops. Women earn income but often toil in dangerous conditions: in sweatshops in many countries of the Global South, making minuscule wages that often are cut further for allegedly flawed work, or exposed to strong pesticides cultivating and processing non-traditional agricultural exports (NTAEs), from flowers to broccoli (Blumberg and Salazar-Paredes 2011). Super-farms (and mega-dams) are created by driving smallholding peasants off the land – leaving them to migrate to slums to work in menial employment. The expansion of resource extraction into pristine frontier areas can have devastating ecological impacts. The most efficient governments for achieving development are often dictatorships. The human rights abuses that have been perpetrated by dictatorships set on achieving and retaining power no matter what have been appalling. Even in non-dictatorships, development has led to mass rape, war and genocide, notably in patriarchal nations (Wartenberg 2012) The list of the adverse side effects of development could be extended indefinitely.

On balance, though, the effect of development has been positive. It is hard to argue with Firebaugh and Beck's argument that development has dramatically reduced hunger in the world and given an ever-increasing share of the world's population access to modern medical care.

What matters is that it is important to reduce adverse side effects that have been unpleasant accompaniments to development.

If development were to ever produce side effects that were truly catastrophic, this would be a *Crisis in Development*.

Development produces robust economic growth – but it has vulnerabilities

At the global level, how robust is the economic growth produced by development? If one considers the long-term history of the world economy, it is striking how the world economy has just kept growing and growing.

Table 1.1 shows the GDP per capita of the world from 1820 to 2013. The data for the most part come from the Maddison Project: an attempt by Angus Maddison, a prominent economic historian, to measure the GDP for every nation in the world going back to AD 0. The estimates for early periods are very speculative and the reader should view the estimate for 1820 with caution. The data for the remaining years are more or less accurate.

The table shows that GDP per capita increased steadily from 1870 to the present day. There was a mild dip in the 1940s due to the destruction associated with World War II. Maddison's data are incomplete for the period of the Great Depression, but

TABLE 1.1 World GDP per capita in 1990 US dollars

Year	GDP ($)
1820	712
1870	884
1913	1,543
1940	2,181
1950	2,104
1960	2,764
1970	3,725
1980	4,511
1990	5,149
2000	5,850
2010	7,814
2013	8,069

Sources: 1820–2010: Maddison Project (2014). 2013: World Bank (2014a). The authors have adjusted the 2013 data to conform to the Maddison metrics used in the rest of the table.

data for that period would probably show another dip. Essentially, however, the story is one of standards of living increasing by leaps and bounds for most of the last two hundred years. The transition from an average real income of $700 per person to $8100 per person is an overwhelming shift. The last twenty five years has seen particularly dramatic economic improvement – with world personal income growing by over 50 percent. Even though this income is unequally distributed, its impact has been enormous.

The good news for the world as a whole does not mean that every region of the world has received the same benefits or that the process of economic growth is necessarily smooth. Table 1.2 contrasts the evolution of GDP per capita in sub-Saharan Africa with that of the world as a whole. Global rates look great in part because of the positive experiences of India and China, which have been growing dramatically. Africa has not been as fortunate. We include data only for 1980 to 2010. The older data for sub-Saharan Africa are suspect due to the limited data collection capacity of some of those nations; very new data may contain errors that will require revision later (Jerven 2013).

TABLE 1.2 World vs. sub-Saharan African GDP per capita for selected dates

Year	World GDP ($)	Sub-Saharan Africa GDP ($)
1980	4,511	1,369
1990	5,149	1,221
2000	5,850	1,161
2010	7,814	1,601

Sources: World: see Table 1.1. Sub-Saharan Africa: Inequality Watch (2014). The authors have adjusted the African data to conform to the Maddison metrics used for the world data.

The statistics tell a strong story. While the global GDP per capita grew substantially from 1980 to 2000, in Africa, per capita income actually fell. Growth returned in 2000–2010, but the rate of improvement in standards of living in Africa was far less than that experienced elsewhere in the world as a whole. It is not hard to find other nations and regions that have had similar adverse experiences.

In the wake of the debt crisis of the 1980s and early 1990s, the strict austerity and Structural Adjustment Programs (SAPs) imposed on debtor nations by the International Monetary Fund (IMF) and the World Bank resulted in a "lost decade of development" – or more – for most of Latin America and sub-Saharan Africa. Southeast Asian economies took a hard hit from the financial crisis that began in 1997 with a speculators' run on the Thai baht, then in September 2008 Wall Street plunged not only the United States but virtually the entire world into the Great Recession, from which many countries – and individuals – still are struggling to emerge (Standing 2011).

What does this combination of the positive and the negative mean?

It means that despite the robust long-term economic development of the world, the development process itself is challenged, with constant obstacles in every historical era and in every nation. It has overcome these obstacles in the past; there is no guarantee it will overcome these obstacles in the future.

The economic health of the world is like the medical health of human beings. Many of the readers of this book will be in perfect health. Some of you are young and are probably in peak physical condition; if you are currently training you may even become stronger in the future. This does not mean you will live forever or that you will never have health problems. You drive cars and manage to avoid auto accidents. You get infections, which you overcome either naturally or with antibiotics. You enjoy recreational food and drink without having heart attacks or cirrhosis of the liver. At some (hopefully distant) point, you encounter *the* auto accident, or *the* infection or *the* attack on an organ that your body can't cope with, and you slide into illness and death.

Development is no different. It has survived the bank failures of the nineteenth century, low levels of education throughout the world, world wars, the population bomb and any number of international debt crises – and somehow come out on top. Every nation has seen some growth – even in the areas facing the worst exploitation by the wealthy nations or the worst innate ecological or social obstacles. But there is no guarantee that either the challenges of the present day, or the challenges of the future, will produce benignly beneficent outcomes. Just as the prosperity of the Roman Empire was followed by the Dark Ages with 800 years of poverty, the current growth associated with the rise of capitalist development in our modern age may be followed by its own Dark Ages if we encounter an obstacle to development that cannot be overcome.

If development were to ever face such severe obstacles and to produce sustained long-term stagnant or declining economic growth, this would be a *Crisis in Development*.

Potential sources of crisis in development

This book, and this chapter, are about potential sources of crisis in development. The crises may involve savage, unpleasant side effects of development. They may involve threats that could severely limit future rates of development. The list of side effects of development is vast; the list of threats to long-term economic growth is vaster still. Just on the subject of economic growth alone, there are entire textbooks of hundreds and hundreds of pages listing all sorts of different causes and potential limits to economic development (Szirmai 2005). The authors in this book describe a wide range of problems and a wide range of solutions. In this chapter, we do not cover the standard, well-known side effects and limits to development that can be found in traditional development textbooks. It is easy to find discussions of limits to growth such as insufficient investment, predatory actions by multinational capital, indebtedness, corruption, mismanagement of scarce valuable resources, uncontrolled fertility and side effects such as displacement of indigenous populations, despoiling of ecosystems, ethnic conflict and sustained internal and international warfare. This chapter covers what we consider to be the *Four Great Constraints*: four fundamental determinants of long-term growth that tend to receive insufficient attention in the literature – but represent critical and fundamental choke points which could severely constrain economic development in future generations, possibly in both Global South and North.

The Four Great Constraints are:

1. limits to the state's capacity to provide the physical and human infrastructure essential for growth;
2. limits to societal capacity to recover from the exhaustion of technological product cycles;
3. entrepreneurial stagnation caused by excessive class inequality;
4. limits to economic/entrepreneurial activity and social reproduction/well-being caused by excessive female economic *dis*empowerment.

We consider each of these four in turn.

Limits to state capacity to provide physical and human infrastructure

Many people think the best strategy to produce enduring economic growth is to have the smallest amount of government possible. In this view, economic value is produced by private capitalists who invest in the future while big government wastes money on consumption now. In a world where government expenditure is useless, and private companies are the sole engine of economic development, one would want to set the tax rate to nearly zero. This would allow the maximum amount of money to go to capitalist wealth creation, and the minimum amount of money to be wasted by spendthrift bureaucrats with political agendas.

These views vastly underestimate the positive contribution made by government to economic development:

> Government provides the physical and human infrastructure essential to economic development that the private sector cannot and will not provide itself. The private sector cannot and will not invest in projects that are intrinsically unprofitable.

Capitalists and private corporations are excellent at wealth creation – when that wealth creation takes the form of a project that can make a short-term profit. Grow more wheat? Make better steel? Sell home mortgages? These all generate immediate financial returns; these are all projects that capitalists do willingly and well.

What about building interstate highways? Building highways is insanely expensive. You have to acquire vast amounts of real estate. If the highway is to connect cities, this includes extremely expensive downtown real estate. The builder can expect that the price of all of the land that has to be acquired will skyrocket once the owners discover their property is essential to completing the project. You have to hire huge armies of workers and buy vast amounts of concrete and industrial earth-moving machinery.

Highways are massively unprofitable. A recent review of the handful of privately built toll roads that exist in the United States found that all of them were losing sizable amounts of money and many were near bankruptcy (Long 2013). The revenues from tolls don't come anywhere near to remunerating the heavy costs of initial construction. Yet how could America's economy survive without highways?

Airports are equally unprofitable. Once again, you buy massive amounts of real estate and pour massive amounts of concrete. What are your revenue flows? Landing fees, aviation fuel sales and renting slots in the food court. You are not exactly drilling for oil here. As with highways, of the handful of privately constructed airports, all have been major money losers (Gordon et al. 2007). Yet how is it possible to be a player in the global economy without airports?

Running primary schools for the general population is unprofitable. Middle-class and poor families cannot afford private tuition. Could any economy become developed with a population that cannot read or write?

Basic research is expensive and unprofitable. How much money did the University of Copenhagen make from Niels Bohr's discovery of quantum mechanics? Yet how many of our technologically advanced products are dependent on building blocks that came from basic research?

Economic development requires basic physical and human infrastructure: transportation, energy, education, science. Private sector capitalists rarely provide roads, airports, mass transit, mass education or basic research because there is no way to make these activities economically profitable. To be sure, they are delighted if someone else, such as the government, builds the infrastructure and then gives it to them for nothing in a strategy of privatization. However, private corporations rarely build full-fledged highway systems, fully built major airports or mass transit systems, or enough schools to educate the general population.

If the economy is to have these vital prerequisites for growth, those prerequisites must be provided by some institution motivated by something other than short-term profit. The state – with its concern over long-term national prosperity – has been critical to the provision of physical and human infrastructure. Governments build roads, build airports, build schools and pay for science. This is a gigantic contribution to economic development.

What evidence is there that infrastructure produces growth? Let's consider the case of airports; specifically Atlanta and New Orleans. In the nineteenth century, New Orleans was the economic center of the South. It was at the mouth of the Mississippi River, which made it the nexus of the South's biggest business, the export cotton trade. Atlanta in contrast had no particular geographical advantages. It was just a rail junction indistinguishable from Chattanooga, Knoxville or any other rail junction. Nowadays, Atlanta is the dominant city in the American Southeast, while New Orleans is economically struggling.

What allowed Atlanta to surpass New Orleans? The city built Hartsfield-Jackson International Airport. The city of Atlanta invested early in airport development. The attractiveness of the facility made two airlines, Eastern and Delta, choose the airport as their hub. The airport got a lucky break just before World War II when the US Air Force decided to expand Atlanta Airport for military reasons. Atlanta became the busiest airport in the United States although Atlanta was hardly the richest or the largest city in the country. Postwar, the City of Atlanta worked to maintain Atlanta's airport advantage over the rest of the country by dramatically expanding the airport in the 1970s in what was the biggest construction project in Southern history up to that time. Atlanta invented and introduced the system of "multi-building" terminals connected by underground train-lines. This made Hartsfield Airport a national leader in airport size and efficiency (Atlanta Department of Aviation 2010). Atlanta parlayed this major advantage in infrastructure into becoming a major center for corporate headquarters.

In contrast, New Orleans was significantly slower in developing airport capacity. Some of this was due to geographical disadvantages. The lake and marshes around New Orleans limit the supply of land that would make for a good airport; the low elevation has given the New Orleans airport a history of flooding. In the 1940s, while Atlanta was celebrated for its relatively large airport, the original New Orleans airport was viewed as being too small. It later had to be relocated. Even today, New Orleans-Louis Armstrong has only two runways to Atlanta's five, and one of those two runways is smaller than any runway at Chicago-O'Hare or Dallas-Fort Worth (Airport Owners and Pilots Association 2014).

New Orleans' marginal airport status has severely constricted its economic growth. One indicator of this is the number of Fortune 1000 companies that choose to base their operations in the city. In 2014, fully 27 Fortune 1000 companies were headquartered in Atlanta. What was the number of Fortune 1000 companies headquartered in New Orleans? Exactly one (Geolounge 2014)!

What happened to Atlanta and New Orleans is typical of what happened to American cities as a whole. John Kasarda has found that economic growth in American cities is highly correlated with the number of flights in and out of that city's airport (Irwin and Kasarda 1991). That would sound logical since places with a lot of activity generate a lot of air traffic. However, in reality, the American hub and spoke system means that some cities get far more air traffic that would be expected from their general size since they are intermediate stopovers where air connections are made. The takeaway from Kasarda is cities that built large airports suitable for being air-hubs grew more than would have been expected from the size of their local population alone.

There is comparable statistical evidence for the effects of growth of other forms of infrastructure provision. Cohn (2012) reviews the studies showing the relationship between infrastructure and growth both for wealthy nations such as the United States and nations in the Global South such as South Africa and India. Growth is linked to the government provision not only of airports but of railways, paved roads, electricity, sewage, water supply systems, public buildings (generally an index of school construction), postal service and government banking.

What about the effect of public education on development? Mass literacy is a prerequisite for development. A review of European industrialization in the nineteenth century found that reaching a male literacy rate of 40 percent was a necessary precondition for achieving sustained economic growth (Bowman and Anderson 1963). Durlauf et al. (2005), in an article claiming that few variables correlate systematically with economic growth, made an exception for levels of overall education; education in every study they examined had a strong positive effect on rates of growth. Girls' education tends to have even higher rates of return than boys' (King and Hill 1993; Schultz 1998; King and Mason 2001).

What about the effect of higher education on growth? The effect of this has been mixed. In some nations in the Global South, the university systems aren't very good (Altbach 2013). As a result, the statistical relationship between higher education and growth has often been weak (Durlauf et al. 2005). In the developed Global North, however, in settings where government support of higher education has been strong, and the universities themselves have been distinguished, the effect of higher education support on growth has been dramatic.

Jonathan Cole (2009) has done an analysis of the economic impact of the eight major research universities in the Metropolitan Boston area: Boston has been blessed with a large number of universities, many of which are internationally renowned. A student who wants to study in the Boston area would have a choice of Harvard, MIT, Boston College, Boston University, Tufts, Northeastern, Brandeis and the University of Massachusetts in Boston. These universities put $7.4 billion into the local economy every year. They produce 32,000 trained graduates every year; most go directly into the local economy. They generate 264 patents every year.

They stimulate the granting of 280 high-tech commercial licenses every year. Out of every 50 start-up firms in the Boston area, 25 are associated in some way with the eight major research universities (ibid.).

Significantly, these universities are supported by $1.5 billion in federal funds every year. These funds come in the form of direct grants for scientific research, federal subsidies for university expenses (generally linked to research grants and referred to as "indirect costs") and federal grants and loans for student financial aid. Let's do the math: The Federal government spends $1.5 billion per year on university support. The universities produce $7.4 billion a year of economic growth. A return of $7.4 billion of growth for an investment of $1.5 billion is an extremely dramatic rate of return. This means the American taxpayer gets a return of almost 400 percent on what is spent for the support of higher education in Boston. It is hard to think of any other private sector investment that produces a 400 percent rate of profit.

The state's funding support for physical infrastructure and education has a substantial positive effect on economic growth and development. If these ever were to shrink, the effects on growth would be noticeable and adverse. Unfortunately, the current political environment is characterized by widespread attempts to reduce the role of the state and minimize state expenditure in the interest of reducing tax burdens. These movements have significant popular and electoral support. Both the Tea Party in the United States and the new right-wing political parties in Europe have mobilized broad swathes of voters who are alienated from "politics-as-usual," welfare payments to ethnic groups other than their own and, especially, government regulations that apply to themselves. The grassroots shrink-the-state movement has significant support from corporations and the wealthy: both groups stand to have their own tax burdens reduced significantly if anti-governmentalism prevails. It is hard to see the direct economic benefit of "getting the state out of people's lives." The costs of eliminating public provision of education and infrastructure alone could be catastrophic.

Limits to societal capacity to recover from the exhaustion of technological product cycles

Economic development is extremely dependent on having new products to sell. Yes, some growth can be achieved by selling basic goods to more and more people. Population growth produces more customers for the world and these customers need food, clothing and shelter. However, the major dramatic expansions in the world economy have been associated with the introduction of a new must-have product – whose arrival created a global shopping spree. These great world-wide expansions are called "Kondratieff Cycles" after the Soviet economist who first discovered them (Kondratieff 1935).

The Industrial Revolution – which was the origin of the prosperity we now enjoy in the modern world – was really a case of new product development. Previously, clothing had been handmade. Handmade clothing is labor intensive and

TABLE 1.3 The five great Kondratieff Cycles

Cycle number	Boom	Bust	Product base
I	1790–1820	1820–1840	Machine textiles
II	1840–1870	1870–1890	Railroads
III	1890–1920	1920–1940	Structural steel
IV	1940–1970	1970–1990	Automobiles
V	1990–?	?	Computer/Internet

Source: Lines I–IV adapted from Berry et al. (1993).

expensive to make. As a result, most people owned very few clothes, possibly one everyday outfit and one outfit for special occasions. Machine spinning and weaving reduced the price of clothing dramatically; now even poor people could afford whole wardrobes. The world went on a clothes-buying binge, leading to one of the greatest economic expansions in history.

The clothing boom particularly benefited Great Britain, which had invented most of the new machinery. However, obstacles soon presented themselves. Other nations learned how to make factory clothing – and they even had better machines and cheaper labor than Britain. Britain was no longer the monopoly producer, and the market was becoming saturated. The British and world economy, however, were rescued by railways.

The building of the railways was a tremendous source of world growth in the 1840s and 1850s (although some important lines had been built before then). However, the mid-nineteenth century saw an explosion of railway construction as nearly every major city was connected with everywhere else in the world. The railway boom required not only the buying of a lot of land and laying a lot of rails. It required constructing vast numbers of railway engines and passenger cars, building railway stations in every city and digging enough coal mines to keep all those steam engines running. Coal became a giant secondary source of growth and the world economy hummed.

Ultimately, this boom too ran its course. All the lines that made sense had been built, and now private companies were duplicating tracks or building lines out into unpopulated and unprofitable hinterlands. After the railway boom, the world saw a significant financial slowdown. Then the world economy was rescued again – this time by structural steel.

The invention of modern steel led to a reconstruction of every large structure in the Global North. Wood buildings became steel-framed buildings and the modern skyscraper was born. Wood boats and bridges became iron boats and bridges. Cheap, high quality steel facilitated the use of heavy machinery and of large amounts of wire, paving the way for the electrical revolution.

Unfortunately, much of the transformation of world structures from wood to steel had been accomplished by 1920. The 1920s saw depression throughout Europe, followed by the Great Depression of the 1930s. Then the world economy was rescued again – by the much-improved automobile.

Cars in the 1910s had to be started by cranks and had a maximum speed of 30 mph. The four successive breakthrough improvements of keyed ignitions, more powerful engines, power steering and power brakes caused the world to completely replace an older fleet of cars with newer better more efficient cars – producing massive sales and massive prosperity.

Companies kept fleets of trucks; meanwhile, automobile ownership spread across the class structure.[1] After World War II, real US family income doubled between 1947 and 1974 (Meyerson 2013: 1). Even many working-class people were able to buy cars. The now more affluent middle class began buying first one automobile and later two automobiles. There was also a sharp rise in female labor force participation: by 1970, 50 percent of American women in prime labor force years, (18–64), were working (Oppenheimer 1973). This was a factor that boosted not only family income but also the need for a now more affordable second car.

Furthermore, the automobile generated a huge number of by-product industries. Highways had to be built to accommodate the new vehicles. The cars needed gasoline – dramatically expanding the petroleum industry. In the US in particular, cars made commuting to work feasible, making it possible for people to live in suburbs and drive to the city. This led to a restructuring of North American cities with the creation of vast new suburbs and the shopping facilities to go with them. Restaurants became economically viable as an industry; people might not walk fifteen miles to have a fried clam dinner, but in the US and Canada they would drive fifteen miles to have a fried clam dinner. The insurance industry thrived since all of the vehicles needed to be insured.

Ultimately, however, shoppers in the developed world had all the cars they needed. Worse, the great new innovations stopped coming, so there was no need for people to jettison older generation cars for better models (the one exception to the no-innovation dead-end may have been the SUV). Furthermore, during the good years of the 1950s and 1960s the Americans and Europeans had a relative monopoly on automotive technology. Every subsequent decade has seen new producers enter the market: first Japan, then Korea, then Mexico, Brazil and China. The world is flooded with automotive capacity and the nations that are favored are those able to exploit cheap labor. The 1970s and 1980s were years of economic stagnation and slow growth in the Global North – although growth was better in the poorer nations that could capitalize on the demand for cheap labor. Fortunately the world economy was saved again – this time by the personal computer and the internet.

The average reader of this book knows the history of the computer/internet era – so there is no need to review that here.

There is a common pattern in all of these stories – a pattern that has been noted by world systems theorists (e.g. Chase-Dunn 1998):

1. a breakthrough innovation produces a global increase in economic growth as everyone buys the new product;
2. the production of these goods is typically concentrated in the wealthy nations;

3. market saturation leads to a global slowdown in growth;
4. production migrates from the wealthy core to less developed nations that can combine cheap labor with some ability to copy the technology once dominated by the core;
5. a new product comes out of nowhere – and becomes the next great engine for global growth.

Item 5 – a new product coming to generate the next wave of global growth – is the linchpin for determining the future prosperity of the world economy. There is no magic guarantee that any new product will develop. New products depend on inventions that haven't happened yet. If no one thinks of anything new, standards of living in the world stagnate.

Thus, development depends on a critical mass of innovative capacity that maximizes the chance of coming up with the next new breakthrough product.

High educational capacity and scientific research capacity are critical to creating the seedbed where such strategic innovations can occur. Mechanical spinning and weaving came out of Great Britain, which was a world leader in levels of education at the time. High levels of British literacy and education also allowed them to invent the railway. The next two innovations – high quality steel and the automobile – were joint inventions of the United States and Germany. At the beginning of the twentieth century, these nations were world leaders in university education and scientific research. This gave them a global advantage in engineering and manufacturing technology – and increased the odds that both countries would become the dominant economic powers of the twentieth century (Landes 1999). The computer and internet revolution was based on the extraordinary quality of the electrical engineering and mathematics of two university complexes in the United States. Stanford engendered Silicon Valley. The Boston Big 8 Universities (and particularly MIT) engendered the Route 128 High Technology complex.

Both Stanford and the Boston research complex depended on substantial economic and financial support from society as a whole, in the form of both federal funding for scientific research and alumni contributions to their former universities. The United States has led every other nation both in the amount of government support for scientific research, as well as in the size of its alumni donations to universities as a whole. This allowed the United States to be the primary source of the computer/internet revolution (Cole 2009).

Global growth depends on the willingness of societies to defend their technological base by financing the educational and research capacities to make the next new wave of products. If one nation chooses not to do so and some other nation steps up to provide that support, then that other nation becomes the dominant power in the next Kondratieff Cycle. If no nation steps up to provide that innovation, then the sixth or seventh Kondratieff Cycle may never come into existence.

Entrepreneurial stagnation caused by excessive class inequality

Discussions of economic inequality tend to be highly politicized. Liberals want less inequality because morally they don't like poverty. Conservatives want fewer programs to transfer wealth from rich to poor because morally they don't like to reduce the incentives for hard work and saving. These moral questions make for good debates. But they are not the critical issue in considering the relationship between inequality and development. What matters is the effect of income distributions on entrepreneurial activity.

In general, economies grow when there is a strong foundation of vibrant small businesses. The small businesses produce products that increase the GDP. They buy supplies from other companies, increasing those companies' sales. They hire workers and pay wages. The managers spend their profits and the workers spend their wages on consumer goods and services. Consumption accounts for up to 70 percent of the US economy, boosting it through increased sales. Furthermore, a small number of micro-businesses are going to turn out to be amazingly successful. Most will do this through some sort of engineering or commercial innovation. They will develop the next awesome technology. They will make the product everybody has to have. The small businesses that turn into mega-businesses are the "winning lottery tickets" of economic development. They create whole new industries, whole new niches – and produce vast amounts of profits that produce vast amounts of wealth. Henry Ford founds Ford Motors; Sam Walton founds Walmart – and the world changes.

More recently, women have been creating significant numbers of labor-intensive small businesses. There are some 8.6 million female-owned firms in the United States, generating $1.3 trillion in revenues and employing nearly 7.8 million people; between 1997 and 2013, the number of women-owned businesses rose by 59 percent, 1.5 times the rate of US businesses overall (Isele 2013). They comprise about 29 percent of all non-farm businesses (National Women's Business Council 2015) and employ 35 percent more people than all the Fortune 500 companies combined (Society of Professional Women 2015).

Extreme inequality, however, interferes with the capacity of small businesses to produce economic growth. So it should be of considerable concern to us that inequality has been growing around the world in recent years. In the United States, it is now higher than at any point since 1929, the year the "Black Friday" October 29 crash of the stock market ushered in the Great Depression. In fact, since the September 2008 financial crisis hit Wall Street and triggered the Great Recession, the worst global downturn since the Great Depression, income concentration has increased: about 95 percent of income gains in 2009–2012 went to the wealthiest 1 percent (Cronin 2013).

Extreme poverty shrinks the supply of local entrepreneurs by keeping some qualified people from getting the capital they need to start businesses. Potential entrepreneurs can come from any social class. All one needs is an idea, a passion, the willingness to learn a skill – *and money*. Getting start-up capital can be an enormous obstacle for poor people. Societies with a large middle class have a lot of people with moderate amounts of savings. They have the resources to act on their dreams. For the very poor in a Pakistani, Ethiopian or Laotian slum, buying a used industrial-quality sewing machine to start a small tailoring or garment microenterprise might be a total impossibility.

Note that the argument here is not our own original creation. It is the intellectual foundation of the microfinance movement. Nowadays development agencies put substantial money into microcredit organizations designed to provide the very poor with small, short-term working capital loans to launch or expand their own microenterprises – and, hopefully, to create a pathway out of poverty. By 2011, there were roughly 200,000,000 clients of Microfinance Institutions (MFIs), the great majority of them female (Maes and Reed 2012: 9). Some of these programs have been great successes (Daley-Harris 2009; Blumberg 2001).

Societies with large middle classes have lots of entrepreneurs who do not need microcredit. They have families with resources, personal assets and access to banks. Societies with small middle classes and large poverty population have large numbers of people with none of those three. More equal income distributions mean more start-ups.

Inequality reduces the size of the market. Economic development needs strong local markets in order to succeed. If businesspeople can't sell anything, then businesses will not survive and the economy will stagnate. To be sure, export markets exist. South Korea in the 1970s was an exception to the strong local markets rule (Koo 2001). It grew quickly under an intentional strategy of selling *everything* it made overseas and not developing its own purchasing capacity at all. But nearly every other case of successful development in the world has counted on local customers to support local business – including the other East Asian economies and, for that matter, South Korea itself today.

Customer support for local business decreases under conditions of extreme inequality. This happens for two reasons. If the poor are really, really poor, they lack the money to consume almost anything at all. People who find food and clothing by scavenging through garbage dumps can't buy a brand new pair of shoes from the locally-owned/locally-sourced shoe store; the super-rich, on the other hand, can afford imported luxuries. They also are likely to spend a disproportionate percentage of their income overseas. They buy overseas real estate. They go on foreign vacations. They purchase Italian sports cars and French designer dresses. They send their children to study at MIT or Harvard rather than at the local university. Even though very rich locals patronize local vendors of services somewhat – they hire lots of security guards and maids and they buy fresh produce from local farms – they still spend a lot of their money overseas where it does little to help the local economy. The middle class, however, makes an ideal consumer base. It has money to spend but lacks the ability to purchase foreign luxuries. Middle-income households buy from local merchants and manufacturers – and thus contribute to building the local economy.

Inequality allows elites to use political influence to shelter their own inefficient firms from competition. Capitalist free markets produce growth by allowing efficient firms to grow at the expense of their less competent competition. Firms facing a challenge from more advanced, more capable rivals either have to raise their standards of production up to the level of the trendsetter – or they will go out of business. This is what motivates firms to upgrade their products and their services.

In highly unequal societies, however, politically connected elites can protect their own firms from market competition. They go to the government and ask for legal monopolies to artificially handicap the opposition, ask for tariffs to keep foreign products out of their country, or ask for government handouts to compensate for their lost sales and profits. Crony capitalism can lead to a nation's wealthy making fantastic fortunes for themselves without actually having to run their firms well or make their companies efficient. Promising companies run by middle-class entrepreneurs without special connections end up being driven out of business because the playing field is most decidedly not level.

What evidence is there that inequality hurts growth?

1. Slave societies and former slave societies have slow rates of economic growth.

Slavery represents the ultimate in social inequality. A large percentage of the population receives no wages and no income. Wealth is concentrated among a small set of slaveholders. Societies with wage labor are much more egalitarian.

In the United States, the Southern states had slavery, while the Northern and Western states were free. In both the slave period itself, and for 100 years after the abolition of slavery, the Southern states were much poorer than states in the North and West.

Western Europe had free labor. Eastern Europe had slave labor. The slaves were called serfs; they were tied to the land and were forced to work for local nobles. From the heyday of slavery in the 1700s to the present day, Eastern Europe has been poorer than Western Europe.

Brazil maintained a slave economy in its northeastern provinces, where they were used to harvest and process sugarcane. While slavery was legal in the southern provinces, it was much less prevalent. The northeast of Brazil continues to be a poverty zone, while the south of Brazil approximates European standards of living.

2. Reducing the purchasing power of the wealthy in Latin America led to a substantial increase in Latin American manufacturing.

Jeffrey Williamson (2006) notes that the Great Depression of the 1930s was a period when manufacturing growth was higher in Latin America than it had been during the good years of the world economy. More surprisingly, whenever the cash value of local export crops decreased – which should have hurt the economy – local manufacturing grew rather than contracted. How does one explain this?

When local agricultural elites had lots of ready cash, they used it to buy imported European luxuries. When their currency crashed or economic times were hard, the local elites simply did not have the money to go shopping for consumption goods overseas. They were forced to buy local. Local business – which had been starved for markets in the "good years" – now had wealthy local customers. Perversely, these "crises" caused Latin economies to thrive.

3. Historically, egalitarian American and Scandinavian economies substantially outperformed the formerly wealthy but elitist Spanish economy

Between 1600 and 1950, the United States and Scandinavia rose from being essentially outback frontier economies to being some of the wealthiest nations in the world. Spain, the globe's dominant military power in the 1500s, declined economically to the point of being practically an underdeveloped nation. What did the United States and Scandinavia do right that Spain did wrong? Dieter Senghaas (1985) argues that the relatively egalitarian structure of the United States and Scandinavia was the secret of their success.

Growth in the nineteenth century came from technological excellence in agriculture. The United States became a super-producer in wheat, dairy and meat. It grew more than any other country; its products were better. The United States flooded world grain markets with vast amounts of excellent and inexpensive wheat in the nineteenth century, driving farmers in many other countries out of business. Denmark adjusted by moving into butter production. Norway adjusted by moving into canned fish. Senghaas argues that American wheat, dairy and meat, as well as Danish butter and Norwegian fish, all shared one common property. Their success was due to the efforts of middle-class farmers who invested their own money in technological improvements that raised their product to world-class levels.

Conversely, Spain declined because it lacked a middle class. Its farmers were too small and debt-ridden to invest in new agricultural technology. Spain lagged behind most of Europe in adopting any kind of agricultural change. There were very large and powerful landlords, associated with the nobility or with the Church, who had enough money to invest in anything they liked. They also, however, had massive political influence – something the American and Scandinavian small farmers lacked. They responded to international competition by having the government raise tariffs – so that the Spanish landlords themselves would not have to spend money on new technology (Tortella 2000). American farmers of the Great Plains could not give orders to Washington the way the Spanish magnates gave orders to Madrid. Americans *had* to adjust in order to survive the rollercoaster of world markets. The Spanish did not. Spain fell behind technologically, leading to literally centuries of economic stagnation.

Limits to economic/entrepreneurial activity and social reproduction/well-being caused by excessive female economic disempowerment

In preview, the argument will be women's economic empowerment as a "magic potion" for development: their *dis*empowerment as a "poison potion" for development

Women's economic empowerment is virtually a "magic potion" for development. Specifically, it results in both more economic growth and greater well-being at levels ranging from micro to macro (Blumberg 2009b, forthcoming). Conversely, women's economic *dis*empowerment is akin to a "poison potion" that depresses growth and is linked to various negative outcomes (including for the environment: see Scanlan this volume; Blumberg 2008). The most poisonous potion is war, with which female economic disempowerment is strongly linked (Caprioli 2000, 2005; Blumberg this volume).

So let's start with a rather extreme and unusual comparison involving two poor countries that have known conflict in recent decades: Laos and Afghanistan. Laos represents a case of development improving after a long period of poverty and conflict. Women have been essential to this development. The case of Afghanistan has been just the opposite.

The following quotation is by a male village leader in one of the roadside villages beside a newly built road in Laos, as he discussed women entrepreneurs who have been able to use to their advantage the opportunities created by the new highway:

> Women travel more than men. They are selling and buying. They keep the money. They are responsible for the economy. They give money to their husbands when husbands ask for it.
>
> *cited in Ireson 1996: 201*

Women's economic activities have remained the backbone of the economy. This has been true through all the years of conflict, first when Laos was the target of the US "secret war" as part of the Vietnam War, then during the years of internal war that led to it becoming a People's Democratic Republic in late 1975, and subsequently during all the ups and downs of changing policies by the PDR regime. Now the country is ramping up export production of textiles and clothing and again it will be women who will be the mainstay of the emerging economy. In short, economically empowered women kept things going in the face of vacillating government policies and, prior to that, conflict – and now their economic empowerment provides both an avenue to further development and a cushion in case things don't work out (they still dominate most trade).

Let's now compare that glimpse of Laos with the situation in Afghanistan, a country where women are economically disempowered and that is and long has been at war. There, women have virtually *zero* economic power. As one consequence, they have greatly restricted mobility. This is further intensified by the fact that the country has been at war for 37 years (starting in 1978) and in many places, it's too dangerous to go out. Women with no income or mobility, and who lack the "voice and vote" in household decisions that female economic power repeatedly has been found to promote, have no way to control their fertility. The country's Total Fertility Rate (TFR) is among the world's "top 10" (Afghanistan, with a TFR of 5.43, is the only nation on the top 10 list – it has the 9th highest fertility in the world – that is not from sub-Saharan Africa [CIA 2015]). Afghanistan's high fertility, in turn, exacerbates the problems of too many young men with little or no economic prospects that don't involve use of arms, corruption or cultivation of opium poppies.

All in all, Afghanistan is doing worse than Laos with respect to development, and not only because of 37 years of ongoing war. It is the almost complete economic disempowerment of women and the often related manifestations of subordination – the high fertility, low mobility, the still-wide gender gap in education, the poorly nourished children born to poorly nourished (often too-young) mothers – that feed both its underdevelopment and its patriarchal bellicosity.

Before further explicating how women's economic empowerment/disempowerment is linked to a magic potion/poison potion for development argument, three hypotheses. First, as argued in Blumberg's general theory of gender stratification, the most *important* (although not the sole) variable affecting the relative equality of men and women is economic power, defined as control of income and other economic resources such as land, access to credit, etc. (Blumberg 1984, 1991, 2004, 2009a, 2015). (It is also argued that economic power is the most *achievable* by women of the major forms of power – political, force/violence, economic, ideological, information [Blumberg 1984, 2009b, 2015, forthcoming].)

The main dependent variable of that general theory of gender stratification theory involves "life options" that exist in every known society (e.g. marriage, fertility, divorce, freedom of movement, etc.). So the second proposition is that with more economic power, women are able to exert more control over/have more say in their destiny. Fertility is seen as especially important in affecting their lives.

Third, a principal proposition of the theory of gender and development (Blumberg 1988, 1989a, 1989b, 1995, 2009a, forthcoming) is that women and men with provider responsibilities generally spend income under their control differently, with women spending disproportionately on children's human capital: education, nutrition and health.[2] On to the potions:

Women's economic empowerment as a magic potion for development

Control of income or other economic resources by women has been found to create greater wealth and well-being for their country. The greater wealth generated by women's income-generating activities has been measured and is supported by research.

Claudia Goldin, an economist who has researched the impact of women's rising labor force participation (LFP) on US national income, has found that the LFP "rate of prime-aged females (15–64 years old) rose from 19.6% in 1890 to 59.9% in 1980 and the female component of the labor force increased from 17% to 43%" (1986: 557). She concluded that "[t]he expansion of the female labor force ... and the rise in the female/male earnings ratio were associated with a growth of national income per capita that exceeded the growth in male earnings by 28%" (ibid.).

Within India, the "states that have the highest percentage of women in the labor force have grown the fastest as well as had the greatest reductions in poverty, according to the World Bank" (Faiola 2008: A12).

Analyzing global GDP growth between roughly 1985 and 2005, an analysis by *The Economist* came up three factors that were the strongest in raising world GDP, concluding:

> The increase in female employment in the rich world has been the main driving force of growth for the last couple of decades. Those women have contributed more to global GDP growth than has either new technology or the new giants, China and India.
>
> The Economist *2006: 16*

In fact, the article's headline was: "Forget China, India and the Internet: Economic growth is driven by women."

So it is quite important that the world recently passed a historic tipping point: Now, fully 53 percent of the globe's women are in the measured labor force, based on the average of each nation's female LFP (World Bank 2014b; Blumberg's calculations), and most work in the measured labor force is remunerated monetarily. (There are data also showing that nations where women's LFP is low *lose* considerable income. These will be presented under the "poison potion" heading [see p. 21].)

In sum, these findings demonstrate the importance of women's *economic* power at the macro level. Later in the chapter, the strength of female economic power and female education will be compared, with economic power proving stronger. Before that, however, other ways that women's economic empowerment contributes to the wealth and well-being of their homelands merit consideration. Here, we'll examine two: fertility and women's vs. men's spending patterns and how they affect human capital.[3] Each proves to be very important for both national income growth and national welfare.

Fertility

Fertility can be considered the most crucial "life option" for women. Without control of their childbearing, women can be turned into veritable baby-making machines, thereby greatly reducing their possibilities for economic advancement and robust health – and even their ability to leave the house and participate in public sphere activities. Since research by Weller 1968 in Puerto Rico, many studies have found a link between women earning income and their using modern contraception (e.g. United Nations 1987, 2010; Engelman 2008). Often, this is the first thing they do for *themselves*, rather than for their children (see p. 139). Most women who have control over their fertility opt for fewer children and with wider spacing between births. Clearly, the rising proportion of the world's women who earn/control income has played a crucial role in the decline in fertility that began in the 1970s; fertility fell in 131 of 132 nations with data from the early 1970s and early 2000s (United Nations 2010).

More importantly, fertility is negatively related to national income growth (Hess 1988; Das Gupta et al. 2011; Nolan and Lenski 2011).[4] When the impact of more individual women taking control of their own fertility and choosing to have fewer children is aggregated, we come to an important predictor of a country's national income growth: its Total Fertility Rate (TFR). Similar processes are at work with respect to women's support of their own children's education, diet and health: at the macro level, they contribute to both national income growth and national well-being.

Human capital

Human capital, as generally used in the world of international NGOs and agencies promoting social development, refers to education, nutrition and health. The third hypothesis – that women who control income tend to spend disproportionately more of it on their children's human capital than male counterparts – is now practically a truism, with a large number of empirical studies in support (see Blumberg 2015, forthcoming for discussion and extensive bibliographies of this research). This is a true "win-win": the children benefit and, in aggregate, so do both their societies' national income growth (which rises with rising human capital) and national well-being indicators (including those for education, nutrition and health). In addition, it is worth citing a couple of the earlier studies showing that poor women with provider responsibilities who earn their own income also held back less for themselves than counterpart men: Mencher (1988) found this in 20 villages in Tamil Nadu and Kerala, India, as did Roldan (1988) in Mexico City.

Education has been extensively studied as a factor in development. As noted earlier, girls' education is seen as especially important for development, often showing higher rates of return than boys' education. Here, let's look at some of the consequences of educating girls and then at a study comparing the relative importance of female education and labor force participation for national development.

The benefits of female education are enormously positive and affect the whole society (King and Mason 2001). These benefits include (see Blumberg 1989a, which also provides supporting evidence):

- higher age of marriage;
- greater use of contraception;

- lower fertility (e.g. as measured by TFR);
- lower infant/child mortality;
- higher female paid modern sector employment;
- greater female earnings (empirically, for example, Pscharopoulos [2002] found that providing an extra year of schooling for girls beyond the national average boosts eventual wages by 10–20 percent; also, greater female income usually results in increased education of sons and daughters, i.e. a "virtuous circle");
- increased national development (e.g. Dollar and Gatti [1999] found that increasing the share of women with secondary education by 1 percent boosts per capita income growth by 0.3 percent on average).

In point of fact, almost all the benefits of educating girls are associated with lower fertility.

Now, turning to the relative strength of female economic empowerment vs. education, overall, women's economic position remains the more consequential in affecting the wealth of nations. Comparing losses due to inequality in female employment vs. in education, a UN Economic and Social Survey of Asia and the Pacific estimated that the region lost $42–$47 billion annually because of women's limited access to employment, vs. only $16–$30 billion lost annually because of inequality in education (United Nations 2007: 103).

This is only a partial presentation of the magic potion side of the links between female economic position and national development (others include Blumberg 2009b, 2015 and forthcoming). Now, a consideration of the poison potion side is in order.

Women's economic disempowerment as a poison potion for development

Essentially, all we have to do is flip the positive outcomes of women's economic empowerment. Let's begin with the macro impact of low female labor force participation.

The region with the lowest female LFP is the Middle East-North Africa (MENA). Recently, the President of the World Bank, Jim Yong Kim, wrote that "women's low economic participation created income losses of 27 percent in the Middle East and North Africa" (Kim 2014). His column also mentioned that raising female employment and entrepreneurship to male levels could improve average income by 23 percent in South Asia and 15 percent elsewhere (his figures came from Cuberes and Teignier 2012).

There is more at stake than a rise of GDP. Let us consider the extremely strong *inverse* correlation between women's LFP and armed conflict. Caprioli makes the case that low female labor force participation – taken here as a partial proxy for women's economic power – is linked to much higher levels of international armed conflict (2000) as well as internal armed conflict (2005). In a study of most of the world's nations, she found that every 5 percent drop in women's LFP was linked to an almost 500 percent increase in both internal and international armed conflict. Let's look at the nations/places with the world's lowest female LFP to see if they have recent or ongoing armed conflict. The lowest have female LFP rates of 13–18 percent. Alphabetically, they are: Afghanistan, Algeria, Iran, Iraq, Jordan, Saudi Arabia, Syria and West Bank/Gaza (all but Afghanistan are in MENA). Based on Caprioli's findings about both internal and international armed conflict and using an average of 15 percent women's LFP for the group, they have an almost 3,500 percent greater likelihood of armed conflict than a country near the world average for female LFP, with, say, 50 percent of women in its labor force. This is a seven-fold difference. In reality, 100 percent of them have been involved in armed conflict in recent years or are involved now (at the time of writing in March 2015).

It also turns out that there is a reason all of the above nations have such low female labor force participation. But first, we must add another proposition from Blumberg's general theory of gender stratification (1984, 2015). There is a prerequisite to women acquiring economic power; without it, they remain economically disempowered: They must be importantly involved in the group's key production activities. In all of the low female LFP countries enumerated above, women do *not* have that prerequisite. This is because the traditional techno-economic base of each of them is rain-fed plow agriculture, with herding in the drier parts. The "historical mainline" of Homo sapiens with respect to making a living off the planet – the techno-economic base (e.g. Blumberg 1984) or "mode of subsistence" (Lenski 1966; Nolan and Lenski 2015) – is comprised of hunting and gathering (foraging), hoe horticulture, plow agriculture and industrial societies (herding is considered an "ecologically specialized type" [Nolan and Lenski 2015]). Boserup (1970) found that non-irrigated plow agriculture was a male farming system. In such systems, women are, at best, very marginal participants at peak periods in the main cultivation activities from plowing through harvest (the work they do in post-harvest processing and storage is invisible to the men, since it takes place in or near the house). In such systems, most women lack a viable route to economic power.

Making it even worse, every one of the countries designated above has a male-dominated kin/property system so women inherit little if at all. Moreover, when they marry, they generally go to the husband's village where they live with his male kin (father and, possibly, other male relatives). As non-earners/non-producers, they arrive at the bottom of the pecking order.

The results have reverberations for both the woman and her children. She has almost no say in her life options, e.g. marriage choice, divorce, fertility or freedom of movement (including the right to leave the house without formal permission and, often, an accompanying male). Her sexuality is so controlled that even the slightest suspicion of misconduct can result in her being killed: Honor killings are still found in significant numbers in these societies and their diasporas (Cooney forthcoming). She has little, if any, say in her children's education, nutrition and health. Additionally, if her people are involved in armed conflict (as is frequently the case) and that conflict is close to home, her options are even more circumscribed (Collins 1971; Blumberg this volume).

Not surprisingly, nations such as these that don't have oil revenue tend to be among the poorest. Even the oil producers are sacrificing a good deal of their economic potential by making so little use of half the population. Many of the oil countries, as well as most others in MENA and South Asia, traditionally have had – and still have – rain-fed plow agriculture with males as the primary farmers, as well as male-dominated kin/property systems. Most continue to have low levels of women's labor force participation to this day. But a number of them now are making fast progress toward eliminating the gender gap in education. On the Persian Gulf, oil-rich Saudi Arabia, Kuwait and the United Arab Emirates already have done so. By 1998 women even predominated in higher education in all three countries: Saudi Arabia 56.98 percent, Kuwait 67.66 percent and the UAE 70.44 percent (Holian 2003: 18). But to this day, they permit few of their well-trained female university graduates to work. So there is no significant countervailing force of female economic power that might soften the negative impacts of patriarchy and armed conflict – and lead to stronger, less distorted development.

Afghanistan, overwhelmingly rural, patriarchal and war-torn (Blumberg, this volume), is a case in point: most people live from non-irrigated plow agriculture, with herding increasing in importance in dry, rocky or badlands areas. Women are considered non- or marginal producers, leaving them few options for acquiring economic power. And where women lack economic power, it is argued, there is a level of gender inequality so high that it reduces economic advance, entrepreneurial activity, the social reproduction of the labor force and well-being at levels ranging from the household to the state. Furthermore, Afghanistan has been riven by waves of warfare since 1978, with grim prospects for enduring peace. Meanwhile, shutting almost all women away from economic power and the public sphere (quite literally, keeping them largely housebound, especially in the areas of the dominant and especially patriarchal Pashtuns), means that the country is left without the economic contributions of almost half its prime age population. Should they raise their voice for peace, it would be too weak to be heard.

Blumberg (this volume) also discusses the Acholi of Northern Uganda. They suffered 23 years of horror and atrocities from the Lord's Resistance Army (LRA), which displaced some 2,000,000 from their homes. But during the years in the Internally Displaced Persons (IDP) camps, many women acquired new income-generating skills and were permitted to leave the camps for day labor as skilled farmers. The farming system there had devolved from plow agriculture back to hoe horticulture, which is a largely female farming system according to Boserup (1970). While the men were forced to stay in camp, for fear they might join the LRA, and many soon had sky-high rates of alcoholism, women's economic power often rose. After the ceasefire, the government quickly emptied most of the IDP camps (only the worst-off – elderly, disabled, orphaned, destitute or disturbed – remained by March–April 2010 [Blumberg 2010]). In our fieldwork area (ibid.), the rest of the people went back to devastated villages. There, they found war-induced deforestation had caused the water table to drop below the depth of the bore wells. As a result, women had to walk up to several miles twice a day, hauling a daily average of 110 pounds of water – barely enough for a household's minimal needs –from often filthy creeks (ibid.). Yet, the women continued to be the economic mainstays, and the level of healing observed in Northern Uganda is inconceivable in Afghanistan, should its current span of 37 years of war actually come to an end. It's tough to pursue peaceful, sustainable development with half the population. Whereas the Acholi case indicates the positive effects on livelihoods, well-being and recovery from war that even a small amount of female economic empowerment can provide, the much more patriarchal Afghanistan case, where women have near-zero economic power, indicates that the country's prospects for peace, healing, recovery and development are much more remote.

Poison potion for development indeed: places where women are economically disempowered share such development-retarding characteristics as high fertility, low human capital (education, health, nutrition), high likelihood of armed conflict, high likelihood of environmental destruction, and more. Further adding to the potion's toxicity, less female economic empowerment often spells more development-sapping corruption (King and Mason 2001, citing Dollar, Fisman and Gatti 2001 and Swamy et al. 2001; see also Rivas 2006). In a nutshell, the more complete women's economic disempowerment, the worse the consequences at both the micro and macro level: for the woman, her family, community and its environment – and her nation.

In conclusion, women's economic empowerment vs. disempowerment lines up quite well with the labels of "magic potion for development" vs. "poison potion for development." Considerable data find female economic power (or its weaker but more widely measured proxy, female labor force participation) to be the single strongest gender-linked stimulus to development. Female education also proves extremely good as a development promoter but women's economic empowerment is even stronger – and women with economic power overwhelmingly encourage the schooling of their girls as well as their boys. For the countries of the Global South – as is also the case in the Global North – there is no better potion to stimulate the wealth and well-being of nations than women's economic empowerment.

Overview of the book

The present volume illustrates these themes with a set of new and exciting contributions from American development sociologists and other scholars doing unusual and important work in development. Many of the chapters are drawn from the 2012 American Sociological Association Sociology of Development Section Conference at the University of Virginia co-organized by the editors. However, a significant number of other chapters were recruited from other sources to supplement the over-arching theme of the four pillars of development in crisis.

Fatton, in Chapter 2, illustrates the importance of state capacity to the promotion of growth by considering a case of gutted state capacity: Haiti. The Haitian state has been consistently weakened by the United States and other Western nations, which supported a foreign occupation of Haiti 1915–1934, stifled all forms of endogenous national development and have used NGOs to administer that nation's social welfare programs. Foreign-imposed economic agendas have been neoliberal and ineffective; non-governmental poverty programs have been minimalistic and ineffective. A neutered state has led to neutered development.

In Chapter 3, Cohn addresses the threats to development that are associated with the US Tea Party and the other shrink-the-state social movements that exist in other capitalist nations. The conservative case for shrinking the state is that tax cuts create jobs. Cohn challenges this assertion by reviewing the theory and evidence for the claim that lower taxation produces economic growth. Both are lacking. Current attempts to shrink the state destroy infrastructure and educational programs that are critical for growth while the associated tax cuts produce negligible compensating increases in jobs.

In his chapter, Kerbo shows that development is affected not only by contemporary state capacity but by ancient state capacity. He traces the variations in state capacity in the hereditary kingdoms of pre-colonial Southeast Asia. Legitimating ideologies that induced kings to improve their countries and subjects to participate in public projects were important. Ancient state capacity explains much of the growth of modern Thailand and Vietnam and the lack of same in Laos. Cambodia squandered its old-kingdom advantages by mismanagement in the modern era.

Schwartz, in Chapter 5, documents the importance of the knowledge-based economy by demonstrating the threat to traditional cheap labor forms of Global South sweatshop manufacturing posed by three dimensional printing. Technological cycles are fundamental to the renewal of capitalism, but there have always been some firms that choose labor exploitation as a strategy for producing low cost merchandise. Schwartz shows how 3-D printing will likely overrun the sweatshop operators of the future. With low wage/low productivity strategies becoming increasingly non-viable, nations in the Global North and the Global South will have to turn to the high-tech high-productivity sector – making science and education essential.

In Chapter 6, Weitzman shows the importance of the empowerment of women for development, by showing the pathological effects of the preferences for male children. Not only China and India, but Vietnam, Pakistan and many nations in the Caucasus have parents who selectively abort female children. The resulting male-heaviness of the population produces a wide variety of pathologies. An absence of care-taking, as well as the rise of a permanent underclass of unattached males who cannot find marriage partners, starts to create a lasting culture of violence and rogue male predation. It is hard to build an economy in a world of constant warfare and crime.

In his chapter, Scanlan highlights an important component of the relationship between gender equality and development: – the relationship between the empowerment of women and protecting the environment. Using a large international dataset, he shows that societies with high female status have superior performance on a number of ecological indicators. Empowered women have the capacity to start labor-intensive businesses that are essentially clean and sustainable.

Furthermore, women's political rights help to promote ecologically responsible legislation and governmental policy.

The effects of gender inequality on the ability of countries to recover from civil war is considered in Chapter 8. Blumberg contrasts highly patriarchal Afghanistan, cursed by nearly four decades of war and extremely stringent limits on female employment and autonomy, with the Acholi in Northern Uganda who had to recover from the devastating effects of 23 years of atrocities committed by the Lord's Resistance Army. Women were the key to recovery. Even in the refugee camps, the women earned income from day labor in farming and began new microenterprises. Back in their villages after the ceasefire, they continued providing day labor income, despite a new burden: spending hours a day hauling water because war had made village wells unusable. No such economic options are available to women in Afghanistan. There, overwhelmingly, they are barred from working for income and have no rights to the land.

Life would be too simple if all the societies that had strong states and good education also had gender egalitarianism. Sometimes you have active, mobilized women in nations with ineffective states, terrible governance and horrific social inequality. Zukas writes about this extremely uncomfortable crossed-wire scenario in Chapter 9. Zimbabwe has a long tradition of economically and politically active women who were instrumental in leading the nation to independence. They have had to confront the Mugabe regime, which has become anti-developmentalist and predatory during 35 years of power. Zukas documents the struggles of women to promote growth and justice in this harsh setting and provides important new material on the dysfunctionality of the Zimbabwean state. It is like watching a train wreck, but the heroines do what they can.

Vom Hau shows in Chapter 10 that even in the face of adverse developmental trends, small gains are possible for disadvantaged groups that are willing to organize. He considers the case of indigenous populations in Argentina, that are often the victims of land grabs by aspiring mega-farmers and dam builders. Such dispossession increases economic inequality, impoverishes populations with previously viable economic strategies of their own and often creates under-consuming slum dwellers. The indigenous activists who fought land grabs in Argentina did not get everything they wanted; however, they were able to set the groundwork for future campaigns to promote their land rights, equality and the rights of the poor.

Chapter 11 is the most sobering chapter in the volume. Handler considers not development per se, but the teaching of development and global studies in American universities. He argues that universities focus very little on the real crises causing underdevelopment and conflict. More often, they present lots of vague platitudes about leadership and internationalism. Students create great vitae showing leadership capacity but learn little about actual foreign cultures, actual foreign problems or about what rich nations do, intentionally or not, that perpetuate these problems. The students show up in government or NGOs with inadequate understanding of what is really wrong, and therefore, with new ideas of how problems could actually be solved.

Reynold's chapter provides a beacon of hope. For 15 years, she served on the Board of Directors of Physicians for Human Rights. In 1992, it joined with five other organizations to launch a global campaign to ban landmines. These efforts led to a grand coalition of 1100 organizations – the International Campaign to Ban Landmines (ICBL) – that won the Nobel Peace Prize in 1997 for its work. In that same year, 122 nations signed the Mine Ban Treaty, a breathtaking accomplishment: the fastest treaty ratification in history. The campaign against landmines represents a bona fide effective international intervention which reduced the adverse effects of war on economic development and human well-being. Strong NGOs were able to design the treaty, which the world's nations signed in record time. This was a case where organizations and states achieved a sophisticated understanding of one of the most unnecessary causes of misery in the Global South and were able to unite to make a dramatic humanistic difference.

We start with Robert Fatton on Haiti, where NGOs were the instruments of the reproduction of poverty and imperialism. And we close with Preston Reynolds, where NGOs led the way to hugely consequential reforms. The sophisticated local knowledge called for in Handler's discussion of universities may be one way to move from a world of neo-colonial dependency and distressing gaps in equality, growth and well-being to a world of genuine international cooperation. With greater state capacity – as well as fully empowered citizens of both genders – the people of the both the Global South and Global North will be able to make the most of new opportunities for development and enhanced well-being.

References

Airport Owners and Pilots Association. 2014 Airport Database. Available at: www.aopa.org/airports/

Altbach, Philip. 2013. *International Imperative in Higher Education*. Rotterdam: Sense.

Anseeuw, Ward, Mathieu Boche, Thomas Breu, Markus Giger, Jann Lay, Peter Messerli and Kerstin Nolte. 2012. *Transnational Land Deals for Agriculture in the Global South: Analytical Report Based on the Land Matrix Database*. Bern: Centre for Development and Environment. Available at: www.oxfam.de/sites/www.oxfam.de/files/20120427_report_land_matrix.pdf

Atlanta Department of Aviation. 2010. *Airport History*. Available at: www.atlanta-airport.com/Airport/ATL/Airport_History.aspx

Berry, Brian, Edgar Conkling and D. Michael Ray. 1993. *Economic Geography: Resource Use, Locational Choices and Regional Specialization in the Global Economy*. Englewood Cliffs, NJ: Prentice Hall.

Blumberg, Rae Lesser. Forthcoming. "The Magic Money Tree? Women, Economic Power and Development in a Globalized World." In *Handbook of the Sociology of Development*, edited by Gregory Hooks et al. Berkeley, CA: University of California Press.

———2015. "'Dry' Versus 'Wet' Development and Women in Three World Regions." *Sociology of Development* 1(1): 91–122.

———2010. "Measuring the Rebuilding of Hope in Northern Uganda." Kampala, Uganda and Washington, DC: Winrock International and USAID.

———2009a. "Mothers of Invention? The Myth-Breaking History and Planetary Promise of

Women's Key Roles in Subsistence Technology." Pp. 227–259 in *Techno-Well: Impact of Technology on Psychological Well-Being*, edited by Yair Amichai-Hamburger. Cambridge: Cambridge University Press.

——2009b. "The Consequences of Women's Economic Empowerment versus Disempowerment: From the 'Magic Potion' for Development to the 'Four Horsemen of the Apocalypse'?" Keynote paper for the UNESCO Women's Studies and Gender Research Networking Conference, Bangkok, February.

——2008. "Gender, Environment and Environmental Ethics: Exploring the Critical Role of Economic Power in Thailand, Ecuador and Malawi." Presented at the UNESCO Conference on Ethics of Energy Technologies: Ethical Views of Nature; held in conjunction with the World Congress of Philosophy, Seoul, South Korea, August.

——2004. "Extending Lenski's Schema to Hold up Both Halves of the Sky: A Theory-Guided Way of Conceptualizing Agrarian Societies that Illuminates a Puzzle about Gender Stratification." *Sociological Theory* 22(2): 278–291.

——2001. "'We Are Family': Gender, Microenterprise, Family Work and Well-being in Ecuador and the Dominican Republic – with Comparative Data from Guatemala, Swaziland and Guinea-Bissau." *History of the Family: An International Quarterly* 6: 271–299.

——1995. "Introduction: Engendering Wealth and Well-being in an Era of Economic Transformation." Pp. 1–14 in *Engendering Wealth & Well-being: Empowerment for Global Change*, edited by Rae Lesser Blumberg, Cathy A. Rakowski, Irene Tinker and Michael Monteon. Boulder, CO: Westview Press.

——1991. "Introduction: The 'Triple Overlap' of Gender Stratification, Economy and the Family." Pp. 7–32 in *Gender, Economy, and the Family*, edited by Rae Lesser Blumberg. Newbury Park, CA and London: Sage.

——1989a. *Making the Case for the Gender Variable: Women and the Wealth and Well-Being of Nations*. Washington, DC: US Agency for International Development/Office of Women in Development.

——1989b. "Toward a Feminist Theory of Development." Pp. 161–199 in *Feminism and Sociological Theory*, edited by Ruth A. Wallace. Newbury Park, CA: Sage.

——1988. "Income under Female vs. Male Control: Hypotheses from a Theory of Gender Stratification and Data from the Third World." *Journal of Family Issues* 9(1): 51–84.

——1984. "A General Theory of Gender Stratification." *Sociological Theory* 2: 23–101.

Blumberg, Rae Lesser and Andres Wilfrido Salazar-Paredes. 2011. "Can a Focus on Survival and Health as Social/Economic Rights Help Some of the World's Most Imperiled Women in a Globalized World?" Pp. 123–156 in *Making Globalization Work for Women*, edited by Valentine Moghadam, Suzanne Franzway and Mary Margaret Fonow. Albany, NY: State University of New York Press.

Blumberg, Rae Lesser, Vivienne Brachet-Marquez, Fernando Cortes and Rosmaria Rubalcava. 1992. "Women's 'Purse Power' in the Household: Reducing Favoritism toward Boys' Schooling in Santiago, Chile." Presented at the meetings of the American Sociological Association, Pittsburgh, PA, August.

Boserup, Ester. 1970. *Woman's Role in Economic Development*. New York: St. Martin's Press.

Bowman, Mary Jane and C. Arnold Anderson. 1963. "Concerning the Role of Education in Development." Pp. 247–269 in *Old Societies and New States*, edited by Clifford Geertz. Glencoe, IL: Free Press.

Caprioli, Mary. 2005. "Primed for Violence: The Role of Gender Inequality in Predicting Internal Conflict." *International Studies Quarterly* 49: 161–178.

——2000. "Gendered Conflict." *Journal of Peace Research* 37(1): 51–68.

Chase-Dunn, Christopher. 1998. *Global Formation: Structures of the World Economy*. New York: Rowman and Littlefield.

CIA. 2015. *Factbook*. Washington, DC: Central Intelligence Agency.
Cohn, Samuel. 2014. "O'Connorian Models of Peripheral Development: Or How Third World States Resist World-Systemic Pressures By Cloning the Policies of States in the Core." Pp. 336–344 in *Routledge Handbook of World Systems Analysis*, edited by Salvatore Babones and Christopher Chase-Dunn. New York: Routledge.
——2012. *Employment and Development Under Globalization: State and Economy in Brazil*. Basingstoke: Palgrave Macmillan.
Cole, Jonathan. 2009. *Great American University*. New York: Public Affairs.
Collins, Randall. 1971. "A Conflict Theory of Sexual Stratification." *Social Problems* 19: 3–21.
Cooney, Mark. 2014. "Death by Family: Honor Killings as Punishment." *Punishment and Society* 16(4): 406–427.
Cronin, Brenda. 2013. "Some 95% of 2009–2012 Income Gains Went to Wealthiest 1%." *Wall Street Journal*, September 10.
Cuberes, David and Marc Teignier. 2012. "Gender Gaps in the Labor Market and Aggregate Productivity." Economic Research Paper 2012017, Department of Economics, University of Sheffield, June.
Daley-Harris, Sam. 2009. *State of the Microcredit Summit Campaign Report 2009*. Washington, DC: The Microcredit Summit. Available at: www.microcreditsummit.org/SOCR/SOCR2009_English.pdf
Das Gupta, Monica, John Bongaarts and John Cleland. 2011. "Population, Poverty and Sustainable Development: A Review of the Evidence." Washington, DC: World Bank Working Paper.
Dollar, David and Roberta Gatti. 1999. "Gender Inequality, Income, and Growth: Are Good Times Good for Women"? World Bank Policy Research Report on Gender and Development, Working Paper Series No. 1. Washington, DC: World Bank,
Dollar, David, Raymond Fisman and Roberta Gatti. 2001. "Are Women Really the 'Fairer' Sex? Corruption and Women in Government." *Journal of Economic Behavior and Organization* 46(4): 423–429.
Durlauf, Steven, Paul Johnson and Jonathan Temple. 2005. "Growth Econometrics." Pp. 555–667 in *Handbook of Economic Growth*, Volume 1A, edited by Philippe Aghion and Steven Durlauf. Amsterdam: North Holland.
The Economist. 2006. "Forget China, India and the Internet: Economic Growth Is Driven by Women." April 15: 16.
Engelman, Robert. 2008. *More: Population, Nature, and What Women Want*. Washington, DC: Island Press.
Faiola, Anthony. 2008. "Women Rise in Rwanda's Economic Revival." *The Washington Post*, May 16: A1, A12.
Firebaugh, Glenn and Frank Beck. 1994. "Does Economic Growth Benefit the Masses? Growth Dependence and Welfare in the Third World." *American Sociological Review* 59: 631–653.
Gana, Alia. 2012. "Rural and Agricultural Roots of the Tunisian Revolution: When Food Security Matters." *International Journal of the Sociology of Agriculture and Food* 19: 201–213.
Geolounge. 2014. "List of Fortune 1000 Companies by Urban Area." Available at: www.geolounge.com/list-fortune-1000-companies-urban-area/
Goldin, Claudia. 1986. "The Female Labor Force and American Economic Growth." In *Long Term Factors in American Economic Growth*, edited by Stanley Engerman and Robert Gallman. Chicago, IL: University of Chicago Press.
Gordon, Cameron, Mark D. Hughes and Andrew Read. 2007. "Is There 'Value for Money' in Transportation PPPs? The Case of Macquarie and Sydney International Airport." *Social Science Research Network*, January 11. Available at: http://ssrn.com/abstract=1522065

Hakangard, Agneta. 1992. "A Socio-Economic Study of Villagers, Transport and Use of Road 13S, Lao PDR." *Development Studies Unit Report No. 23*. Stockholm: Department of Social Anthropology, Stockholm University.

Hess, Peter N. 1988. *Population Growth and Socio-Economic Progress in Less Developed Countries: Determinants of Fertility Transition*. New York: Praeger.

Holian, Laura. 2003. "Gender, Education and Empowerment: A Comparison of Three Arab States." M.A. Thesis, Department of Sociology, University of Virginia.

Inequality Watch. 2014. "Evolution of the Per Capita Income Levels of the World." Inequality Watch. Available at: www.inequalitywatch.eu/spip.php?article102

Ireson, Carol J. 1996. *Field, Forest, and Family: Women's Work and Power in Rural Laos*. Boulder, CO: Westview Press.

Irwin, Michael and John Kasarda. 1991. "Air Passenger Linkages and Employment Growth in US Metropolitan Areas." *American Sociological Review* 56: 524–537.

Isele, Elizabeth. 2013. "The Paradox of Women Business Owners." *Forbes*, June 18. Available at: www.forbes.com/sites/nextavenue/2013/06/18/the-paradox-of-women-business-owners

Jerven, Morten. 2013. *Poor Numbers: How We Are Misled By African Development Statistics and What To Do About It*. Ithaca, NY: Cornell University Press.

Kim, Jim Yong. 2014. "The True Cost of Discrimination: Blocking Productive People from Full Participation Only Hurts Countries." *Washington Post*, February 28: A15.

King, Elizabeth M. and M. Anne Hill (eds). 1993. *Women's Education in Developing Countries*. Baltimore, MD: The Johns Hopkins University Press.

King, Elizabeth M. and Andrew D. Mason. 2001. *Engendering Development through Gender Equality in Rights, Resources, and Voice*. Oxford/New York: Oxford University Press/World Bank. Kondratieff, Nikolai. 1935. "Long Waves in Economic Life." *Review of Economic Statistics* 17: 105–115.

Koo, Hagen. 2001. *Korean Workers: Culture and Politics of Class Formation*. Ithaca, NY: Cornell University Press.

Landes, David. 2009. *Wealth and Poverty of Nations: Why Some Are So Rich and Some Are So Poor*. New York: Norton.

Lenski, Gerhard. 1966. *Power and Privilege: A Theory of Social Stratification*. New York: McGraw-Hill.

Long, Cate. 2013. Are Private Toll Roads a Losing Idea? Reuters, US Edition. January 19. Available at: http://blogs.reuters.com/muniland/2013/01/19/are-private-toll-roads-a-losing-idea/

Maddison Project. 2014. *Maddison Project Database*. Available at: www.ggdc.net/maddison/maddison-project/home.htm

Maes, Jan P. and Larry R. Reed. 2012. *State of the Microcredit Summit Campaign Report 2012*. Washington, DC: The Microcredit Summit. Available at: www.microcreditsummit.org. SOCR/SOCR2012_English.pdf

Mencher, Joan. 1988. "Women's Work and Poverty: Women's Contribution to Household Maintenance in South India." Pp. 99–119 in *A Home Divided: Women and Income in the Third World*, edited by Daisy Dwyer and Judith Bruce. Palo Alto, CA: Stanford University Press.

Meyerson, Harold. 2013. "The Forty-Year Slump." *The American Prospect*, Sept.–Oct. Available at: http://prospect.org/article/40-year-slump

National Women's Business Council. 2015. "Women-Owned Businesses." Available at: www.nwbc.gov/facts/women-owned-businesses

Nolan, Patrick and Gerhard Lenski. 2015. *Human Societies: An Introduction to Macrosociology*, 12th edn. New York: Oxford University Press.

——2011. *Human Societies: An Introduction to Macrosociology*. 11th edn. Boulder, CO: Paradigm Press.

Oppenheimer, Valerie Kincade. 1973. "Demographic Influence on Female Employment and the Status of Women." *American Journal of Sociology* 78: 946–961.
Paige, Jeffery. 1975. *Agrarian Revolution*. Berkeley, CA: University of California Press.
Psacharopoulos, George. 2002. "Returns to Investment in Education: A Further Update." World Bank Policy Research Working Paper. Washington, DC: World Bank.
Rivas, Maria Fernanda. 2006. "An Experiment on Corruption and Gender." Universidad de la República, Departamento de Economía, Facultad de Ciencias Sociales, Montevideo, Uruguay. Documento No. 08/06.
Roldan, Marta. 1988. "Renegotiating the Marital Contract: Intrahousehold Patterns of Money Allocation and Women's Subordination among Domestic Outworkers in Mexico City." In *A Home Divided: Women and Income in the Third World*, edited by Daisy Dwyer and Judith Bruce. Palo Alto, CA: Stanford University Press.
Schultz, T. Paul. 1998. "Why Governments Should Invest More Educating Girls." New Haven, CT: Yale University, Department of Economics. Available at: www.econ.yale.edu/~pschultz/GovtEducatingGirls.PDF
Senghaas, Dieter 1985. *European Experience: Historical Critique of Development Theory*. Dover, NH: Berg.
Shorter, Edward and Charles Tilly. 1974. *Strikes in France 1830–1968*. New York: Cambridge University Press.
Snow, David, Sarah Soule and Hans Peter Kriesi. 2004. *Blackwell Companion to Social Movements*. Malden, MA: Blackwell.
The Society of Professional Women. 2015. "Fast Facts." Available at: www.spwmainline.com/womensfacts.html
Standing, Guy. 2011. *The Precariat: The New Dangerous Class*. London: Bloomsbury Academic.
Swamy, Anand, Steve Knack, Young Lee and Omar Azfar. 2001. "Gender and Corruption." *Journal of Development Economics* 64(1): 25–55.
Szirmai, Adam. 2005. *Dynamics of Socio-economic Development: An Introduction*. New York: Cambridge University Press.
Tortella, Gabriel. 2000. *Development of Modern Spain: Economic History of the Nineteenth and Twentieth Centuries*. Cambridge, MA: Harvard University Press.
United Nations. 2010. *World Fertility Report 2007*. New York: United Nations/Economic and Social Affairs.
——2007. *Economic and Social Survey of Asia and the Pacific 2007: Surging Ahead in Uncertain Times*. United Nations Publication, Sales No. #.07.II.F.4.
——1987. *Fertility Behaviours in the Context of Development*. New York: United Nations Department of International Economic and Social Affairs, ST/ESA/SER.A/100.
Wartenberg, Julia. 2012. "Understanding Mass Rape in Genocide: A New Perspective on a Deadly Weapon of War." PhD Dissertation, Department of Sociology, University of Virginia.
Weller, Robert H. 1968. "The Employment of Wives, Dominance and Fertility." *Journal of Marriage and the Family* 30: 437–442.
Williamson, Jeffrey. 2006. *Globalization and the Poor Periphery before 1950*. Cambridge, MA: MIT Press.
Wolford, Wendy, Saturnino Borras Jr., Ruth Hall, Ian Scoones and Ben White (eds). 2013. "Governing the Global Land Grab: Role of the State in the Rush for Land." Special Issue. *Development and Change* 44: 189–472.
World Bank. 2014a. *World Development Indicators*. Available at: http://data.worldbank.org/data-catalog/world-development-indicators
——2014b. "Labor Force Participation Rate, Female (% of Female Population Ages 15+) (modeled ILO estimate)." In *World Development Indicators*. World Bank. Available at: http://data.worldbank.org/indicator/SL.TLF.CACT.FE.ZS

Notes

1 During World War II, vehicle production was almost wholly for the war effort and it began skyrocketing around 1940. It was this war production that finally got the world out of the Great Depression.
2 These hypotheses from both the gender stratification and gender and development theories have considerable empirical support (Blumberg 2015, forthcoming).
3 Among Blumberg's other propositions about the consequences of women's economic power, at the *micro* level, the following are particularly well-supported empirically (see Blumberg 2015, forthcoming): (a) it increases their self-confidence, often earning them greater respect from their families; (b) it increases their say in household decisions, including those relating to their own fertility, economic issues (including acquisition, allocation and/or sale of assets) and domestic well-being matters (e.g. concerning access to nutrition, health care and/or education of sons vs. daughters – with women proving to be more even-handed with their daughters than male counterparts – see, e.g. Blumberg et al. 1992 for quantitative national household survey evidence from Santiago, Chile that women sent their daughters to high school at rates equal to men – although they had only half the men's income).
4 Nolan and Lenski (2011: 304) show that industrializing hoe horticultural (IH) nations (almost all in sub-Saharan Africa) averaged 2.6 percent annual fertility from 1961 to 2006 versus 2.1 percent for industrializing plow agrarian (IA) countries (the rest of the Global South). They calculate that the higher fertility in IH countries ate up fully 90 percent of economic growth, versus 47 percent in IA countries.

2
THE CRISIS OF INTERNATIONAL DEVELOPMENT AND THE CASE OF HAITI

The making of an outer-periphery

Robert Fatton Jr.

This chapter is an attempt to situate Haiti in what I call the outer-periphery (Fatton 2014).[1] The outer-periphery symbolizes the degradation of the world capitalist economy brought about by more than 35 years of neoliberalism. Neoliberalism has accentuated economic inequalities and exacerbated social polarization scandalously on both a global and national scale (Harvey 2005). Up to the 1980s the world capitalist system was hierarchically divided into three main zones: the core, semi-periphery and periphery (Wallerstein 1979, 2004). I argue, however, that the neoliberal regime has engendered a new zone of catastrophe that fell off from the periphery to become the outer-periphery.

Though founded in 1804 as the first black independent nation in the wake of the only successful slave revolution, Haiti has endured a history marked by recurring patterns of foreign intrusions, political instability and authoritarianism. On the one hand, its modern period is dominated by the harsh Duvalier dictatorship of 1957–86. It began in 1957 with "Papa Doc"; on his death in 1971, his son, Jean-Claude, succeeded him after a dubious referendum ("Baby Doc," who, like his father, had the title of President for Life, was forced to flee in 1986). On the other hand, the period is also marked by the continuous and unending struggle for a democratic society. The fall of Jean-Claude Duvalier inaugurated a moment of popular hope for the creation of a new society. But since 1986 and the rise of Jean Bertrand Aristide's populist Lavalas movement, the country has continued to face political instability and foreign interferences that have prevented the development of governmental accountability and the equalization of life chances. In January 2010 Haiti suffered a massive earthquake that killed some 220,000 people and destroyed much of its already weak infrastructure. The earthquake has exacerbated political tensions and economic destitution in spite of a very hesitant program of reconstruction.

Thus, Haiti's legacy of colonialism and slavery as well as its difficult survival as a black republic in a hostile international environment, have all contributed to its current predicament. In fact, the intersection of the domestic and world economies have further contributed to the country's acute material scarcity and persisting authoritarian rule.

Devastated by natural catastrophes, zero-sum-politics, obscene inequities, neoliberalism and imperial interference, Haiti represents a paradigmatic outer-peripheral state. It is an empty shell lacking the basic bureaucratic apparatus to execute the policies and laws that it promulgates. The cataclysmic earthquake of January 2010 has exacerbated these deficiencies (Farmer, Gardner and Van Der Hoof Holstein 2011; Schuller and Morales 2012; Dubois 2012); the country has turned into a virtual trusteeship of the international community and grown increasingly dependent on its neighbor, the Dominican Republic. Haiti is thus becoming a periphery of the periphery.

I contend that imperialism remains the fundamental organizing principle of the current international conjuncture; what is new, however, in the age of globalization is the dramatic accentuation of world inequalities even if significant economic growth has occurred in regions that had previously been relatively low-wage areas. The magnitude of inequalities is simply obscene; in a briefing paper, Oxfam reports that "almost half of the world's wealth is now owned by just one percent of the population" and "the wealth of the one percent richest people in the world amounts to $110 trillion," which is "65 times the total wealth of the bottom half of the world's population." Moreover, this bottom half of the world's population "owns the same as the richest 85 people in the world" (Oxfam 2014: 2). The tale of gross inequities is unending, but suffice to add that over three billion people, more than 40 percent of humanity, live on less than $2.50 a day and that 80 percent of the world's population lives on less than $10 a day (Shah 2013).

The outer-periphery is confined to low-end production with wages barely sufficient for survival; wages are often not paid at all. The International Labor Organization (ILO) and the International Finance Corporation (IFC) that monitor the activities of the major retailers and apparel brands reported that "*every single one* of the country's 24 export garment factories was illegally cheating workers of pay by failing to comply with the country's legal minimum wage … The majority of Haitian garment workers are being denied *nearly a third* of the wages they are legally due as a result of the factories' theft of their income" (Worker Rights Consortium 2013: 4).

The outer-periphery is not only a region of ultra-cheap wages; it is also dominated by extremely high rates of unemployment and a vast informal sector. In addition, the politics of the outer-periphery are a simulacra of representative democracy in which fraudulent elections are more or less regularly held. These elections are not merely financed but also certified as "free and fair" by outside powers and "pro-democracy" organizations, which are poorly rooted in the local terrain.

Finally, the outer-periphery lacks the state apparatus to establish any real sovereignty over its territory; it is a zone under the control of the international community. While outer-peripheral regions owe much of their existence to their own domestic social forces and processes, they are also the product of the history of their subordinate incorporation into the world capitalist economy (Amin 1974; Baran 1957; Frank 1967; Wallerstein 1979). The outer periphery is on the one hand the specific product of the effects of the long-term imposition of neoliberal policies, and on the other hand of the continued absence of productive capital investments. What James Ferguson (2006: 38) writes about Africa applies to the realities of the outer-periphery:

> Capital does not 'flow' from New York to Angola's oil fields, or from London to Ghana's gold mines; it hops, neatly skipping over most of what lies in between. Second, where capital has been coming to Africa at all, it has largely been concentrated in spatially segregated, socially 'thin' mineral-extraction enclaves ... Capital is *globe-hopping*, not *globe-covering*.

Outer-peripheral nations are thus simultaneously integrated into the world capitalist system and marginalized from its main process of capital accumulation.

The logic of privatization, state withdrawal, and market "rationality" unleashed by neoliberalism on the weakest links of the periphery debilitated further their already fragile governmental capacity, weak economies and tenuous sovereignty. The outer-periphery was thus created; it has become the geographical space occupied and managed by "peace-keepers" and non-governmental organizations (NGOs) of a self-appointed "international community." Promoted by the International Financial Institutions (IFIs) as the substitute of corrupt and failed states, NGOs unwittingly became part of the liberal "assemblage of occupation" (Duffield 2007: 27) not only in post-disaster and post-conflict "nation-building," but also in the aftermath of "regime change."

Regime change has led to electoral simulacra organized by alien forces installing emasculated, unpopular and unaccountable governments. The international community assumes little responsibility for the political dislocation and economic destruction that its takeovers inflict on the outer-periphery. Such dislocations aggravate pre-existing social inequality and poverty. Not surprisingly, most people in outer-peripheral states lack the sense of being full citizens.

Rooted in claims of human universalism, citizenship and egalitarianism, liberalism is besieged by the reality that capitalism is inherently polarizing and hierarchic. Western conceptions of "nationhood" reinforce boundaries, exclusion and racism. This in turn has exacerbated the ideological and political contradictions of liberalism. Nation-states are exclusionary constructs that helped transform peripheral areas into zones of "exotic other" (Fanon 1968; Kapuscinski, 2008; Said 1978; Wallerstein 2006). Until the 1950s, the "other" was infantilized; the moral community of humanity comprised only the self-appointed citizens of the "civilized" Western core.

While at the level of the world system, all human beings are now allegedly equal, some are clearly more equal than others. In fact, the core has given itself the right to determine unilaterally whether the "international community" and its "machinery of occupation" should intervene in peripheral and particularly in outer-peripheral states. Such interventions span a spectrum ranging from saving lives, as in the case of disaster relief, or "terminating them with extreme prejudice."

The core is thus driven to protect itself from the very system it has engendered; it has unfolded a containment strategy against the "surplus population" of "boat people," refugees and asylum seekers of the outer-periphery. Unlike capital, which moves without restrictions across borders, a "cordon sanitaire" provided by the international community's "machinery of occupation" prevents the free circulation of people.

For instance, the United States with the complicity of the Haitian government has the legal right to patrol Haitian waters and compel any Haitian on the sea to return to his country. While this is a quintessential relationship between core and outer-periphery, it extends to interactions between periphery and outer-periphery. Indeed, the Dominican Republic (DR) has exploited Haitian migrant workers as a socially "invisible" and humiliated people for the past 70 years. The Constitutional Court of the DR legalized this "invisibility" when in September 2013 it invalidated the citizenship of unauthorized migrants born in the country between 1929 and 2010 (Abiu Lopez and Coto 2013; Agence France Presse 2013). The ruling renders stateless some 200,000 Dominicans, mainly of Haitian descent. Not surprisingly it generated international condemnation and the furious protests of Haitian politicians and intellectuals (Bell 2013; Groupe d'Appui aux Rapatriés et Réfugiés 2014a). In an attempt to lessen tensions, Dominican and Haitian authorities have initiated negotiations to find a mutually satisfactory solution, but so far they have met little success (Groupe d'Appui aux Rapatriés et Réfugiés 2014b). However, it is likely that some sort of compromise will eventually materialize given geographical realities (Haiti occupies a third of the island of Hispaniola; the DR occupies the rest) as well as the significant economic and political interests uniting the two nations (Groupe d'Appui aux Rapatriés et Réfugiés 2014c).

These ties, however, have become very unequal; they reflect the hegemonic position of the DR in its interaction with Haiti (Agence Presse Média Caraibes 2013). Trade between the two countries has increased significantly since the early 1990s, but it is "nearly unidirectional" as the DR exports to Haiti are estimated to total $2 billion in 2012 (Antonini 2012). Clearly, the Dominican Republic and Haiti have relations that are looking increasingly like those characterizing core and peripheral countries. Thus, economically, Haiti is subservient to the DR, which is now bent on exploiting ultra-cheap Haitian labor in Haiti itself or near the frontier. The new Dominican strategy limits the political costs of massive inflows of Haitian migration into its heartland.

The constricting of the outer-periphery to its own segregated space defies the liberal pretensions of universalism, solidarity and equality that globalization allegedly entails. Thus, Haiti is represented as a bizarre human anomaly; a society so strange and weird that it is rejected by the "civilized" world. In fact, Samuel Huntington calls Haiti a "lone country," that "lacks cultural commonality with other societies." He writes: "Haiti's Creole language, Voodoo religion, revolutionary slave origins, and brutal history combine to make it a lone country ... Haiti, 'the neighbor nobody wants,' is truly a kinless country" (Huntington 1996: 136–137). The globalized "village" has thus spawned a "new racism" that hides its ugly face behind the defense of "cultural difference" and a community's right to exclude those who do not share its "way of life" (Balibar and Wallerstein 1991).

The core's civilization was once untouched, unchallenged and triumphant. Now, the Empire is determined to stop the "barbarians" from penetrating its space fearing that they endanger its very liberal essence. Universalism is thus a mirage, the ideology of those who have the power to claim that their own civilization and only theirs is universal.

These contradictions generate explosive tensions. In the outer-periphery, the desire for a decent living standard in a democratic community where each individual is treated fairly as a citizen clashes with the continuing reality of political exclusion and grotesque inequality. This is not to say that there has been no resistance to the world capitalist economy, nor that social progress is impossible. In the outer-periphery, popular movements have risen to contest the system, but they have failed to change its basic structures. The case of *Lavalas* ('the Flood' – the social movement that carried Jean-Bertrand Aristide to power) illustrates well how popular revolt could not overthrow entrenched patterns of class power. Lavalas *did* however radicalize popular consciousness and facilitated future dissent (Dupuy 2007; Fatton 2002).

The people's revolt against Duvalierism and militarism symbolized one of those rare moments when an excluded majority claimed its citizenship. "Tout moun se moun" – every human being is a human being – the slogan Aristide popularized, entailed a profound cultural shift that nurtured the idea that all Haitians were in fact equal, that they were all citizens. Though the ruling class resisted and still resists accepting this democratic logic, popular pressures compelled it to accommodate itself to the rhetoric of equality.

Clearly, however, the profound inequalities of class, gender, status and wealth prevent the overwhelming majority of Haitians from enjoying the benefits of citizenship. Thus, while the rhetoric of equality, social contract and solidarity has become part of the new political narrative of the country, it clashes with the continuing realities of inequities, exclusion and poverty.

Moreover, to be a citizen is inextricably linked to belonging to a sovereign territorial space, the nation. Without such sovereignty, the very idea of citizenship is moot. Haiti, however, has become a virtual trusteeship of the international community. Its economy is dependent on external assistance and the remittances of its diaspora; and the broad contours of its domestic policies are decided abroad in the headquarters of the major international financial institutions.

Paradoxically then, while the universal franchise is now firmly embedded in the structures of the political system, Haitians are not truly in charge of their own affairs. Haitian elections are not only rigged, but they are funded by foreign powers and under the surveillance of the core's machinery of democratic legitimation, which imposes strict limits on political choice. Currently, these limits are enforced by the presence of over 10,000 troops from the United Nations. Thus, obdurate constraints on the country's sovereignty circumscribe further an already thoroughly incomplete sense of Haitian citizenship.

When the subaltern classes challenge the status quo and take seriously their role as citizens, they confront the domestic opposition of their ruling class and the external "disciplining" of the major powers. The result, as the Lavalas experience demonstrated, is the ultimate exhaustion of the popular forces and the growing opportunism and corruption of their cadres. Cynicism therefore set in, undermined democratic practice, divided the movement and revived Haiti's authoritarian tradition by reawakening the cult of the providential *Chef* (Chief) (Dupuy 2007; Fatton 2002).

Thus, with Aristide, a form of messianic presidency monopolized power and eviscerated the independence and organizational drive of the Lavalas movement. The excluded majority ended up surrendering its citizenship to the Chef and became a disorganized mass awaiting salvation. The personalization of Haitian politics also accentuated the emasculation of the state, which in turn was fueled by the imposition of neoliberal policies. These policies promoted the privatization of the economy and led to the rise of the "NGO Republic" and the dismantlement of the public sector. In the process, governmental institutions that had always been weak collapsed to the point that at the time of the tragic earthquake of January 12, 2010 the Haitian state was utterly incapable of responding to the catastrophe. It was a powerless shell at the mercy of the international community.

And yet, in the aftermath of the earthquake, the pattern of foreign assistance has continued to bypass the government and reinforced state incapacity. According to a 2011 report of the UN special envoy for Haiti:

> Of the $2.43 billion committed or disbursed in humanitarian funding:
>
> - 34 percent ($824.7 million) was provided to donors' own civil and military entities for disaster response;
> - 28 percent ($674.9 million) was provided to UN agencies and international NGOs for projects listed in the UN appeal;
> - 26 percent ($632.5 million) was provided to other international NGOs and private contractors;
> - 6 percent ($151.1 million) was provided (in-kind) to unspecified recipients;
> - 5 percent ($119.9 million) was provided to the International Federation of the Red Cross and national Red Cross societies;
> - 1 percent ($25.0 million) was provided to the Government of Haiti.
>
> United Nations 2011: 15

All told, approximately 99 percent of post-earthquake relief aid was disbursed to non-Haitian actors. Moreover, Haitian NGOs were virtually excluded from relief or recovery funds. Only two – Perspectives pour la Santé et le Développement (Prospects for Health and Development) and Adventist Development and Relief Agency Haiti – received funding. And that amounted to only an embarrassing $0.8 million (United Nations 2011:15–16). In fact, a significant portion of both relief and recovery-assistance funded organizations were located in the donor countries themselves; for instance, more than "75 percent of USAID funds went to private contractors inside the Washington DC 'Beltway'" (Ramachandran and Walz 2012: 13; see also Mendoza and Daniel 2012; Schuller 2012).

This debilitation of the Haitian state was aggravated further by the creation of a supranational body called the Interim Haiti Recovery Commission (IHRC), which displaced the country's already weak and ineffective government. Created in Washington by key figures in the State Department with the help of American private consultants and lawyers, the Commission was parachuted in with little warning to the Haitian government of René Préval (Johnston 2014; Mills 2010; Lundahl 2013: 250–265; Katz 2013: 279–280). While Préval and his administration managed with the help of some other major international players to introduce some changes in the Commission's functioning, these changes could not hide the stark reality of limited Haitian sovereignty. In April 2010, the Haitian Parliament voted for a state of emergency law giving the Commission complete authority to determine the country's future until October 2011.

The Commission aimed to coordinate the recovery from the earthquake. It was also responsible for encouraging investment and development. The Commission was unaccountable to any Haitian representative body. All decisions made by the IHRC were "deemed confirmed" unless vetoed by Haiti's president within 10 business days after formal notification (Interim Haiti Recovery Commission 2010: 23). Thus, the Commission maintained a legal façade of ultimate Haitian authority. But in reality, it placed the country under foreign powers.

The 24 voting members of the Commission were equally divided between Haitian government officials and civil society organizations on the one hand and foreign powers and organizations, on the other (Haiti Libre 2010). Apart from the representative of the Caribbean Community (CARICOM), the other foreign voting members came from institutions or countries that "pledged to donate at least US$100,000,000 for the reconstruction of Haiti over a period of two consecutive years, or that [had] pledged at least US$200,000,000 in debt relief to Haiti" (Interim Haiti Recovery Commission 2010: 9).

The Commission is now defunct, although it has been revived as the Cadre de Coordination de l'Aide Externe (CAED). And Haiti remains dependent on the external community for its financial survival (Michel 2012; Geffrard 2013). The presence of the so-called Mission des Nations Unies pour la Stabilisation en Haïti, (MINUSTAH), a contingent of some 13,000 United Nations peacekeepers, as the primary operating coercive force has further emasculated the Haitian state.

The Commission and MINUSTAH were conceived with very little national debate. They defied the nation's sovereignty and have been unrepresentative of Haitian aspirations. The Commission had neither a peasant nor a refugee camp representative on its board. The Commission was an urban, elite, foreign-favoring phenomenon pretending to speak for the countryside and the poor following the earthquake. MINUSTAH was used by the United States to "pacify" the country in the aftermath of President Aristide's forced departure from office in 2004. While American and French troops occupied the country immediately after Aristide's fall, neither Washington nor Paris was willing to commit its armed forces for the long term. MINUSTAH became their substitute.

In a 2008 cable publicized by Wikileaks, former Ambassador Janet A. Sanderson stated that:

> [without] a UN-sanctioned peacekeeping and stabilization force, we would be getting far less help from our hemispheric and European partners in managing Haiti ... [if MINUSTAH were to leave Haiti] it could lead to resurgent populist and anti-market economy political forces – reversing gains of the last two years ... The UN Stabilization Mission in Haiti is an indispensable tool in realizing core USG [US Government] policy interests in Haiti ... It is a financial and regional security bargain for the USG.
>
> *Sanderson 2008*

The UN troops, however, have never been popular in Haiti except in some sectors of the ruling class. While most Haitians may have initially tolerated MINUSTAH as a necessary evil, it violated their most basic sense of sovereignty. Very soon the population saw MINUSTAH as an occupying force rather than a peacekeeping contingent. MINUSTAH's human rights violations in its fight against the so-called *Chimères* (violent gangs) in the slums of Port-au-Prince (Hallward 2007), its clear connections with the cholera epidemics (Higgins 2012; peacekeeper troops from Nepal proved to be the source) and its soldiers' rape of a young Haitian exacerbated its already tense relations with the local population. Most Haitians shared the feeling of fishermen in the town of Abricots who likened MINUSTAH to the lionfish that have invaded Haitian waters and depleted them of other fish species: "li gen anpil koule e li dezod anpil" – they have many colors and they are extremely destructive.[2]

In fact, nationalistic sentiments and unfulfilled foreign promises of rebuilding the country (Edmonds 2012; Lundahl 2013:250-265) have nurtured an increasingly powerful disenchantment with the international community as a whole. While the programs of reconstruction elaborated by the International Financial Institutions in the aftermath of January 12 have paid lip service to agricultural renewal, economic decentralization, and building state capacity, in reality, they are "old wine in new bottles." These programs continue to privilege the development of both the assembly industry sector because of Haiti's ultra-cheap labor, and agricultural exports, principally mangoes and coffee. In fact, they echo the failed policies of the late 1970s and early 1980s.

The post-earthquake strategies of reconstruction are likely to accentuate rural migrations to urban areas, which will not provide the employment and wages required to avoid the further expansion of slums. Haiti, as it were, is on its way "back to the future." The Western powers and financial institutions funding Haiti's developmental project continue to reject, however, anything departing from the neoliberal model as unrealistic and misguided.

Mats Lundahl, a leading scholar on the political economy of the country, offers a forceful defense of the neoliberal mode of industrialization advocated by these powers. He contends that Haiti has to submit to the discipline of world market prices and take advantage of its cheap labor to engage in production for export, which at this time implies the apparel industry. Lundahl views this strategy as the only viable option (Lundahl 2013: xxiv, 284, 341). He rejects as "utopian" any plan that would privilege the development of agriculture and food sovereignty (283).

Moreover, in Lundahl's view, giving priority to agriculture leads not only to poor economic outcomes; it is also impractical given extreme soil erosion, high man-land ratio and the lack of an effective titling system. He approvingly quotes Uli Locher, who bluntly asserted in his study of land distribution, tenure and erosion that "rural Haiti as we know it is doomed" (Lundahl 2013: 277). In addition, Lundahl contends that feeding Haitians through Haitian agriculture is not feasible: "Increasing food production simply contributes to soil destruction, to 'mining' the soil ... For the process to be reversed, the man-land ratio must decrease, not increase" (277).

Not surprisingly, Lundahl argues that reducing the rural population can only be achieved by creating employment "elsewhere, in the context of an open economy, and then there is only one viable alternative: the manufacturing sector, apparel production, where Haiti has a comparative advantage in terms of wages and privileged access to the American market" (xxiv).

The problem with Lundahl's argument is that the neoliberal strategy he espouses had already been tried by Jean-Claude Duvalier and had failed. Industrialization stagnated, corruption soared, agriculture declined and there was a massive increase in slums. Lundahl offers no reason to believe that this would work any better a second time.

It would make much more sense to promote agriculture. Even Bill Clinton said so when he was the Special Envoy of the United Nations to Haiti (Clinton 2010):

> Since 1981, the United States has followed a policy, until the last year or so when we started rethinking it, that we rich countries that produce a lot of food should sell it to poor countries and relieve them of the burden of producing their own food, so, thank goodness, they can leap directly into the industrial era. It has not worked. It may have been good for some of my farmers in Arkansas, but it has not worked. It was a mistake. It was a mistake that I was a party to. I am not pointing the finger at anybody. I did that. I have to live every day with the consequences of the lost capacity to produce a rice crop in Haiti to feed those people, because of what I did. Nobody else

Clinton's policies contributed to transforming Haiti into one of the countries with the most open trade regime (International Monetary Fund 1999), which resulted in the massive reliance on imported food and the total neglect of agriculture. Oxfam has pointed out the IMF forced Haiti to cut its rice tariff from 35 percent to 3 percent in 1995, leading to imports increasing by more than 150 percent in 1994–2003. Today, three-quarters of all rice eaten in Haiti comes from the United States. Oxfam claims American rice exporters have benefited, with the profits of Riceland Foods of Arkansas, the biggest rice mill in the world, jumping by $123m from 2002 to 2003. This was the result of a 50 percent increase in exports, primarily to Haiti and Cuba. The effects on Haiti have been grim since its rice-growing areas now have some of the highest levels of malnutrition and poverty in the world (Oxfam 2005: 3; see also, Georges 2004).

The neglect of rural areas was clearly reflected in the 2007 budget of the Ministry of Agriculture, which was a measly $1.5 million, a figure that contrasts sharply with the $69 million spent on the UN World Food Program (WFP). The Haiti Support Group deplores the lack of investment in farming in Haiti. It points out that agriculture has been a stable economic base which has always accounted for at least 25 percent of the country's GDP and employed more than 50 percent of its working population. Sadly, in 2012, farming received only 6 percent of the national budget (Haiti Briefing 2012: 1–2). Sadly, in 2012, farming received only 6 percent of the national budget (Haiti Briefing 2012: 1–2).

Thus, instead of reconstructing its rural sector and promoting domestic food production, Haiti has remained a country of malnourished and hungry people alarmingly dependent on external charity and at the mercy of the weather. The Haiti Support Group describes the country's declining food security and catastrophic agricultural decline:

> Haiti, considered very food secure just 30 years ago, now has the third worst level of hunger in the world, according to the current Global Hunger Index (GHI). Haiti's status is considered "extremely alarming," with 57% of the population under-nourished and 18.9% of children under 5 underweight, the key factor in a mortality rate of 16.5% amongst this group.
>
> *Haiti Briefing 2012: 1*

There is every reason to believe that giving priority to the modernization of the countryside and domestic food production would alleviate poverty and equalize life chances. In fact, the launching of a coherent agrarian reform, a transition to higher tariffs on imported agricultural goods and a public plan of re-forestation would do more to employ, feed and equalize life chances of Haitians than any neoliberal industrialization based on cheap labor and uncertain foreign demands for apparel. On the contrary, what is utopian is to believe that after investing the bulk of scarce resources in the apparel industry for more than three decades, it can now miraculously generate the virtuous cycle of development that it has consistently failed to deliver.

Haiti: making of an outer periphery **43**

The Haitian state's incapacity to confront the country's problems is caused by both the domestic political crises and the foreign intrusions that have marked the island's history. The intersection of dominant internal forces and the world economy has made Haiti a full member of the outer-periphery with all the consequences that this entails.

I have proposed the concept of the outer-periphery to help understand Haiti's plight. Yet the outer-periphery is clearly not restricted to the "poorest nation in the Western Hemisphere." The outer-periphery comprises more than a dozen other nations in which the evisceration of state capacity is pervasive, zero-sum politics dominant, life-chances deeply unequal and sovereignty virtually non-existent. The list includes nations such as Somalia, South Sudan and Guinea. Unlike the conventional wisdom, these pathologies are externally induced rather than internally determined. This is not to say that local structures, history and culture are unimportant, but rather that they have been overshadowed by the power of foreign interventions. Imperialist logic compels governments of all ideologies to devise policies that protect the interests of global capital from democracy. Domestic choices are constrained by the power of global capital.

Haiti is a paradigmatic case of how constant imperial intrusions generate catastrophic outcomes. Stuck in the margins of the global economy, starved of direct foreign investments and compelled to engage in ultra-cheap labor activities for exports, the country is at the farthest end of the global production process, trapped in the outer periphery. It has come under the control of NGOs. It lacks the bureaucratic apparatus to execute basic policies. The earthquake exacerbated these conditions and led to further imperial control. My concept of outer-periphery thus opposes the dominant theory of "failed" states. For instance, Paul Collier has argued that countries like Haiti are failing because they are stuck in "the conflict trap, the natural resource trap, the trap of being landlocked with bad neighbors, and the trap of bad governance in a small country" (Collier 2007: 5). While these traps may impede economic growth, they ignore the consequences that a subordinate position in the world system entails. By ignoring the destructive interferences of hegemonic powers into the outer-periphery, "failed state" theorists are blind to the realities of imperial politics and the devastating effects of future interventions.

This interventionism, in Collier's view, "has to do much more to strengthen the hand" of local "reformers" chosen by a self-appointed international community to implement the neoliberal policies that have paradoxically caused the current crisis. Collier argues self-righteously that the international community "has to learn to be comfortable with infringing upon sovereignty" (Collier 2007: 178).

In reality, however, it is this very type of infringement that has undermined Haiti's capacity to deal with its own problems. In the past forty years, the international community and its neoliberal policies have contributed significantly to the emasculation of the Haitian state. This emasculation became clear when the government of President Préval stood completely helpless in the face of the devastation caused by the quake of 2010; it had neither the institutional capacity nor the resources to deal with the catastrophe. Once more, the country was turned into a "laboratory" for humanitarian assistance and worldwide charity. The laboratory is the result of a pattern of decades-long interventionism in Haiti by major world powers – particularly the United States and France – and international organizations. In fact, the most significant moments in the last 30 years of Haiti's history would not have occurred had it not been for a long history of some form of imperial interventionism in its internal affairs, such as the US occupation of 1915–1934.

This interventionism has involved covert support for coups, embargoes, outright military occupation and heavy-handed "humanitarianism" (Farmer, Gardner and Van Der Hoof Holstein 2011). Orchestrated elections have also deeply reflected imperial interests. President Aristide's return to power in 1994 and subsequent forced departure ten years later, would have been impossible without the massive intrusion of the United States, France and Canada (Dupuy 2007; Fatton 2002). More recently, the election of Michel Martelly shows similar influence (Weisbrot and Johnston 2011; Johnston and Weisbrot 2011).

In fact, Martelly himself acknowledged in October of 2012 that his presidency was in essence "coup-proof" precisely because he is the man of the international community. In an interview on the French cable television station, France 24, Martelly declared: "Today, there is this peacekeeping unit maintaining order, this force of the United Nations, the international community that watches over Haiti … Even if there were a coup d'état against my government, I think it would not be tolerated" (Perelman 2012 [my translation]; see also Olivier 2012).

The confluence in Haiti of imperialism and a comprador elite (which occupies a subordinate but mutually advantageous relationship with foreign capital) undercuts the patronizing label of "failed state." The Fund for Peace dubiously explains state evisceration, economic decline, social conflicts and political instability by invoking Haitian mismanagement, corruption and culture. It is as if the unbroken pattern of imperial interventions in Haiti had nothing to do with the country's massive failures. But contrary to the Fund for Peace explanation, the country's dire condition is the product of the inter-related local and global political economies that reproduce the disparities of power of the world-system.

Thus, the structures of the global economy impose strict limitations on what Haitian rulers can achieve. Haiti is not helpless, however. Haiti has diplomatic options it has used, notably with Cuba and Venezuela. The United States strongly opposed the further development of Haitian relations with Havana and Caracas. Between 2006 and 2008, the United States had sought to block, and then undermine, the PetroCaribe agreement that would have allowed Haiti to buy subsidized oil from Venezuela (Coughlin and Ives 2011), even though the American Embassy acknowledged that it "would save [Haiti] USD 100 million per year" (ibid.). Janet Sanderson, the American Ambassador, warned Préval and his senior advisers that "a deal with Chavez would cause problems with us." She cautioned them against "the larger negative message that [the PetroCaribe deal] would send to the international community at a time when the GOH [Government of Haiti] is trying to increase foreign investment" (ibid.). Ultimately, the Préval administration defied the United States and implemented the PetroCaribe plan.

Moreover, to the dismay of Ambassador Sanderson, Préval decided to attend as a "special observer" the summit of the Bolivarian Alternative for the Americas (ALBA) in Venezuela. He went for the express purpose of finalizing a tri-lateral assistance agreement between Haiti, Venezuela and Cuba (Coughlin and Ives 2011). Not surprisingly, Préval's determination to defend Haiti's national interest contributed to the deterioration of his relations with the United States. Ambassador Sanderson lamented that Haitian officials did not understand that the United States was not willing to tolerate a greater regional role for Venezuela and Cuba (ibid.).

In spite of continued American misgivings, Haiti under President Martelly seems determined to follow Préval's friendly foreign policy towards both Havana and Caracas. This policy is more than just a matter of establishing some independence from Washington; it responds to the simple reality that unlike other foreign donors, Venezuela is willing to provide foreign assistance to the Haitian state itself instead of privileging NGO-led development. Whatever may be their ideological differences, Haitians have realized that the results of some 40 years of NGO-led development have been at best meagre. They agree with the analysis of Ricardo Seitenfus, the former OAS special representative in Haiti, when he denounced donors and NGOs for their own corruption and lack of transparency. Seitenfus condemns the placement of vast amounts of money in the hands of the NGOs without social control, transparency or government management. In his view, anti-corruption campaigns are fatuous when they refer to governments that have no money with which to be corrupt. Seitenfus argues (Elizondo 2011):

> We cannot demand from Haiti what we do not demand for ourselves ... All projects that come in to Haiti that weaken even more the weak Haitian state should be discarded ... We cannot make of Haiti a "Disneyland" of the NGOs.

While Haitian rulers have been able to create a limited space of diplomatic autonomy from the United States by forging special relations with Cuba and Venezuela, the constraints imposed by the capitalist world economy on their economic policies are very real and obdurate. This is especially so in an outer-peripheral country like Haiti whose state is not only under siege, but lacks the means to exercise effective sovereignty over its territory. The irony of the dominant and current political science literature is that it has sanctified the concept of the "failed state" on the basis of twelve key indicators that primarily measure internal conditions (The Fund for Peace 2012; see also: Brock et al. 2012). In the reigning analytical perspective, failed states are the creatures of backward domestic political economies that have to be rescued from themselves by foreign interventions. Thus, according to the failed state paradigm, when societies are acutely dependent on foreign assistance and reliant on external peacekeeping operations, it is because of their own internal incapacity to provide material well-being and security for their citizens. That these societies' domestic incapacity might instead be the product of pervasive interferences and manipulations of their political economy by neoimperial powers is never considered.

Instead, in the name of a fictional cosmopolitanism, failed state theorists advocate humanitarian militarism, neoliberal rationality and non-governmental governance as the solution to the problems plaguing the outer-periphery. It is this context that explains the emergence of the concept of the "responsibility to protect," known by its acronym R2P.

R2P is the product of the final report of the International Commission on Intervention and State Sovereignty, which supported the international community's right to intervene forcefully into the internal affairs of a nation-state that violated the basic rights of its citizens (International Commission on Intervention and State Sovereignty 2001; see also, Evans 2008). In that sense, sovereignty is not absolute; it becomes contingent on a state's capacity to protect the human rights of its people. While more than 150 governments at the 2005 United Nations World Summit endorsed R2P, it has a distinctively Western liberal ethos. Moreover, in practice, it can be set in motion only if the major powers so desire. To that extent, R2P is evocative of colonial conquests rooted in Western imperial claims of moral superiority. In fact, as John M. Hobson has pointed out, it is "reminiscent of the nineteenth century 'white man's burden,' requiring not just Western paternalist intervention to rescue Eastern victims, but a subsequent reconstruction of the state along Western lines. In this way R2P reconvenes the conception of Western hyper-sovereignty and conditional Eastern sovereignty" (Hobson 2012).

R2P gives Western powers a license to intervene in the domestic policies of the outer-periphery. It gives juridical backing to old and crude patterns of "regime change," placing strategic considerations above moral principles. Moreover, R2P advocates ignore the historical realities that generated the so-called "failed states" in the first place. It was Western colonialism and the collusion between international organizations, major powers and domestic elites that contributed to the decay of such states (Young 1994) – including Haiti. "Failed state" theorists ignore this history and praise a new imperialism that will miraculously rescue "failed states" from their predicament. I argue instead that this new imperialism is the same as the old imperialism and will have devastating effects on the outer-periphery.

The outer-periphery suffers from acute deprivation and insecurity. Haitians are exposed to violence, policies over which they have no control, imported diseases, foreign occupation as well as to the humiliations of governmental beggarhood (Caple James 2010).

Haitians, however, are not merely resilient in the face of hardship, or resigned in the face of oppression. At its best, the Haitian character embodies a recurring fight for freedom, as evidenced after the world's only successful black revolution against slavery, as well as the successive revolts against foreign occupations and dictatorships. If Haitians are to alter the present trajectory of their country and build a better tomorrow, they must rekindle this spirit of resistance and defiance. Haiti's so-called "international partners" will not change course on behalf of the island nation, because their interests, as the outer-peripheral model makes clear, are too well-served by existing neoliberal policies. In 1804, at a time of unchallenged white supremacy, Haitians did the "unthinkable" (Trouillot 1995). Against all odds, they freed themselves from slavery and created the first independent black republic. Perhaps once more, Haitians will muster the courage and energy to bend seemingly unshakable global structures and begin their long march away from the outer-periphery. Somehow, they must reclaim their capacity to make their own history on their own terms.

References

Abiu Lopez, Ezequiel and Danica Coto. 2013. "Dominican Ruling Strips Many of Citizenship." Associated Press, September 26.
Agence France Presse. 2013. "La République dominicaine 'dénationalise' des milliers d'Haïtiens." *France 24*, October 3. Available at: www.france24.com/fr/20131003-haiti-republique-dominicaine-nationalite-dechenace-transit-immigrants/
Agence Presse Média Caraibes. 2013. "La balance commerciale reste encore trop déséquilibrée entre Haïti et la République dominicaine." Agence Presse Média Caraibes, February 8. Available at: www.maximini.com/fr/news/haiti/economie/-la-balance-commerciale-reste-encore-trop-desequilibree-entre-haiti-et-la-republique-dominicaine--21005.html
Amin, Samir. 1974. *Accumulation on a World Scale*, 2 Volumes. New York: Monthly Review Press.
Antonini, Blanca. 2012. *Relations between Haiti and the Dominican Republic*. Oslo: Norwegian Peacebuilding Resource Centre.
Balibar, Etienne and Immanuel Wallerstein. 1991. *Race, Nation, Class*. New York: Verso.
Baran, Paul. 1957. *The Political Economy of Growth*. New York: Monthly Review Press.
Bell, Lis. 2013. "Rép. Dominicaine: La 'dénationalisation' des Dominicains d'origine haïtienne planifiée par le PLD et la FNP depuis 2008." *AlterPresse*, December 9. Available at: www.alterpresse.org/spip.php?article15624#.Uv2Xgv2_20s
Brock, Lothar, Hans-Henrik Holm, Georg Sorensen and Michael Stohl. 2012. *Fragile States*. Cambridge: Polity Press.
Caple James, Erica. 2010. *Democratic Insecurities*. Berkeley, CA: University of California Press.
Collier, Paul. 2009. *Haiti: From Natural Catastrophe to Economic Security: A Report for the Secretary-General of the United Nations*. Oxford University Department of Economics.
——2007. *The Bottom Billion*. Oxford: Oxford University Press.
Clinton, William Jefferson. 2010. "Testimony, Building on Success: New Directions in Global Health." *US Senate Committee on Foreign Relations*, March 10. Available at: www.foreign.senate.gov/hearings/hearing/?id=3f546a93-d363-da0b-b25f-f1c5d096ddb1
Coughlin, Dan and Kim Ives. 2011. "WikiLeaks Haiti: The PetroCaribe Files." *The Nation*, June 1. Available at: www.thenation.com/article/161056/wikileaks-haiti-petrocaribe-files?page=0,0
Crane, Keith. 2010. *Building a More Resilient Haitian State*. Santa Monica, CA: Rand Corporation.
Dubois, Laurent. 2012. *Haiti, The Aftershocks of History*. New York: Metropolitan Books.
Duffield, Mark. 2007. *Development, Security and Unending War*. Cambridge: Polity Press.
Dupuy, Alex. 2007. *The Prophet and Power*. Lanham, MD: Rowman & Littlefield Publishers.
Edmonds, Kevin. 2012. "MINUSTAH's Upcoming Renewal: A Setback for Democracy in Haiti." *NACLA*, October 11. Available at: http://nacla.org/blog/2012/10/11/minustah's-upcoming-renewal-setback-democracy-haiti

Elizondo, Gabriel. 2011. "An Insider's Critique of What Went Wrong in Haiti." *Al Jazeera*, January 8. Available at: http://blogs.aljazeera.com/blog/americas/insiders-critique-what-went-wrong-haiti

Evans, Gareth. 2008. *The Responsibility to Protect: Ending Mass Atrocity Crimes Once and For All*. Washington, DC: Brookings Institution.

Fanon, Frantz. 1968. *The Wretched of the Earth*. New York: Grove Press.

Farmer, Paul, Abbey Gardner and Cassia Van Der Hoof Holstein. 2011. *Haiti After the Earthquake*. New York: Public Affairs.

Fatton, Robert, Jr. 2014. *Haiti: Trapped in the Outer Periphery*. Boulder, CO: Lynne Rienner Publishers.

——2002. *Haiti's Predatory Republic*. Boulder, CO: Lynne Rienner Publishers. Ferguson, James. 2006. *Global Shadows*. Durham, NC: Duke University Press.

Frank, Andre Gunder. 1967. *Capitalism and Underdevelopment in Latin America*. New York: Monthly Review Press.

Geffrard, Robenson. 2013. "Réunions des Bailleurs de Fonds: Le CAED pour Redéfinir l'Aide Internationale." *Le Nouvelliste*, May 9. Available at: http://lenouvelliste.com/lenouvelliste/article/116609/Le-CAED-pour-redefinir-laide-internationale.html

Georges, Josiane. 2004. "Trade and the Disappearance of Haitian Rice." TED Case Studies Number 725. Available at: http://www1.american.edu/ted/haitirice.htm

Groupe d'Appui aux Rapatriés et Réfugiés (GARR). 2014a. "Position de la Plateforme GARR autour du dossier de la dénationalisation des Dominicains/Dominicaines d'ascendance haïtienne." January 31. Available at: http://reliefweb.int/report/dominican-republic/position-de-la-plateforme-garr-autour-du-dossier-de-la-d-nationalisation

——2014b. "Le GARR se prononce sur la déclaration de la 2ème rencontre binationale entre Haïti et la République Dominicaine Spécial." February 5. Available at: http://reliefweb.int/report/dominican-republic/le-garr-se-prononce-sur-la-d-claration-de-la-2-me-rencontre-binationale

——2014c. "Rencontre haïtiano-dominicaine à Jimani : Le respect des droits humains serait-il troqué au profit des intérêts politiques et économiques ?" February 12. Available at: http://reliefweb.int/report/dominican-republic/rencontre-ha-tiano-dominicaine-jimani-le-respect-des-droits-humains-serait

Haiti Briefing. 2012. "Disastrous Food Policy Bites Hands that Feed: Haiti's Hunger Games." *Haiti Support Group* 72: October.

Haiti Libre. 2010. "Haïti - CIRH : Liste officielle et complète de tous les représentants." June 18. Available at: www.haitilibre.com/article-390-haiti-cirh-liste-officielle-et-complete-de-tous-les-representants.html

Hallward, Peter. 2007. *Damming the Flood: Haiti, Aristide, and the Politics of Containment*. New York: Verso.

Harvey, David. 2005. *A Brief History of Neoliberalism*. Oxford: Oxford University Press.

Higgins, Michael. 2012. "UN Peacekeepers to Blame for 7,500 Cholera Deaths in Devastated Haiti: Public Health Expert." *National Post*, October 24. Available at: http://news.nationalpost.com/2012/10/24/haiti-cholera-that-has-killed-7500-blamed-on-un-troops-from-nepal/

Hobson, John M. 2012. *The Eurocentric Conception of World Politics*. Cambridge: Cambridge University Press.

Huntington, Samuel. 1996. *The Clash of Civilizations and the Remaking of World Order*. New York: Simon and Schuster.

Interim Haiti Recovery Commission (IHRC). 2010. *By Laws*. Available at: http://en.cirh.ht/about-us.html

International Commission on Intervention and State Sovereignty. 2001. *The Responsibility to Protect*. Ottawa: International Development Research Centre.
International Monetary Fund. 1999. *Haiti Staff Report*. Washington, DC: International Monetary Fund.
Johnston, Jake. 2014. "Outsourcing Haiti: How Disaster Relief Became a Disaster of its Own." *Boston Review*, January 17. Available at: www.bostonreview.net/world/jake-johnston-haiti-earthquake-aid-caracol
Johnston, Jake and Mark Weisbrot. 2011. *Haiti's Fatally Flawed Election*. Washington, DC: Center for Economic and Policy Research.
Kapuscinski, Ryszard. 2008. *The Other*. London: Verso.
Katz, Jonathan M. 2013. *The Big Truck that Went By: How the World Came to Save Haiti and Left Behind a Disaster*. New York: Palgrave MacMillan.
Lundahl, Mats. 2013. *The Political Economy of Disaster*. London: Routledge.
Mendoza, Martha and Trenton Daniel. 2012. "US Pledge to Rebuild Haiti Not Being Met." *Associated Press*, July 21. Available at: http://news.yahoo.com/us-pledge-rebuild-haiti-not-being-met-170346036.html
Michel, Carlin. 2012. "Le CAED Remplace la CIRH, des Organisations sont à l'Avant Garde." *Le Nouvelliste*, November 29. Available at: http://lenouvelliste.com/lenouvelliste/article/111227/Le-CAED-remplace-la-CIRH-des-organisations-sont-a-lavant-garde.html
Mills, Cheryl. 2010. "Concept Note: Haiti Development Authority." Unpublished Document. Washington, DC: United States Department of State.
Olivier, Djems. 2012. "Haïti-Politique: Martelly s'Estime à l'Abri des Coups d'Etat, La communauté internationale 'Veille' sur le Pays, dit le Président." *AterPresse*, November 1. Available at: www.alterpresse.org/spip.php?article13624
Oxfam. 2014. "Working for the Few." Oxfam Briefing Paper No. 178. Oxford: Oxfam International.
——2005. "Kicking Down the Door: How Upcoming WTO Talks Threaten Farmers in Poor Countries." Oxfam Briefing Paper No. 72. Oxford: Oxfam International. Perelman, Marc. 2012. "L'Entretien: Michel Martelly, Président Haïtien." *France 24*, October 29. Available at: www.france24.com/fr/20121027-2012-lentretien-michel-martelly-president-haiti-seisme-crise-alimentaireeconomique
Ramachandran, Vijaya and Julie Walz. 2012. "Haiti: Where Has All the Money Gone?" Policy Paper No. 004. Washington, DC: Center for Global Development. Available at: www.cgdev.org/content/publications/detail/1426185
Said, Edward. 1978. *Orientalism*, New York: Random House.
Sanderson, Janet. 2008. "Why we Need Continuing MINUSTAH Presence in Haiti." Cable from US Ambassador to Haiti, October 1. Available at: http://wikileaks.org/cable/2008/10/08PORTAUPRINCE1381.html
Schuller, Mark. 2012. *Killing with Kindness: Haiti, International Aid, and NGOs*. New Brunswick, NJ: Rutgers University Press.
Schuller, Mark and Pablo Morales. 2012. *Tectonic Shifts*. Sterling, VA: Kumarian Press.
Schwartz, Timothy T. 2010. *Travesty in Haiti*. Lexington, KY: BookSurge Publishing.
Shah, Anup. 2013. "Poverty Facts and Stats." *Global Issues: Social, Political, Economic and Environmental Issues that Affect us All*, January 7. Available at: www.globalissues.org/article/26/poverty-facts-and-stats
Smith, Terence. 1969. "Beret Case Details Reported in Saigon." *The New York Times*, August 14.
The Fund for Peace. 2012. *Failed State Index*. Washington, DC: The Fund for Peace. Available at: www.fundforpeace.org/global/library/cfsir1210-failedstatesindex2012-06p.pdf

Trouillot, Michel-Rolph. 1995. *Silencing the Past: Power and the Production of History*. Boston, MA: Beacon Press.
United Nations. 2011. "Has Aid Changed? Channeling Assistance to Haiti Before and After the Quake." New York: United Nations Office of the Special Envoy for Haiti.
US State Department. 2011. "Fast Facts on US Government's Work in Haiti: Interim Haiti Recovery Commission." Factsheet, January 8. Available at: www.state.gov/p/wha/rls/fs/2011/154141.htm
Wallerstein, Immanuel. 2006. *European Universalism: The Rhetoric of Power*. New York: The New Press.
——2004. *World-Systems Analysis*. Durham, NC: Duke University Press.
——1979. *The Capitalist World-Economy*. Cambridge: Cambridge University Press.
Weisbrot, Mark and Jake Johnston. 2011. "Analysis of the OAS Mission's Draft Report on Haiti's Election." *Center for Economic Research, Issue Brief*, February 1. Available at: http://fr.scribd.com/doc/47037329/Analysis-of-the-OAS-Mission's-Draft-Final-Report-on-Haiti's-Election
Worker Rights Consortium. 2013. *Stealing from the Poor: Wage Theft in the Haitian Apparel Industry*. October 15. Available at: www.workersrights.org/freports/WRC%20Haiti%20Minimum%20Wage%20Report%2010%2015%2013.pdf
Young, Crawford. 1994. *The African Colonial State in Comparative Perspective*. New Haven, CT: Yale University Press.

Notes

1   Some parts of this paper are excerpted from *Haiti: Trapped in the Outer Periphery* by Robert Fatton Jr. Copyright © 2014 by Lynne Rienner Publishers. Used with permission of the publisher.
2   Jessica Hsu, personal communication, October 9, 2011.

3
WHY CUTTING TAXES DOES NOT INCREASE EMPLOYMENT
Or why shrinking the state does not provide compensating economic development

Samuel Cohn

Many nations today face a political debate between a right that wants to cut taxes and a left for whom this is a lesser priority. The right and the left also disagree about the size of government. The right wants to shrink big government. The left, generally on the defensive, is trying to maintain traditional levels of government services in areas such as supporting education, providing a social safety net for the distressed and building infrastructure. Conservatives justify their position intellectually on the grounds that cutting taxes stimulates long-term economic growth and creates jobs. Liberals are more skeptical of this position. They see tax cuts as a thinly veiled attempt to increase the incomes of wealthy corporations and rich individuals since under most tax reduction plans, it is these groups that see the largest reductions in their tax bills. The average voter is indifferent to the question of whether the top 1 percent gets more or less money, since this does not have that much of an effect on the daily life of normal people. However, the average voter cares passionately about the creation of jobs, since unemployment is a very real issue for lots of people.

So the public debate on this issue generally focuses on the relationship between government provision of tax cuts and the creation of jobs. The right says that tax cuts create jobs. The left says … *nothing about the relationship between taxes and jobs whatsoever (!!!)* … and then tries to defend the government programs that are in danger of being cut. In other words, when the conservatives claim that the evidence shows that reducing taxes helps to create employment, the liberals roll over and play dead. By their silence, they implicitly agree with the conservative position. This is basically an all-out intellectual surrender.

Surrender is perfectly reasonable when the data support the position of the opposite side. Surrender is lunacy when the opposite side does not have a defensible position. Unfortunately, the logic and evidence for the argument that cutting taxes creates economic growth and jobs is tenuous at best and shows the opposite at worst. Most of the literature on the subject – both in traditional economics and in the sociology of development – argues that tax cuts have *no* effect on aggregate employment and in fact, that the only observable consequence of reducing tax rates is to reduce the money available to the government programs that actually *do* have an effect on creating jobs.

This chapter is a review of the literature on taxes and employment. Some of the research and a few of the more minor arguments are my own. However, most of the case made here has been made by other scholars. Since most development sociology scholars and students have not seen this material, I bring those materials together here in a generally accessible form.

The case for tax cuts

The case for lowering taxes is intuitive.

1. Employers hire more workers when their firms are growing and profitable.
2. Taxation raises employers' costs.
3. High costs reduce the amount of money employers have to invest.
4. Less investment means fewer jobs both now and in the future.

You can find basic statements of this position in McBride (2012), Barro and Redlick (2011) and Rabushka and Bartlett (1985).

It is possible to make more elaborate versions of this argument. High US corporate income taxes induce American companies to invest overseas and discourage foreign companies from investing in the United States (Schuyler 2013; Hines 2001). Taxes on profits decrease the incentive of corporations and individuals to save because their investments will be worth less. Because companies make less money, both stocks and bonds become less attractive options, reducing overall incentives to invest (Mitchell 1999). Taxes can reduce "predictability" because tax levels might change (Fichtner and Christ 2010). Strangely, the predictability argument is rarely invoked to oppose tax cuts – merely tax increases.

It is possible to object to exactly what gets taxed.

Q   Would you like to tax the revenues of web-based retail companies such as Amazon?

You can't tax the Internet! It is the secret of American competitiveness! Amazon won't be able to create jobs!

Q   Would you like to tax the proceeds of financial transactions?

You can't tax the financial sector! It will hurt Wall Street relative to the City of London and Zurich and banks won't be able to create jobs!

Q   Would you like to use payroll taxes – taxes that employers pay on the salaries of workers and which appear as "deductions" on a worker's paycheck (used

to finance Social Security and Workman's Compensation) ?
Payroll taxes tax employers for creating jobs!

Q   Would you like to tax capital gains?
Capital gains taxes tax savers for investing which makes jobs!

Many of these arguments sound nice in theory; however all of this assumes taxation really reduces jobs. Is that in fact actually the case?

The case against tax cuts

I

Consider the following two stories: one from Morocco, the other from the United States.

Currie and Harrison (1997) looked at a set of wealthy, well connected firms in Morocco. These companies were facing a substantial tax increase. This tax increase came from a neoliberal reform in Morocco that was forcing the government to balance its books by taxing whatever sources of revenue they could get – in this case proceeds from local big business. The companies had the money to pay but they were not enthusiastic about having their profit margins reduced. Their response was to invest heavily in new machinery, management consulting and a re-engineering of the shop-floor. The plan was to increase their competitiveness, efficiency and product quality so that they could get more revenues from local and international sales. The new investments were phenomenally successful and the companies were far more profitable than they had ever been before. They were able to pay the taxes with ample money left over, funds that were used to increase production and create more jobs. In this case, the tax increase was the wake-up call that induced management to move their engineering and business practices to the next level. The companies responded to a tax not by cutting jobs – but by investing more in order to maintain their original rate of profit. This created more jobs in the longer run.

Vroman (1967) tells a similar story for American firms in the 1960s. He studied American corporations that were faced with increases in their payroll taxes. Few of them cut employment. The more typical response was to raise prices in response to the new taxes. Revenues stayed roughly the same; employment stayed roughly the same.

This story is slightly out of date, which in this case is a plus rather than a minus. Vroman's story takes place in the 1960s. These were the glory years for American manufacturing. The economy was booming. American automobile and steel companies faced almost no foreign competition. Japan was still putting the finishing touches on its knowledge about how to manufacture automobiles – although Japanese cars would show up later in the decade. The foreign car Americans bought was the VW Beetle, which in those days was (and still is) a terrible car. So

Americans could sell all the cars they wanted at whatever price they wanted. Somebody taxes a company? Jack up the prices of the goods! Customers paid more, but profits and employment were just fine.

The Moroccan firms and American firms in these studies were pretty well off; we will consider today's environment of global competition and struggling companies later in the chapter. But for now, think about how these wealthy firms responded to taxation. They did not shut down. They did not go overseas. They did not lay off workers. They did not lose money. They invested more if they were in a competitive market (as the Moroccans were) or raised prices if they were in a protected position (as the Americans were). Investment and price increases were alternative responses to new taxes.

What is being described here is the real-life equivalent of how economists treat tax matters in the literature on public finance. What follows is the theoretical argument from Musgrave's classic 1959 textbook on the *Theory of Public Finance* and Joseph Stiglitz's work on taxation that earned him the Nobel Prize (Stiglitz 1988). Both Musgrave and Stiglitz argue that there are two possible employer responses to a tax increase, an "income" effect and a "substitution" effect. Those names come from basic terms in microeconomics (Mankiw 2014). In the substitution effect, when an employer has to pay a higher tax in Business A, he pulls his money out of Business A and puts it into Business B. Business A shrinks as a result. In the income effect, the employer tries to maintain his original income and profitability in Business A. He increases his investment in resources in Business A to compensate for the taxes. This is what we saw in the two previous case studies. Musgrave and Stiglitz argue that it is impossible to know which will be dominant – the income effect or the substitution effect. Therefore, the effects of taxes on employment is indeterminate.

II

Consider the two following facts.

(1) Some very large American companies paid no Federal taxes whatsoever between 2008 and 2012. These include General Electric, Verizon, Boeing, Priceline, MetroPCS and a number of very large energy companies such as Duke Energy and Consolidated Edison (*Huffington Post* 2014). None of this is illegal, or if one wants to be political, particularly immoral. Congress has passed laws explicitly allowing corporations to take deductions for various expenses of doing their business. Those fully sanctioned deductions lower the legal tax rate qualifying companies have to pay.

(2) Tax evasion is widespread in many countries. Many firms simply pay no taxes whatsoever. They do so by not registering with the tax authorities, so the officials don't know that their company exists at all. If need be, business people bribe the appropriate authorities to keep the company off the tax

rolls. These clandestine firms are known as the *informal economy* or the *shadow economy* (Portes et. al. 1989). The size of the shadow economy is massive. Two Turkish economists have estimated the size of the shadow economy for most of the nations in the world. In most poorer nations, the figure is pretty high: 41 percent of Albania's economy is informal, in El Salvador this figure is 43 percent and in Haiti 57 percent (Elgin and Oztunali 2012). Of course, all of this tax evasion is completely illegal; however, that does not stop it from happening.

The lesson here is that high tax rates do not necessarily translate into high tax burdens for corporations. Companies can avoid paying taxes, regardless of the nominal rates. If companies pay only a fraction of the tax rates on the books, then cutting those rates will have a diminished effect on boosting employment. This is one reason why the claims that American employment is hurt by the United States having a higher corporate tax rate than other nations should be viewed with some skepticism. One can only know the true tax burden after one adjusts for deductions and evasion. Evasion is low in the American system, but deductions are high.

III

Do tax cuts help to keep American jobs from going overseas? Let us consider the case of the Bush tax cuts. George W. Bush passed two significant tax cuts during his presidency: the 2001 Economic Growth and Tax Relief Reconciliation Act and the 2003 Jobs and Growth Tax Relief Reconciliation Act. What happened after these cuts?

The Congressional Research Service found that after the tax cuts of 2001 and 2003, American investment overseas rose dramatically. The flow of foreign investment in the United States was far less than that of American investment going overseas. So the tax cut did not lead to a net inflow of capital (Jackson 2012).

Stranger still, more of America's post-tax-cut investment went to Europe than to any other region. Europe is an extremely high-tax environment. To be sure, nominal corporate income tax rates in Europe are generally lower than those in the United States (whether this is true after deductions is an industry-specific question). However, most of Europe's other taxes are extremely high. Europe has extremely high payroll taxes – which are used to finance their national health care systems, their job training programs and their welfare programs. Europe also has extremely high personal income tax rates. In the United States, the highest tax rate for individual tax returns is 35 percent. In Germany it is 57 percent. In France it is 60 percent. In Sweden 61 percent. In Denmark it is 66 percent. Ireland is considered to be a tax haven where you can get a break from the high rates of Continental European taxation. Their highest rate of personal income tax is only 48 percent (Trading Economics 2014) – still 13 percent higher than the US tax rates! Europeans have a hard time understanding how American Tea Party members can complain that they have the highest taxes in the world.

So, despite the government cutting corporate taxes dramatically, American companies moved money *out* of the United States into other nations. Even more against the conservative case, they moved to places with higher taxes than in the United States. Furthermore, companies in other nations were not impressed by US tax cuts. They did not move money into the United States in a volume sufficient to counteract the loss of American money. Why did the tax cuts have so little power to attract either foreign or domestic investors?

Discussions of tax policy often seem to imply a closed world in which tax cuts in America will produce jobs in America. In a globalized economy there is no guarantee that the profits obtained from tax cuts in the United States will be reinvested in the United States. Most large firms are multinational – and they allocate investments among subsidiaries around the world. Multinational resource allocation is based on far more than just tax considerations.

Labor is far cheaper in China than it is in the United States (Lin, Cai and Li 2003). Marginal tax differences will not make the United States a less expensive place to manufacture than China. Environmental regulation is far less severe in the China that it is in the United States (Fazio and Strell 2012). Marginal tax considerations will not provide a haven from the liabilities associated with toxic manufacturing processes.

Multinationals often need to locate in expanding markets with population growth and increasing propensities to consume. American markets for many products are mature. If corporations need sales over and above what American markets can provide, they will have to reach prosperous consumers overseas – which generally means Europeans and Japanese. Marginal tax considerations will not keep companies from putting their new factories and warehouses near the customers to whom they actually want to sell. A few percentage points of tax break in the United States will not make McDonald's lose interest in the profitable markets of Germany or China.

The logic of global enterprise dictates investment on a worldwide rather than a local scale. This makes it increasingly unlikely that a tax cut in the United States would produce jobs in the United States. What is the point of reducing public revenue for services provided to its own population – if the effect would be to build the economic strength of the countries that are its primary international competitors?

IV

Four stories: two from Brazil and two similar ones from the United States.

Years ago, when I was just starting my career in development sociology, I sincerely believed that big government and big taxes were the source of slow economic growth in the underdeveloped world. I was heavily under the influence of a famous pro-laissez-faire book, Hernando de Soto's *The Other Path* (1986). This book claims that corrupt officials prey on small business to get bribes for themselves – and they use high taxes as the tool to shake the businessmen down. De

Soto's argument implies that taxes are just as bad or even worse than the corruption. The reason presumably the owners are better off paying the bribe than paying the taxes is because the taxes would be higher.

Convinced that de Soto was right, I looked for an ideal test case for his theory. I needed to find a set of small struggling businesspeople who could would be highly vulnerable to arbitrary increases in their costs. The businessmen had to be poor and on the very edge of survival, so that high taxes and high payoffs would kill companies and kill jobs. I also needed a place with a big, cumbersome, nasty tax structure; with lots of taxes, the taxes being complicated and the tax rates high.

Studying taxes and small business in Brazil seemed ideal. The Brazilian tax code mandates very high tax rates – rates that are high even by Latin American standards (Pastore 1998). Of particular note is their system of sales taxes, which is not a value-added tax, rather, Brazil charges full tax on the market value of every item even if it is an intermediate good in a production chain (a value-added tax exempts what a firm paid to acquire the raw materials used to make the final product being sold). The effect of this is that unlike the rest of the world, Brazilian firms pay sales tax on the same item multiple times. This effect is known as the "cascade"; it is the subject of vehement and outspoken criticism by Brazil's anti-tax writers (Leite 1972; Martins 2004).

Brazil also has a substantial burden of payroll taxes. These include previdência (Social Security), paid vacations, holiday bonuses, provision against medical infirmity, unemployment insurance, workers compensation and union dues, vocational training, support of the small business promotion association and a thirteenth month of salary before Christmas (Campanhole and Campanhole 1983; dos Santos 1996).

I picked two sectors that I thought would be extremely vulnerable – restaurants and barber or beauty shops. These are typically small mom-and-pop operations that are often operating on negligible amounts of reserve capital. In Brazil, a cafe can be a woman with a barbecue grill, a canopy, a sound system and an ice chest, sitting in an empty lot in a slum selling shish-kebab to the neighbors. A hairdressing salon can be a woman with a beauty parlor chair in the driveway of her mother or her aunt's home. I added hotels as a contrast case. Many hotels belong to large national or international chains and are well financed – although there are also some *pousadas*: modest bed and breakfasts located in people's homes. I had data on the amount of taxes these firms actually paid. I had checked these data for reliability and found that the estimates were remarkably free of bias.

So it came as quite the shock to find that tax burdens were uncorrelated with jobs in any of the three industries. Neither payroll taxes, non-payroll taxes nor total tax burden had any effect on employment!

It turned out that taxes were a very small component of total firm costs in any of these enterprises. Other expenses of doing business were simply more important. Hotel and restaurant budgets were driven by raw material costs. Restaurants buy a lot of food; in many ways, they are simply grocery stores with a different manner of delivering the groceries. Labor and rent were also major concerns. Hotels were also driven by food expenses; their dining operations made up more than half of all expenses. Barber and beautician budgets were heavily determined by rent. Barber/beauticians use few raw materials, and rent chairs to fellow hairdressers rather than pay wages. Therefore, real estate makes up their most important cost; location matters if a hairdresser is to attract a reasonable volume of walk-up trade. Employment turned out to be sensitive to "most important strategic" costs. Taxes were not a most important strategic cost (Cohn 2012).

A second Brazil story, actually a type of story, comes from scholars who have studied business failures in Brazil, including business failures among the marginal small businesses and microenterprises such as the ones I examined. The studies are straightforward; one interviews owners of such enterprises that have died and you ask them what killed them. Almost no one in these studies mentions taxes. The most common problem faced by small businesspeople is lack of sales. The second most common is cash flow problems related to an inability to get credit. Taxes rarely make it into the top ten complaints that the Brazilian small businesspeople had. Surprisingly, this is in a nation with a particularly cumbersome and expensive tax system – and these are the most underfunded and economically vulnerable businesses (SEBRAE 2005; Durand and Rodrigues 1979).

If you study small businesses by observing them ethnographically rather than asking about their problems after they die, similar findings emerge. Schmitz (1982) studied a variety of informal, unregistered businesses in São Paulo. Informal means not paying taxes; it is a matter of speculation what would have been the effect of taxes if these firms had actually been paying. The main point here is that what was make or break for these tiny firms was access to raw materials. The big companies could buy their supplies wholesale and paid lower prices as a result. The micro-operators had to buy their inputs at retail level, making it hard for them to compete with larger established companies. The key to survival was finding some way to get raw materials at a discount. Almost nothing else mattered: labor costs, rent, insurance, whatever. Schmitz argues that taxes would have been in the irrelevant column. If the small operators could get raw materials at a good price, they could make enough money to pay taxes. If not, they weren't going to be paying any creditors, government or private.

Studies of American firms have made similar observations. Gaskill et al. (1993) interviewed owners in a large sample of failed retail stores in Iowa. Once again, the former owners reported that taxes had little to do with the failure of their business. As was the case in Brazil, insufficient sales or lack of access to credit accounted for most of the closures. In some cases, the owners confessed to managerial errors either on their own part or on the part of key employees.

Stafford (1974) showed that taxes were the *least* important of thirteen other variables that explained firms moving out of the state of Ohio. Kieschnick (1981) found that there was no statistical relation between a state's relative share of an industry and how heavily that industry was taxed in the state. He followed up his statistical analysis with interviews of corporate executives who were in charge of locating plants in one state or another. In these discussions, taxes were not a particularly important consideration. The executives listed access to customers, availability of capital, availability of skilled labor and the quality of the transportation network as being the driving factors in the choice to invest in particular states.

To be fair to the scholars who advocate tax cuts, taxes may be more important in the contemporary environment than they were historically, or even thirty or forty years ago. Some of the previous studies were done in the 1970s and 1980s – including the Kieschnick survey mentioned above. These studies examined heavy manufacturing with a lot of transportation costs. The American economy has evolved out of heavy manufacturing into services, where transportation costs are less of an issue. Firms that seek cheap labor have left the United States entirely and have relocated in Asia, Latin America and Africa were their workforces are particularly cheap. The companies that remain in the United States are relatively indifferent to labor costs and relatively indifferent to transportation costs. For these companies, their tax bill probably does make a difference.

However, this is the exception that illustrates the general point being made here. Industrial location decisions and decisions to hire workers are not just based on taxes. They are based on the full range of business considerations that owners and managers have to deal with. They have to think about nearness to market, access to skilled labor forces, the price of energy, proximity to raw materials, labor costs in general, unionization issues in particular, and even the quality of life for the managers who would be actually living in the town where the plant is to be located. Taxes may be a factor, but they are not the only issue in determining whether an employer decides to expand and create jobs. If an employer needs skilled games programmers, he or she will locate the firm in Silicon Valley, San Francisco or Boston. Those locations all have high costs and high taxes. However, if this is where the firm needs to locate to get the people it needs, the company will go there and create jobs, and just pay California or Massachusetts taxes as a cost of doing business. If high taxes were the dominant consideration in deciding to open or expand a firm, then there would be no offices or economic activity in New York City.

What about scientific statistical tests?

What does the evidence show about the relationship between taxes and economic growth? There are macro-level studies that use regression models to examine the statistically controlled relationship between taxation and growth. Such econometric studies of the economic effects of taxation are either cross-national (comparing nations at a single point in time), time-series (looking at many years of data for one nation) or time-series cross-section (comparing multiple countries with multiple years of data for each nation). One would think this would be the gold standard in testing the relationship between taxation and development – or any theory of growth: systematic data, rigorous statistical methodology, sophisticated controls for exogenous factors.

In fact, this quantitative literature is a complete morass. The number of studies that have been done examining the relationship between taxes and growth is massive. You would think that given such a large body of literature, there would be general agreement as to what that literature says. No such agreement exists. Partisans of each position claim that the literature overwhelmingly supports their view. One can find "comprehensive reviews" of the literature that claim the dominant result is that high taxes reduce growth. (McBride 2012). One can find "comprehensive reviews" of the literature that claim no effect (Durlauf et al. 2005; Huang and Frentz 2014). The Huang and Frentz review is particularly interesting because it considers pretty much the same studies that McBride reviewed, but reaches precisely the opposite conclusion.

One can also find comprehensive reviews of the literature that claim that results are completely inconsistent from study to study (Wasylenko et al. 1997; De Mooij and Ederveen 2008). These analyses tend to be the most convincing. I concur with the Wayslenko team that the findings are highly inconsistent. The same studies will sometimes report different effects for different taxes (Arnold et al. 2011; Gemmell et al. 2011) or different effects for equally desirable dependent variables such as employment, investment and growth (Katz et al. 1983; Tomlanjovich 2004). The explanations of the deviations tend to be ad hoc and vary from study to study.

De Mooij and Ederveen do a meta-analysis of the literature where they do a statistical analysis of the findings of many other people's previous research analyses. They report an enormous range of findings ranging from high taxes having negative effects on growth, to taxes having no effects on growth to taxes even having positive effects on growth! They find that regardless of what measure you use half the time taxes have no effect on growth. The other half the time is a split between positive and negative effects. Furthermore the effect of tax differences between US states is much larger than the effect of tax difference between nations – which is hard to reconcile with any traditional argument about why taxes hurt job growth. Their larger conclusion was that there was no robust significant effect of taxation on growth.

Why the different perceptions of the literature? Some of this comes from pure partisanship. Much of this literature is advocacy, designed to legitimate tax cuts (or not giving tax cuts) by showing seemingly scientific support for the position. Lobbying organizations that want to see tax cuts passed (or more rarely, that oppose tax cuts passing) will pay think tanks to write "scientific" reports to justify the position the lobbying organization espouses. However, not all of the participants in these debates are unprincipled hired guns. Much of the conflicting work is done in good faith by economists who sincerely believe in the scientific validity of their position.

The real problem is that it is possible to massage the data to turn tax effects on or off by manipulating the technical specification of the model. Why are results prone to such relatively easy manipulation?

Warning to the reader: A technical statistical discussion follows. If this is not what you like to read, skip ahead to the conclusion.

Regression analysis is generally stable when applied to large samples of individuals such as those that are studied in scientific surveys. Regression results are *not* stable at the macrosocial level when the unit of analysis is a nation observed over a number of years. This is a new methodological argument – made not by qualitative ethnographers or historians who don't like working with numbers – but by sophisticated econometricans and sociological statisticians who know their mathematical methods backwards and forwards. The leading advocate of this position is Steven Durlauf, an econometrician at the University of Wisconsin-Madison (Durlauf et al. 2005). The parallel argument has been made in sociology by Salvatore Babones in his latest graduate methodology textbook, *Methods in Quantitative Macro-Comparative Research*.

Why are regression coefficients stable for people but not for nations? There are dozens of causes that explain any form of behavior either for people or for nations. To statistically determine the effect of each, one can use statistical control but one needs lots and lots of cases to get a solid estimate of the effect of each variable. In random sample surveys, one can interview thousands of people, giving the investigator plenty of cases to sort out the effects of all twenty or thirty variables in their models. However there are only 20 rich countries, only 50 US states and only 100 or 120 countries in the world with really high-quality data on their complete economies. Adding more years does not really give you more cases because consecutive years are not completely independent from each other. Any data for the United States in 2010 is likely to be heavily shaped by the United States in 2009 and not be independent of that case. So, one's sample of advanced economies still in essence has 20 cases, maybe 40 if one considered decades to be really independent from each other. This is simply not going to be enough cases to consider a full model of ten variables. Yes – statistical techniques exist that allow for the correction for period specific error – and techniques exist that allow for the correction of regionally correlated errors – and for autocorrelation. But one also has to correct for backwards causation of the independent variable by the dependent variable, regional autocorrelation, multicollinearity among the predictors in the model, correlated error linked to being in common trading networks, correlated error linked to similarities of industrial structure, lags in the operation of every causal variable, non-linearities in the operations of every causal variable, etc. etc. One runs out of cases long before one runs out of things to fix; although any one source of error can be corrected – you can't correct for them all. Any one source of error that does not get corrected will lead to biased mis-specified coefficients. The Durlauf and Babones position is that most regression equations of national level data are mis-specified.

The presence of invisible errors causes findings to change wildly every time one makes a minor re-specification of the model. This is what causes research studies to report wildly different findings for similar analyses of the same variable. Durlauf shows the severity of the problem by listing the findings of *every* multivariate regression analysis of GDP growth that had been done up to 2004. His summary is a sickening sea of inconsistency. Virtually every variable he reports was positive in some settings, negative in others and zero in the rest. Every time technical specifications of the equations were changed, findings changed. Nothing was constant.

So how do you rig a cross-national or time-series equation to get a negative relationship between high taxes and economic growth? Run the model a zillion ways until you get the findings you need. If contemporary data don't work, lag the data different ways. Put in control variables. Take out control variables. Add years to the analysis. Add cases to the analysis. Drop years or cases that don't fit. Change the denominator of the tax variable. Change the regression estimating technique. (There are a large number of different cross-section time series-techniques and they produce different results.)

Time-series of single nations – such as the United States – are particularly subject to this type of manipulation. In the American case, there is a lot of interest in estimating the effects of the Bush tax cuts. The two primary cuts occurred in 2001 and 2003. Any variable that is high in 2001 and 2003 and low in 2000 will look to have the same predictive power as the Bush tax cuts. These kinds of considerations should make the reader very skeptical about the cross-national or time-series findings about the effects of taxation on growth.

Conclusion

So why doesn't cutting corporate taxes create more jobs in the United States? Because employers do not always respond to tax increases by reducing investment or to tax cuts by raising investment. Managers can make many adjustments to tax increases, and not all involve moving money out of their firm. If a business is basically good, management responds to tax increases by raising prices or by investing in technology to maintain margins. If a business is basically weak, management responds to tax cuts by investing elsewhere. The fundamentals of job growth are based on product quality, access to markets, access to capital, access to skilled labor and access to transportation. Taxes are a small component of total costs and a minor component of total business viability.

Advocates of cutting taxes can generate impressive-looking statistical equations that make it seem like high taxes are linked to lower employment and lower growth. However, this is a field for which for every equation there is an equal and opposite equation – and there are a lot of equations that show no effects for taxes whatsoever. Since statistical methodology is very suspect on the kind of comparative cross-section time-series data on which these analyses are founded, it is best to be suspicious of nearly all of these equations – whether they favor one's own pre-existing position or not.

The bottom line is that there is neither convincing theoretical nor empirical evidence linking tax cuts to job growth. Development academics are all too silent about this critical policy issue. They should speak up more. Since the government programs that are supported by taxes are generally essential not only to long-term economic growth but to human development and the general quality of life overall. We are being asked to trade what is known to work – sensible government programs – for a promise of future jobs that is extremely unlikely to materialize.

References

Arnold, Jens, Bert Brys, Christopher Heady, Asa Johansson, Cyrille Schwellnus and Laura Vartia. 2011. "Tax Policy for Economic Recovery and Growth". *Economic Journal* 121: F59–F80.
Babones, Salvatore. 2013. *Methods for Quantitative Macro-Comparative Research*. Thousand Oaks, CA: Sage.
Barro, Robert and C. J. Redlick. 2011. "Macroeconomic Effects of Government Purchases and Taxes." *Quarterly Journal of Economics* 126: 51–102.
Campanhole, Adriano and Hilton Lobo Campanhole. 1983. *Consolidição das Leis da Previdência Social*. São Paulo: Atlas.
Cohn, Samuel. 2012. *Employment and Development Under Globalization: State and Economy in Brazil*. Basingstoke: Palgrave Macmillan.
Currie, Janet and Ann Harrison. 1997. "Sharing the Costs: Impact of Trade Reform on Capital and Labor in Morocco." *Journal of Labor Economics* 15: S44–S71.
de Soto, Hernando. 1989. *Other Path: Invisible Revolution in the Third World*. New York: Harper and Row.
De Mooij, Ruud and Sjef Ederveen. 2008. "Corporate Tax Elasticities: A Reader's Guide to Empirical Findings." *Oxford Review of Economic Policy* 24: 680–697.
Dos Santos, Anselmo Luis. 1996. "Encargos Sociais e Custo de Trabalho no Brasil." Pp. 221–252 in *Crise e Trabalho No Brasil*, edited by Carlos Alonso de Oliveira and Jorge Eduardo Levi Mattoso. São Paulo: Scritta.
Durand, Jose Carlos Garcia and Leonicio Martins Rodriguez. 1979. "Evolução das Empresas Observadas." Pp. 57–97 in *Pequena e Media Empresa no Brasil 1963/76*, edited by Henrique Rattner and José Carlos G. Durand. São Paulo: Simbolo.
Durlauf, Stephen, Paul Johnson and Jonathan Temple. 2005. "Growth Econometrics." Pp. 555–677 in *Handbook of Economic Growth*, Volume 1A, edited by P. Aghion and S. N. Durlauf. Amsterdam: New Holland.
Elgin, Ceyhun and Oguz Oztunali. 2012. "Shadow Economies Around the World: Model Based Estimates."Working Paper 2012/5, Department of Economics, Bagacizi University. Available at: www.econ.boun.edu.tr/public_html/RePEc/pdf/201205.pdf
Fazio, Christine and Ethan Strell. 2012. "Comparing and Contrasting US and Chinese Environmental Law." *New York Law Journal* February 23. Available at: www.clm.com/publication.cfm?ID=366
Fichtner, Jason and Katelyn Christ, 2010 "Uncertainty and Taxes: A Fatal Policy Mix." Working Paper, Mercatus Center at George Mason University, Arlington, VA. Available at: http://mercatus.org/sites/default/files/publication/Economic%20Impact%20of%20increases%20in%2
Gaskill, Luann Ricketts, Howard Van Auken and Ronald Manning. 1993. "Factor Analytic Study of the Perceived Causes of Small Business Failure." *Journal of Small Business Management* 31: 18–31.
Gemmell, Norman, Richard Kneller and Ismael Sanz. 2011. "Timing and Persistance of Fiscal Policy Impacts on Growth: Evidence From OECD Countries." *Economic Journal* 121: F33–F58.

Hines, James. 2001. *International Taxation and Multinational Activity*. Chicago, IL: University of Chicago Press.
Huang, Chye-Ching and Nathaniel Frentz. 2014. *What Really is the Evidence on Taxes and Growth? Reply to the Tax Foundation*. Washington, DC: Center on Budget and Policy Priorities. Available at: www.cbpp.org/files/2-18-14tax.pdf
Huffington Post. 2014. "These 26 Companies Pay No Federal Income Tax." December 11. Available at: www.huffingtonpost.com/2014/02/25/corporation-tax-rate_n_4855763.html
Jackson, James. 2012. *US Direct Investment Abroad: Trends and Current Issues*. Congressional Research Service, Washington, DC. Report 7-5700. Available at: http://digitalcommons.ilr.cornell.edu/key_workplace/1202/
Katz, Claudio, Vincent Mahler and Michael Franz. 1983. "Impact of Taxes on Growth and Distribution in Developed Capitalist Countries: Cross-National Study." *American Political Science Review* 77: 871–886.
Kieschnick, Michael. 1981. *Taxes and Growth: Business Incentives and Economic Development*. Washington, DC: Council of State Planning Agencies.
Leite, Antonio de Oliveira. 1972. *Impostos no Brasil*. Rio de Janeiro: n.p.
Lin, Justin Yifu, Fang Cai and Zhou Li. 2003. *China Miracle: Development Strategy and Economic Reform*. Hong Kong: Chinese University Press.
Mankiw, Gregory. 2014. *Principles of Microeconomics*. Boston, MA: Cengage.
Martins, Marcelo Guerra. 2004. *Impostos e Contribuições Federais*. Rio de Janeiro: Renovar.
McBride, William. 2012. "What is the Evidence on Taxes and Growth?" Special Report #207. Washington, DC: Tax Foundation. Available at: http://taxfoundation.org/article/what-evidence-taxes-and-growth
Mitchell, Daniel. 1999. "How Taxes Reduce Savings." Backgrounder #1309. The Heritage Foundation. Available at: www.heritage.org/research/reports/1999/07/how-taxes-reduce-savings-backgrounder
Musgrave, Richard. 1959. *Theory of Public Finance: Study in Public Economy*. New York: McGraw-Hill.
Pastore, Jose. 1998. *O Desemprego Tem Cura?* São Paulo: Makron.
Portes, Alejandro, Lauren Benton and Manuel Castells (eds). 1989. *Informal Economy: Studies in Advanced and Less Developed Economies*. Baltimore: The Johns Hopkins University Press
Rabushka, Alvin and Bruce Bartlett. 1985. *Tax Policy and Economic Growth in Developing Nations*. Washington, USAID Bureau for Program and Policy Coordination, Office of Economic Affairs.
Schmitz, Hubert. 1982. *Manufacturing in the Backyard: Case Studies on Accumulation and Employment in Small Scale Industry*. Allenheld, NJ: Osmun.
Schuyler, Daniel. 2013. "Growth Dividend From a Lower Corporate Tax Rate." Special Report #208. Washington, DC: Tax Foundation. Available at: http://taxfoundation.org/sites/taxfoundation.org/files/docs/sr208_0.pdf
SEBRAE. 2005. *Fatores Condicionantes e Taxa de Mortalidade de Empresas no Brasil*. Available at: www. sebrae.com.br/br/mortalidade_empresas
Stiglitz, Joseph. 1988. *Economics of the Public Sector*. New York: Norton.
Tomljanovich, Marc. 2004. "Role of State Fiscal Policy in State Economic Growth." *Contemporary Economic Policy* 22: 318–330.
Trading Economics. 2014. *List of Countries By Personal Income Tax Rate*. Available at: www.tradingeconomics.com/country-list/personal-income-tax-rate
Vroman, Wayne. 1967. Macroeconomic Effects of Social Insurance. Ph.D. Dissertation, University of Michigan.

Wasylenko, Michael, Timothy Bartik, Michael Duncan and Therese McGuire. 1997. "Taxation and Economic Development: State of the Literature." *New England Economic Review* (March/April): 37–52.

4
THE STATE AND ECONOMIC DEVELOPMENT IN EAST AND SOUTHEAST ASIA

The advantage of an ancient civilization

Harold R. Kerbo

Introduction

The data are clear that in the Global South, democracy is related to neither economic nor human development (United Nations 2002: 27, 60). China today is not a democracy, neither were South Korea and Taiwan in the 1960s, yet they have all grown very quickly. India's form of democracy is widely seen to have been a drag on economic development (Kohli 2012; Chibber 2002). Japan was not democratic during its growth spurts in the late 1800s or – despite a US-imposed pro-democracy constitution – immediately after the Second World War. To this day, unelected government ministries wield disproportionate power (Kerbo and McKinstry 1995; Johnson 1982, 1995). Indeed, Collier's data on Africa (2009: 20) suggests that below about $2,700 per capita GDP, more democracy is negatively related to economic development.

In fact, the historical data strongly indicate the correlation is the other way around: that economic development at a certain level leads to democracy (Jackman 1975; also see data in United Nations 2002). Moreover, most recent research suggests that some authoritarian governments are more able to prevent "veto groups" of traditional elites from blocking economic policies that would harm the elites' interests. Such authoritarian governments thereby avoid a threat to long-term national economic development (Evans 1995; Kohli 2004, 2012; Chibber 2002; Doner 2009). In other words, if democracy is the goal, under certain circumstances a period of civic-minded authoritarian government may provide a way-station.

But the unanswered question is this: How do you end up with authoritarian governments that work to protect the long-term development interests of the nation and its people versus ending up with authoritarian governments concerned mostly with making themselves and their elite friends rich at the expense of the long-term development interests of the nation and its people? This puzzle will be taken up below. It is a key question related to the origins of a successful development state.

The "development state" with a Weberian bureaucracy

In his now-classic work, *Embedded Autonomy*, Evans (1995: 13) describes three categories of states in less-developed countries today: predatory states, development states and intermediate states. In 1995, he classed most nations in sub-Saharan Africa, and even some in Southeast Asia (such as Cambodia, Burma and the Philippines) as predatory states – seeking to extract wealth and resources from the population for elite enrichment. Development states are those that can direct and promote long-term economic development, such as those in rapidly developing Asian nations in recent decades. Intermediate states are those that have experienced some economic development but have not been able to move the country to a more advanced industrial society; their own domestic industries still are not connected to corporations from advanced industrial nations. Doner (2009), for example, has described how Thailand so far has remained only an intermediate state, unable to move its economy into more advanced levels of production because it relies on joint ventures with corporations from the United States, Europe or Japan – rather than creating their own export brands, as did South Korea.

A development state implies the existence of state institutions capable of carrying out policies with some success. Again, it is Evans (1995) who has focused on how a Weberian rational bureaucracy is required to achieve state-directed development. In subsequent research, Evans and Rauch (1999) developed what they refer to as a "Weberianness" scale measuring relatively efficient bureaucracies with less corruption in 31 less-developed nations. This scale was shown to have a strong correlation to economic development in recent decades. And it is important to note that countries from East and Southeast Asia were generally ranked the highest on this Weberianness scale. Evans and Rauch (1999) also used traditional measures of levels of democracy to demonstrate that a more rational Weberian bureaucracy is not significantly correlated with democracy. In more qualitative comparative research, Kohli (2004, 2012) has shown that a Weberian bureaucracy behind a development state helps explain differing levels of economic development success in South Korea, Brazil, India and Nigeria, as well as among different states within India. Chibber (2002) also demonstrated the importance of a Weberian rational bureaucracy in his case studies of economic development in South Korea compared to India in recent decades. But little research has focused on how a nation has acquired an efficient rational Weberian bureaucracy and a development state.

The origins of the development state

In short, the evidence points clearly to the importance of both competent governmental institutions and a development state if less-developed nations are to have any – let alone sustainable – economic development in today's global economy.

Countries that have a development state with extensive autonomy and effective governmental institutions can push through development policies which can lead to long-term and sustainable economic development, even against the resistance of domestic "veto groups" and multinational corporations demanding conditions unfavorable to a country's long-term development. Evans (1995) calls this "embedded autonomy" because the authoritarian state elites must be able to work through, but have influence over, key economic elites able to carry out their economic policies. This is also to say that these authoritarian political elites must be *benevolent dictators* who are not overly corrupt and are not simply working for their own short-term self-interest. The unanswered question now becomes, where do these efficient governmental institutions and benevolent dictators come from? How does a country get them?

> Scholars recognize that one must look to world history to answer these questions; no one has yet provided complete answers.

Case studies of the "economic miracles" in East and Southeast Asian countries are clear in showing that these countries began their "economic miracles" under authoritarian governments. Only later did they achieve at least some degree of democracy. But the tricky part needs to be restated: How does a country end up with authoritarian governments working to protect the long-term development interests of the nation and its people versus ending up with authoritarian governments concerned mostly with making themselves and their elite friends rich at the expense of the long-term development interests of the nation and its people?

As indicated in Table 4.1 below, I will begin with an updated model of Asian economic development I have presented in a more simple form elsewhere (Kerbo 2005, 2006). Then I'll demonstrate the logic of this model with an historical-comparative analysis and findings from recent fieldwork in Thailand, Cambodia, Laos and Vietnam. This field research extended over several years. It included two years of focused fieldwork with interviews in over 50 villages and slums in the region, plus interviews with NGO officials, academics and government officials.[1] A comparative analysis of these four Southeast Asian nations is useful because they all have Buddhist religious traditions. Moreover, these neighboring countries include both two of the most rapidly developing nations in recent decades (Thailand and now Vietnam) and two of the poorest countries in the world (Laos and Cambodia).

I used a mini version of a "three-tiered nested research design," which first employs large quantitative data sets to show relationships among variables in scatter plots and correlations. Then I used qualitative historical analysis for the outlier countries (see Lange 2009 for an example of this methodology). As it turned out, the quantitative analysis showed the only negative outlier among these Southeast Asian Buddhist countries: Cambodia (Kerbo 2011). Because of space limitations, however, I will describe only the findings of some of the large quantitative data sets and refer the reader to these primary sources for more details.

TABLE 4.1 Origins and sustainability of the development state in late-late developing nations

Ancient civilizations leading to:
- A history of some governmental complexity and institutional capacity in the nation
- A history of elite identification with national interests
- The development of norms of elite responsibility
- Relatively high ethnic homogeneity and a relatively high degree of unity forged over many generations

Making a modern development state more likely with:
- Fewer veto groups
- Relative state autonomy
- Institutional capacity on national and local levels – and some Weberian bureaucratic efficiency

Ancient civilizations and traditions of government complexity

In contrast to Africa, throughout Asia we find countries which are the *direct descendants* of what were once central parts of ancient state-level civilizations. To be sure, few of these were as dominant as the Chinese or Indian civilizations. But many other Asian nations today (including Japan, South Korea, Vietnam, Cambodia, Burma and Thailand) have strong roots in ancient civilizations dating back a thousand years or more.

Analyzing historical data from a large data set (which I term the "Zurich data set") that encompasses all less-developed regions of the world (though with less historical data from Latin America), one result is striking: We find that most less-developed countries with more efficient and less corrupt governments today had more complex states before the high point of colonialism in the nineteenth century (Mueller et al. 1999; Ziltiner and Mueller 2007; also see Kerbo 2006: 35–38, 121, 127). In another study with similar measures of levels of government going back to 1500, Chanda and Putterman (2005) found much the same thing. In essence, if a country did *not* have a somewhat complex state before Western colonial dominance (or it was eliminated, as in Spanish and Portuguese conquest and genocide in South America), today it is less likely to have efficient and effective government or reasonably equitable economic development. Furthermore, it is also very likely to be ranked lower on the "Weberianess" scale (Evans and Rauch 1999). Of underlying importance is that this Zurich data set, as well as others, show that today, many measures of government effectiveness also are strongly related to economic development and poverty reduction (also see Kerbo 2006: 127; Kerbo and Ziltener 2015). We now turn to our four Buddhist countries of Southeast Asia for more explanation.

Cambodia

The temples of Angkor were built by the Khmer civilization that dominated the mainland of Southeast Asia from the ninth to the fourteenth centuries. The grandeur of the Khmer civilization some 1,000 years ago is found in the more than 100 temples around the old capital in what is present-day Cambodia. But the most spectacular evidence is the main Angkor Wat temple complex – the largest religious structure in world history. These Khmer kingdoms were the first to dominate large areas of Southeast Asia. Ancient Chinese records indicate there were numerous smaller kingdoms in what came to be Angkor from the second century to the eigth century. In the late sixth and early seventh centuries, two brothers united almost all of the Khmers, but it was not until the rule of Jayavarman II during the early ninth century that the kingdom of Angkor emerged with a strong central polity able to exert control over a wider area. Given this history of a strong ancient civilization and a complex government that over 1,000 years ago was able to coordinate the building of hundreds of temples, not to mention manage a population of over one million people in the area around Angkor Wat (according to the large data sets noted above), one might think Cambodia would be one of the most rapidly developing countries today – an "Asian tiger." As we will see, however, Cambodia today represents an exception to historical conditions leading to a strong development state. The reasons for this exception will be taken up later in this chapter.

Laos

Laos did not exist as a single nation before it was created by the French during their colonial domination starting in the 1870s (Invarsson 2008). As in the other nations of Southeast Asia, there have been humans in the area for thousands of years. But in the landlocked area we call Laos today there were no kingdoms able to unite people and exert regional power at anywhere close to the level of ancient Burma, Cambodia, Thailand or Vietnam. Up through the 1400s, the area was controlled by the Khmers (from their heartland in present-day Cambodia). Following Khmer dominance, there was a brief period of relative independence in the region roughly corresponding to today's Laos. This permitted some small kingdoms to develop. However, unlike Cambodia (or Vietnam, as discussed next), Laos lacked an ancient civilization with traditions of complex state organization upon which it could build – before or after European colonial domination.

Vietnam

Vietnam was flooded with people leaving southern China some 3,000 to 2,000 years ago (as was the rest of Southeast Asia during that time, although to lesser extent). From the second century AD to the tenth century, Vietnam was a nation controlled by China. From the tenth to the eighteenth centuries, though, Vietnam was mostly independent. It became one of the dominant countries in the region, competing for dominance first with Cambodia and then Thailand. But by the 1870s, all of Vietnam had lost its independence again, this time to the French. Indeed, it was not completely independent again until the United States finally withdrew from the country and South Vietnam fell to the North Vietnamese communists in 1975. Along with Thailand, however, Vietnam was one of the strong and ascending nations of Southeast Asia *before* the Western colonial powers came in to the region. In addition to having a rather complex state long before the European colonial period, Vietnam (much like China) also had complex educational institutions as well as traditions of training government officials. For example, in Hanoi today one can find a large compound of 1,000-year-old buildings. They now are called the "Temple of Literature." This Temple of Literature once was one of the first universities in Vietnam, a university older than those claimed to be among the first in Europe. In contrast, the first university in the capital of Laos was founded in the 1970s.

Thailand

The Thai state dates from approximately 1250, when the Thais obtained relative independence from Burmese and Cambodian overlords. Their first capital, Sukothai, was in the north-central area of present-day Thailand. In 1350, it was decided that the capital city should be moved further south for better access to trade routes on the Chao Phraya River and away from Burmese attacks. It was moved to Ayutthaya. And it was from there that Thailand continued its nation-building between 1350 and 1767. One of the most important aspects of this nation-building during the Ayutthaya period was the strengthening of the king's power as well as that of the whole central government. By 1782, after more wars with Burma, the capital was moved and rebuilt in what is now Bangkok. Within relatively short order, Thailand regained its power to counter Burma and dominate what is now Cambodia as well.

Traditions of authority and elite responsibility

As Lange (2009: 40) puts it in his recent study of the development chances of former British colonies, a "development will" must go along with any state capacity for economic development and poverty reduction. Where does this "will" among national elites come from? In addition to old traditions of governmental institutions, a look through Asian history suggests there is a greater sense of national identity among a population that descends from ancient civilizations. The older civilizations of Asia are more likely to have retained ancient traditions of authority and elite responsibility, as well as elites who identify with national interests. In Myrdal's (1970: 212) description, European colonialism in Asia was less likely to harm "the indigenous system of rights and obligations among the population." Extensive research from the world system perspective (see Kerbo 2006, 2011, for a summary), shows that outside intervention by rich multinational corporations often presents a situation in which wealthy and powerful elites within less-developed nations can enrich themselves, often at the expense of long-term economic development and the continued poverty of people in their country. In contrast, when faced with the dilemma of pleasing outside multinationals or pushing for some protection and benefits for their nation and the common people, elites in countries with these ancient traditions of obligations will more likely temper their narrow self-interests to protect the nation and people.

Many scholars argue that norms of elite responsibility have been common in Asian history. The strongest example is China's concept of a "heavenly mandate" (Morris 2010; Keay 2009). New evidence shows that around 1,000 BC, the phrase "heaven's mandate" first surfaced in China's early Western Zhou period: "the power on earth derived from a supreme and impersonal entity called 'heaven,' and came in a form of a devolved 'mandate' whose term was finite and in some way contingent on the virtuous conduct of the holder" (Keay 2009: 54). Other scholars add that the concept of "a mandate from heaven" was more constraining on Asian rulers' exercise of power than Europe's "divine right of kings" (Jacques 2009: 219). Recent research, for example, indicates that over the centuries there has been a strong correlation between famines in China and the fall of imperial dynasties (Chung 2008). Widespread famines, it is suggested, indicated to the Chinese people that the current imperial dynasty had lost the "mandate from heaven" and should be overthrown. Around 500 BC, Confucius added his philosophy of rights and obligations between rulers and subjects in response to almost 200 years of social disorder in China. These old traditions of rights and obligations in China held the nation more or less together and maintained emperor rule for nearly three millennia until emperors began to have greater difficulty meeting their obligations, due to social change and European near-colonialism. These were the changes that led eventually to massive revolution in China throughout most of the twentieth century until the Communist victory in 1949.

Japan's emperor, unlike China, Korea or Vietnam, was not seen as under a mandate of heaven: He was a god and in charge of heaven. Even before 700 AD, however, the Japanese emperor had no real power. It was people below the emperor in status, most importantly the *daimyo*, powerful feudal lords, who had real power; it was they who were seen as responsible for the needs of the people (Eisenstadt 1995: 252). If a local daimyo was not perceived to be carrying out those responsibilities at an acceptable level, his subjects were likely to switch allegiance and support a daimyo who was attacking him.

It can be easy to pass off a "benevolent dictator" as simply Machiavellian, pretending to be benevolent simply to stay in power. Collier (2009) almost humorously describes how recent African dictators have come up with ways of looking sufficiently benevolent to keep the rich donor countries, the World Bank and the United Nations appeased – so the aid money keeps flowing. But what separates these Machiavellian pretenders from dictators who are, in fact, somewhat benevolent, is that the latter actually must provide benefits for their people or the "mandate to rule" will be violated. In that case, these leaders would lose the real legitimacy they once had and their hold on power would become precarious.

Compared to China and India, most kingdoms in Southeast Asia are relatively recent. But the "Buddhist kingdoms," along with Vietnam's overlay of Confucianism inherited from China, also had strong traditions of obligations and rights developed and amended over the centuries. We now return to our four Southeast Asian countries for further explanation.

Thailand and Laos

Both were Theravada Buddhist from the beginning of their kingdoms (though, as noted above, the many kingdoms in Laos were much smaller than their counterpart in Thailand). Their Theravada Buddhism incorporated a philosophy of benevolent kings. But, as stated above, Laos is a nation recently created by French colonial rulers; it lacks a long history of large-state organization. This means that even if the philosophy of a benevolent king existed, there were no centuries-old traditions of a complex government able to implement this "will."

In Thailand, on the other hand, there was a lengthy history of governmental organization, beginning with the Sukothai period from 1253 until 1350. This period was an extremely important 100 years for Thais because it established the kingdom as a political system dominated by a king with strict obligations to the people. It was during this period that King Ramkamheng established the written language Thailand has today. He also established a philosophy of justice, which some claim was first inscribed on a stone lintel found in the ruins of Sukothai (Wyatt 1984).

In Thailand today, even though the absolute monarchy was eliminated in 1932, the sense of obligations rulers have to the common people remains strong. Years of fieldwork in a northern Thai village by Walker (2012) closely supports what I found during my fieldwork in villages in Northeastern Thailand. As Walker describes it, "there is an informal rural constitution" that goes along with Thai Buddhism. It creates collectivist "moral obligations" in which those who sacrifice something for the good of the community are seen as good leaders (Walker 2012: 173). This means that political elites in Thailand need to show "moral norms of benevolence" if they are to hold legitimacy (21).

My fieldwork and long-term experience in the country lead me to suggest that these moral obligations are in large part related to the current "red shirt" versus "yellow shirt" conflict. At times, it has become relatively violent (that is, relative to the very low levels of political violence in modern Thai history). The country is almost evenly divided between "red shirt" supporters (mostly rural people in the northeast and north, as well as the urban working class) and "yellow shirt" supporters (mostly the urban middle class, traditional elites and some people from the south). The "yellow shirt" supporters struck first in the early 2000s, shutting down much of Bangkok and blockading the international airport for several weeks. The main motivations for their anger were perceived corruption in the Thaksin government, as well as policies they claimed were leading to more foreign influence in the Thai economy at the expense of Thailand's future.

The charge of allowing too many foreign multinational corporations to take over Thai assets actually predated the Thaksin government, which took power in 2001. During the 1997 Asian economic crisis (which began with a run by speculators against the Thai baht), the IMF forced Thailand to undertake their "structural adjustment" policies. This required them to be more open to foreign direct investment (FDI). Another result was that some weak Thai banks were sold to foreign corporations. But during Thaksin Shinawatra's terms as Prime Minister (he was forced out by a military coup in September 2006), old laws preventing foreign investors from holding more than 49 percent of the stock in a Thai company (the laws required foreign corporations wanting to open factories in Thailand to have a Thai corporate partner that owned at least 51 percent of the operations) were continually flouted. As I walked through crowds of thousands blockading three main sections of Bangkok just before the 2014 coup, I heard "yellow shirt" leaders rallying their followers with complaints that Thaksin-dominated governments (his sister Yingluck was Prime Minister until she too was overthrown by a military coup in May 2014) illegally permitted foreigners to own more than 49 percent of joint ventures.

Thai rice farmer peasants, especially in the northeast and north of Thailand, have been increasingly political for two or three decades (Walker 2012). But their "red shirt" movement exploded on the scene especially after the first military coup of the twenty-first century overthrew the Thaksin government in 2006. The main motivating factor was the fear that many of Thaksin's new policies helping rural people and the urban working class would be taken away. They viewed the 2006 military coup as sponsored by the old elite establishment to stop benefits going to the common people. There had been increasing government support for rural people (a majority in Thailand) from the King's projects to help farmers since the 1960s. Many see these agricultural development projects as a means for the King to regain moral authority lost by Thai kings since the 1932 coup eliminated the absolute monarchy. In fact, the king is widely revered and loved. But from 2001, Prime Minister Thaksin was the first major politician to run his political campaigns in an American populist style: he promised rural and working-class Thais many new programs, including the "30 baht health care program" (about $1 per doctor or hospital visit) and micro loans for low-income people. Fears that these would be abolished were voiced in every village and by every family I interviewed during 2006 and 2007. It was in large part because of these Thaksin programs that once new elections were held in 2008 and subsequently, Thaksin-supported political parties won a majority each time: Thaksin's brother-in-law became Prime Minister for a while; later, Thaksin's sister was elected. Knowing they could not win at the polls, the "yellow shirts" blockaded Bangkok in 2014. This led to another military coup. Both "yellow shirts" and "red shirts," in other words, have been motivated by fear that a benevolent authoritarian government protecting the interests of the nation and people was being taken away. But they define the interests of the people quite differently, based on their social class, urban-rural residence and region.

Cambodia

In the earliest history of what came to be Cambodia, the first dominant religion, and the religion of the kings, was Hinduism. It is a much more hierarchal religion than Buddhism, with less emphasis on what one can call a benevolent ruler. However, as the Khmer empire matured some 1,000 years ago, the kingdom moved back and forth from Hinduism to Theravada Buddhism with Theravada Buddhism eventually becoming dominant. It was during the first 200 years of Theravada Buddhism under kings such as Jayavarman VII that the kingdom greatly expanded and saw its greatest development.

It is important to note, however, that after the high point of the Angkor civilization around 1,000 years ago, the nation went into a steep decline. Over the centuries, the sense of nationhood and traditions of benevolent authoritarian leaders died off. Recent evidence shows ecological disaster was the beginning of the end of these Khmer civilization traditions (Higham 2001). A city of one million people in the forests of the Angkor area was only possible because of the massive water infusion from the Mekong River during the rainy season: it was channeled to the city through a series of canals. As the city grew, the nearby forests were cut down to build more and more housing. Unfortunately, the trees had been absorbing rainwater, which otherwise would have made vast amounts of mud during the rainy season. After the forests were cut down, every rainy season clogged the canals with mud. No canal meant no water, no agriculture and no food. Over the next few hundred years, the Khmer empire was constantly chipped away by the emerging Thais and Vietnamese. In response, the Cambodian capital was moved further and further away from Angkor Wat until it reached its current location in Phnom Penh, considerably farther south. Historians suggest that the Khmer civilization lost most of its old government traditions and organization over these centuries.

Finally, not long after the fall of Saigon in 1975, the most radical and extreme form of Communism was imposed by the Khmer Rouge, under the leadership of Pol Pot. About a quarter of the population died from overwork, starvation and executions in the notorious "killing fields." The horrific Khmer Rouge rule from 1975–79 destroyed what might have remained of old Khmer civilization and its moral order. I was told by several social service workers in Cambodia that from 50 to 60 percent of Cambodians alive during the Khmer Rouge years even today experience some kind of mental problems. Several studies by North American psychologists have agreed with these figures. The most recent UN *Human Development Report* (UN 2014) includes a new measure of "trust in fellow humans" for almost 200 countries between 2009 and 2011. Only 9 percent of Cambodians said they trust other people; Syria had the same low score. Only two other countries of the almost 200 nations surveyed ranked lower than 9 percent: Albania and Lebanon at 7 percent. A lack of trust can mean less cooperation for common goals and a greater focus on short-term individualistic goals, as well as more corruption. Government officials and academics in Cambodia told me again and again that a lack of trust and cooperation permeates the entire society and that corruption is found throughout, not only among high government officials.

Vietnam

Though for the past 1,000 years, Vietnam was mostly independent from China, it still has a culture, a Confusion philosophy and a Buddhist religion that are very similar to that of China. Thus, the concept of a "mandate of heaven" described above remains important in Vietnam. And unlike in Cambodia, neither European colonialism nor its aftermath destroyed Vietnam's sense of a moral economy: Elites generally feel a strong obligation to national rather than narrow interests. There continued to be a strong sense of national identity among both the North and the South that could be rejuvenated after the North won the war in 1975 and united the country. This meant the psychological scars of war between North and South could be healed. It was actually this violation of the norms of elite responsibility that contributed to the demise of the South Vietnamese government soon after the Americans began a large-scale pull-out after 1972. The division between North and South after the French were defeated was never strongly accepted by Southern Vietnamese – especially because the Southern governing elites propped up by the United States were seen as in violation of national interests, ruling with a high level of corruption for short-term individual interests.

Finally, I was told repeatedly by Vietnamese academics and even some minor government officials that it was a sense of what I call elite responsibility (though they never used the exact term, "mandate of heaven") that brought about *doi moi* (or economic reform) at the end of the 1980s. The Vietnamese Communist government leaders finally realized that their old Stalinist economic policies (such as collective farms) were not working and only bringing more poverty and hunger. These Communist officials recognized that if the standard of living among the Vietnamese people did not start to improve, they could be thrown out, as were many imperial dynasties in early Chinese history during conditions of famine.

Ancient civilizations and relative ethnic homogeneity

The "Zurich data set," along with others, shows that ethnic diversity is related to less economic development and greater poverty, in both developed, and especially less-developed, nations (see Kerbo 2006; United Nations 2004; Collier 2009; Haller and Eder 2014). Most current national boundaries in sub-Saharan Africa were created by the Europeans at the Berlin Conference in 1895 with little regard to ethnic or tribal divisions. Today, many sub-Saharan African countries are mired in ethnic conflict that retards chances of economic development.

Less recognition has been given to the relationship between ancient civilizations and relative ethnic homogeneity throughout world history. As Collier (2009) reminds us, almost all nations in their early history had ethnic divisions, certainly his native Great Britain and virtually all of Europe. But through a long history of modern nation states, national identities were forged among these various ethnic groups so that, for example, Scots and Welsh could work with the English. These national identities, when more superficial and more recently imposed, can be broken, as happened in the old Yugoslavia after the fall of Communism. It took millennia for most Chinese to perceive of themselves as Han Chinese, given the many ethnic divisions in their early history (Keay 2009), many of which persist to the present day. It was much the same for most old civilizations in East and Southeast Asia that have achieved extensive economic development today, or are moving toward it. The relationships between their ethnic minorities, however, tend to be less problematic than the those in a country like Yugoslavia.

In addition to traditions of governmental organization, in contrast to Africa, colonialism in Asia was also less likely to result in new countries with boundaries cutting across old ethnic or tribal divisions. Most Asian nations today are therefore more likely to make "sociological sense" with respect to relatively natural societal and cultural boundaries. There are nations in Asia today that do not fit this general rule, such as Burma and Indonesia. But these are in most cases precisely the Asian nations with the highest levels of post-colonial ethnic instability.

Thailand

Some 95 percent of Thais today identify themselves as both Thai and Buddhist. There was extensive Chinese immigration in the late nineteenth and early twentieth centuries. But these Chinese immigrants have been almost completely integrated into the dominant Thai culture. Some estimate that about half of all Thais today (especially in the cities and the north) have some Chinese ancestry. In the far south of Thailand a majority of the people are Muslim, with Malay ancestry common. In the four southern provinces just above Malaysia some 90 percent of the people are Muslim. In fact, before the early twentieth century, these provinces were considered part of the Malay Federation, but they were given to Thailand in 1902 under a treaty with Great Britain. Not surprisingly, this is where we find most political violence in Thailand today. Still, the political violence (with some jihadism) in the south has remained almost completely isolated from the rest of Thailand. To date, it has not proved harmful to Thai unity and economic development.

Laos

The country put together by the French during the colonial period has significant ethnic diversity. Only about 60 percent of people living in Laos today identify themselves as Lao. The other 40 percent are various hill tribe peoples, mostly still living in remote mountains. This is one reason the economic development and poverty figures in Laos today remain some of the worst in the world. However, the 60 percent of Lao people identifying themselves as Lao are "lowland" (*lum*) people and ethnically homogenous. My fieldwork and a recent anthropological survey indicate that these lowland Lao people can be described as a "nation of themselves," with higher levels of economic development and greater poverty reduction than the overall figures for Laos indicate. The lowland Lao are actually at higher levels of economic development than a majority of Cambodian rural people (Kerbo 2011).

Vietnam

Despite the division between the North and South created after the French withdrawal in 1953, lowland Vietnam had been a culturally mostly unified land for hundreds of years. There is a small percentage of the population who are hill tribe people – who are not as well integrated – and there has been a significant number of the population with more Chinese identification. But during the political violence created during and soon after French and then US domination, most of these ethnic Chinese were forced out of Vietnam. It is interesting that Ho Chi Minh during the war against the Americans continued to promote archeological projects he thought would help create even stronger national identification and unity in Vietnam by showing the Vietnamese people how old their civilization was, with an ethnic unity going back thousands of years (Keay 1997: 3).

Cambodia

Today, Cambodia continues to have a highly homogenous population. There is a small Vietnamese presence but it is clearly a minority. There are some hill tribe peoples, but far less than found in Laos and even Thailand. Less than 5 percent of the population is Muslim, remnants of the small Champa civilization that existed in central Vietnam centuries ago. The infamous "killing fields" massacres that occurred during the 1975–79 Khmer Rouge years technically were not genocide because they involved rural versus urban as well as class divisions among a population that was culturally homogeneous.

The state of the development state in the four Buddhist countries of Southeast Asia today

During a recent visit to Thailand and Cambodia for follow-up observations, I was in the Si Saket region in the northeast of Thailand, just across the Cambodian border. In earlier stages of my fieldwork, I had been not far from this area, but on the Cambodian side of the border. In Si Saket, a large percentage of the people have rather recent Cambodian ancestry and many can speak only Khmer and not Thai. We often hear and read descriptions of contrasting conditions in cities close to each other, but on opposite sides of the US and Mexican border. The contrasts are equally striking between villages in this area on different sides of the Thai–Cambodian border. On the Thai side, most village people have pickup trucks, motorbikes, electricity, TVs with satellite dishes, clean running water and irrigated farm land. There is none of this on the Cambodian side. Thailand today has at least a rudimentary development state, what Evans calls an *intermediate development state*. When Thailand started the drive for modernization in the late 1800s, about the time Japan was doing the same with the Meiji Restoration that began in 1868, both began to develop government bureaucracies staffed with well-educated ministry elites. In Thailand, however, this development didn't reach the level of efficiency and relative autonomy achieved by the Japanese government bureaucracy during the twentieth century. But to the extent that Cambodia ever had any efficient government ministry in modern times, it was destroyed by the Khmer Rouge in 1975–79 and has yet to recover.

In the aftermath of colonialism in Southeast Asia, the Cambodians were sucked into the Vietnam War and devastated. Then the Khmer Rouge finished off any functioning government Cambodia had before 1975. There were only some 300 college-educated Cambodians left alive in the country after the Vietnamese pushed the Khmer Rouge to the fringes of Cambodia in 1979. An American lawyer who was part of the United Nations team trying to rebuild Cambodian governmental institutions during the early 1990s (Gottesman 2003) ran across discarded records kept by the Vietnamese from the beginning of the 1980s when the Vietnamese were trying to bring Cambodia out of anarchy. They estimated only 15 percent of the remaining Cambodian population had any significant education at all, and almost no one with any government experience survived the Khmer Rouge "killing fields": they left almost two million dead, nearly a quarter of the Cambodian population of roughly eight million.

The Vietnamese ended the Pol Pot regime in 1979 and began searching the labor camps for anyone with enough education to help run the new Cambodian government. This is how they found a few talented Cambodians now in government, such as the middle-aged man I interviewed in his Planning Ministry office during the summer of 2006. He had hidden his educated background from Khmer Rouge guards, for example, by not responding to them when they quietly came up behind him and quickly spoke to him in English or French. But neither the Vietnamese in the 1980s nor the UN task force in the early 1990s could find enough educated and talented people to build anything like an efficient government to bring Cambodia out of its current desperation.

Early into my fieldwork, I began noticing that village and local government officials in Cambodia were far less skilled, organized and knowledgeable about government policies than anyone I interviewed in Thailand or Vietnam. Of the 50 villages where I spent time for many interviews, I would always ask for interviews with headmen and district government officials. Those in Thailand and Vietnam were well-trained. Over the course of a year, they met frequently with central government officials to learn about policies and central government support for these policies; I found none of this in Cambodia. Local political leaders in Cambodia were mainly put in place by the Cambodian People's Party (in power since the 1980s) to make sure they pressure peasants to vote for the Party in elections that were mandated by the UN from the early 1990s. The World Bank and United Nations have programs in countries around the world to give better training to local government officials in hopes of producing better governance, but with little success. I interviewed the head of "Seila" in Phnom Penh, one of these UN agencies charged with this task. He sadly told me their training programs for local government officials have had little if any impact in Cambodia. The UN was closing his Seila office down in 2008.

According to indicators of government corruption used by the World Bank and Transparency International, Cambodia has one of the most corrupt governments in the world. One might assume that because of an abundance of natural resources, Cambodia would have the funds to increase human capital and infrastructural development. But natural resources can be useless for long-term economic development if there is no development state and no political elites who put national interests above short-term personal interests to keep those natural resources from being stolen. During my fieldwork in Cambodia, I interviewed officials at a European Union-supported office of one of the world's most famous international NGOs. This Phnom Penh office was charged with trying to encourage new laws in Cambodia to make the revenues from newly-found offshore oil transparent. In a later interview with the British head of this NGO office, I was told the office is closing. He said, "It is hopeless, the oil money will be stolen."

In another cross-border comparison, in early 2007 I was in Kampong Chan Province in eastern Cambodia, close to the Vietnam border, interviewing people in some very small villages. What I saw and heard from these people was the usual for rural Cambodia: no electricity, no clean water, no medical clinic in the area – and no kind of aid or assistance from the Cambodian government. But a few more miles further north, we saw something new: There were huge rubber plantations, then large open fields being plowed by big almost American-sized tractors, several in a large field at the same time. At the next village we found out what was happening. Most of the land in this area had been taken away from Cambodian villagers and leased to a major Vietnamese company. The Vietnamese company was planting cassava, a starchy tuber somewhat similar to a potato. Then, a few more miles north, we came to the Vietnamese-owned processing plant where the starch was then shipped to Vietnam to make noodles. Land grabs such as these have been allowed – especially by Chinese, South Korean and Vietnamese companies – through bribes to corrupt Cambodian government officials (see Kerbo 2011, especially chapter 6). The Cambodian villagers had been transformed into mostly landless peasants who labored for the Vietnamese companies.

Just a few weeks later I was on the other side of the border in Vietnamese villages such as Binh Hoa, just west of the Mekong Delta. The contrast was almost as striking as between northeast Thai villages and those across the Cambodian border. There were an impressive number of aid programs from both the Vietnamese government and foreign NGOs. Various small-scale craft industries were set up to provide jobs. There were government schools and clinics in the area and almost all small homes had electricity and fresh water, as wells as TVs and other appliances. Later, in a small provincial city in the area, we met with local Communist party officials, primarily from the Women's Union (which I found to be an important group throughout Vietnam). They gave us information about all government and NGO programs in the area. We found much the same type of government assistance programs in all provinces of the east-central coast of Vietnam. There were some differences – but not many – in levels of anti-poverty and government programs providing such things as irrigation projects. Unlike the common view of communist governments in the West, the Vietnamese Communist government is not so centralized and all-powerful. Local governments had some autonomy, with some local governments having more resources and better leadership than others.

Now to some final cross-border examples: I visited small provincial cities and villages not far from the Mekong River, which forms the border between Thailand and Laos. The Lao capital city, Vientiane, is just across the Mekong River from the Thai provincial city of Nong Khai. Vientiane hardly looks like the capital city of a country. Dozens of provincial cities in Thailand are much larger, more modern, and have far more business activity. There were a few new small buildings in Vientiane since I spent time there in the mid-1990s. Even a few foreign factories had appeared by 2007, but little else. In Lao villages in the lowlands along the Mekong River, however, there were some improvements. I found some government projects expanding electricity into villages and agricultural extension offices teaching small farmers about new crop and livestock methods. Observations and interviews in the Lao villages in 2006–7 indicated that some development progress had begun – much more than I saw in Cambodia – but nothing to compare with similar-sized villages in Thailand and Vietnam.

Conclusions and summary

The focus of the model presented here is how less-developed countries can create the development state that recent research has shown important for sustainable economic progress and poverty reduction in today's global economy. I have argued that states with ancient civilization traditions that have remained intact are more likely to have developmentalist states. These enduring cultural traditions support rational state action by weakening the clout of powerful elites who are more interested in corruption and personal profit than in bona fide national growth. Other factors undoubtedly affect growth too, such as sound macroeconomic management and support of women's economic roles. Still, the ancient culture factor is all too often omitted from discussions of development; I suggest that further research on this is needed.

In no way, however, am I advocating "autocracy forever." After a certain level of economic development, South Korea and Taiwan, for example, began turning increasingly democratic. Their democracy, however, is not necessarily in the Western mold – and this, too, merits further study.

References

Chanda, Areendam, and Louis Putterman. 2005. "State Effectiveness, Economic Growth and the Age of States." Pp 69–91 in *States and Development: Historical Antecedents of Stagnation and Advance*, edited by Matthew Lange and Dietrich Rueschemeyer. New York: Palgrave.

Chibber, Vivek. 2002. "Bureaucratic Rationality and the Development State." *American Journal of Sociology*. 107: 951–989.

Chung Min Lee. 2008. "The Emperor's Famine." *Asia Policy*. 5.1: 189–193.
Collier, Paul. 2009. *Wars, Guns, and Votes: Democracy in Dangerous Places*. New York: Oxford University Press.
——2007. *The Bottom Billion: Why the Poorest Countries Are Failing and What Can Be Done About It*. New York: Oxford University Press.
Doner, Richard. 2009. *The Politics of Uneven Development: Thailand's Economic Growth in Comparative Perspective*. New York: Cambridge University Press.
Eisenstadt, S. N. 1995. *Japanese Civilization: A Comparative View*. Chicago, IL: University of Chicago Press.
Evans, Peter. 1995. *Embedded Autonomy: States and Industrial Transformation*. Princeton, NJ: Princeton University Press.
Evans, Peter and James E. Rauch. 1999. "Bureaucracy and Growth: A Cross-National Analysis of the Effects of 'Weberian' State Structures on Economic Growth." *American Sociological Review*. 64: 748–765.
Gottesman, Evan. 2003. *Cambodia after the Khmer Rouge: Inside the Politics of Nation-Building*. New Haven, CT: Yale University Press.
Haller, Max and Anja Eder. 2014. *Ethnic Stratification and Economic Inequality round the World: The End of Exploitation and Exclusion?* Oxford: Ashgate Press.
Higham, Charles. 2001. *The Civilization of Angkor*. London: Weidenfeld and Nicolson.
Invarsson, Soren. 2008. *Creating Laos: The Making of a Lao Space between Indochina and Siam, 1860–1945*. Copenhagen: NIAS Press.
Jackman, Robert. 1975. *Politics and Social Equality: A Comparative Analysis*. New York: John Wiley and Sons.
Jacques, Martin. 2009. *When China Rules the World: The End of the Western World and the Birth of a New Global Order*. New York: Penguin Press.
Johnson, Chalmers. 1995. *Japan, Who Governs? The Rise of the Developmental State*. New York: Norton.
——1982. *MITI and the Japanese Miracle*. Stanford: Stanford University Press.
Keay, John. 2009. *China: A History*. New York: Basic Books.
——1997. *Last Post: The End of Empire in the Far East*. London: John Murray.
Kerbo, Harold. 2011. *The Persistence of Cambodian Poverty: From the Killing Fields to the Present*. London and Jefferson, NC: MacFarland and Company.
——2006. *World Poverty: Global Inequality and the Modern World System*. New York: McGraw-Hill.
——2005. "Foreign Investment and Disparities in Economic Development and Poverty Reduction: A Comparative-Historical Analysis of the Buddhist Countries of SE Asia." *International Journal of Comparative Sociology*. 46: 425–460.
Kerbo, Harold and John McKinstry. 1995. *Who Rules Japan? The Inner Circles of Economic and Political Power*. West Port, CT: Greenwood/Praeger.
Kerbo, Harold and Patrick Ziletner. (2015) "Sustainable Development and Poverty Reduction in the Modern World System: Southeast Asia and the Negative Case of Cambodia." Pp. 201–220 in *Overcoming Global Inequalities*, edited by Immanuel Wallerstein, Chris Chase-Dunn and Christian Suter. Boulder, CO: Paradigm Publishers.
Kohli, Atul. 2012. *Poverty Amid Plenty in the New India*. Cambridge: Cambridge University Press.
——2004. *State Directed Development: Political Power and Industrialization in the Global Periphery*. Cambridge, Cambridge University Press.
Lange, Matthew. 2009. *Lineages of Despotism and Development: British Colonialism and State Power*. Chicago, IL: University of Chicago Press.

Moore, Barrington. 1978. *Injustice: The Social Bases of Obedience and Revolt*. White Plains, NY: M.E. Sharpe.
Morris, Ian. 2010. *Why the West Rules – For Now*. New York: Farrar, Straus and Geroux.
Mueller, Hans-Peter, Claudia Kock, Eva Seiler and Brigitte Arpagaus. 1999. *Atlas vorkolonialer Gesellschaften. Sozialstrukturen und kulturelles Erbe der Staaten Afrikas, Asiens und Melanesiens* [*Atlas of Precolonial Societies: Cultural Heritage and Social Structures of African, Asian and Melanesian Countries*]. Berlin: Reimer.
Myrdal, Gunnar. 1970. *The Challenge of World Poverty: A World Anti-Poverty Program in Outline*. New York: Pantheon.
United Nations. 2014. *Human Development Report, 2014*. New York: Palgrave Macmillian.
——2004. *Human Development Report, 2004*. New York: Palgrave Macmillian.
——2002. *Human Development Report, 2002*. New York: Palgrave Macmillian.
Walker, Andrew. 2012. *Thailand's Political Peasants: Power in the Modern Rural Economy*. Madison, WI: University of Wisconsin Press.
World Bank. 2013. *World Development Report, 2013: Equity and Development in Cambodia*. Available at: www.worldbank.org
Wyatt, David K. 1984. *Thailand: A Short History*. New Haven, CT: Yale University Press.
Ziltener, Patrick and Hans-Peter Mueller. 2007. "Weight of the Past: Traditional Agriculture, Socio-Political Differentiation and Modern Development in Africa and Asia: A Cross-National Analysis." *International Journal of Comparative Sociology* 48: 371–415.

Note

1   For details about this fieldwork see Kerbo and Ziltener 2015. I first want to thank the Japan Foundation. It awarded me an Abe Fellowship that supported most of the fieldwork upon which much of this chapter is based.

5
DOES A POST-SCARCITY WORLD MEAN AN END TO DEVELOPMENT?

Herman Mark Schwartz

Introduction

Does a post-scarcity world mean an end to development?[1] Prediction, though difficult and dangerous, is sometimes useful if it gives us a sense of how changes in the parameters shaping development today might produce a different world tomorrow. While answering this question takes us a little bit into the realm of science fiction, the answer is largely based not on pure hypotheticals but rather on the logical extension of current trends, keeping in mind that no linear trend continues forever and that many linear social trends bring forth opposing forces.

Joan Robinson's (1962: 45) succinct comment on dependency theory helps answer the question above: "the misery of being exploited by capitalists is nothing compared to the misery of not being exploited at all." Put briefly, a post-scarcity world implies much slower growth of exports and therefore much slower growth of income for developing countries. Simply by exporting, or being chosen as an export platform, developing countries used to enjoy a large, once-only jumpstart on economic development through a huge increment to the deficient local demand that otherwise hinders development. This strategy used to offer what Dani Rodrik (2013) called a path to "unconditional convergence." Exports of manufactured goods provided an opportunity for convergence towards developed-country manufacturing productivity levels.

But a post-scarcity world diminishes the size of that potential export bonus. The increased cost of transportation for physical goods, in both a money and a time sense, will interact with the "third manufacturing revolution" – the application of information technology to all phases of manufacturing – to create localized markets for highly customized, produce-on-demand products. These will substitute for goods made in distant low-wage labor locations, and put a premium on design and quality features that are difficult to find and sustain in developing economies.

The loss of the export motor will deprive developing economies of both unconditional convergence and extra effective demand. Following Robinson, this means slower growth and development.

Economic development historically is a problem of effective demand. Poor countries are poor because they are poor and therefore lack sufficient effective demand. The non-tautological sense of this is that income and investment typically occur in and follow big markets. Poor countries generally don't have big markets. Historically successful developers have overcome the relatively small size of their market by generating huge streams of cheap, low quality exports that enable them to piggyback on rich country demand. These exports fund the creation of physical and human capital. More and better infrastructure dramatically lowers the cost of doing business, freeing up income that can be directed to additional local production, promoting extensive growth. Additional human capital creates productivity growth and thus intensive growth. Rising human capital also creates popular demands for and the ability to produce a more stable and predictable social order, which also is conducive to intensive growth.

Three recent trends threaten these sources of additional effective demand. First, the third manufacturing revolution combines with a second threatening trend, volatile and generally expensive transportation fuel costs; together, they lower the incentives to relocate production to or start production in low-wage areas. Drastically cheaper automation and new manufacturing techniques such as additive manufacturing (e.g. 3-D printing) permit a much greater range of customization for simple products that used to be mass-produced. Higher transportation costs deter long-distance transport at the same time that customization creates a demand for timely delivery. Third, demographic trends in the rich OECD (Organization for Economic Cooperation and Development) countries also comprise a threat. The primary ominous trend is aging but there is also declining interest in physical goods by many of the young, as well as the old. One result will be continuous shifts in demand towards non-traded services and away from manufactured goods. Traded services are unlikely to produce Rodrik's unconditional convergence. Unconditional convergence occurred when multinational firms transferred entire production systems designed for unskilled labor to Asia, obviating the need for Asian managers and firms to develop these from scratch.

If we accept Paul Krugman and Anthony Venables' (1995) argument about the interaction of manufacturing economies of scale and transportation costs, then the first two trends imply that there will be "re-shoring": much manufactured production will return to developed nations. When transportation costs are low and manufacturing economies of scale are high, production tends to concentrate. This occurred first in the nineteenth century concentration of manufacturing in Europe and later in the shift of much manufacturing to Asia in the late twentieth century. But when transportation costs are high and manufacturing economies of scale are low, production disperses toward local markets, in this case, developed country markets. Re-shoring reduces transportation time and monetary (but essentially energy) costs.

Re-shoring will not eliminate all developing country manufactured exports. Rather, it degrades their ability to use exports as an increment to domestic demand, stalling many developing nations at their current level of relative income. Demand for services will continue to expand, but these markets are fragmented and require the kinds of human and social capital that developing economies lack. Service exports cannot substitute for manufactured goods exports. Altogether, these trends mean it is possibly "game over" for the kind of export-led growth we historically saw driving development in nineteenth-century Europe and twentieth-century Asia. Developing countries will have to find some new model for development, just as they did when global markets slid and then abruptly shut down from the mid/latter part of the 1920s through the Depression and until the end of World War II.

This chapter has five sections. The first section elaborates what I mean by development and thus, how development occurs. Section two defines what I mean by a post-scarcity world. This has two aspects: First, there is a substitution towards human-intensive services and second, there is a shift towards digitized production via cheap automation and additive (e.g. 3-D printing) manufacturing. The third section explores what this means for traditional export-led development and makes an analogy with the end of agricultural export-led development in the 1920s to 1980s era. Section four presents an optimistic scenario for middle-income countries, but cautions that the optimistic outcome here is a pattern of slow growth rather than the kind of explosive growth seen in China and some other Asian countries in the past 20 years. The last section provides a conclusion and an attempt to assess the degree to which the overall argument is actually true.

What is development and how does it occur

Development is a highly contested and complicated concept. Development can mean many things, ranging from the accumulation of physical capital all the way through to states of mind such as capitalism and the modern state. The former is easily observed and measured, unlike the latter. This chapter considers only one aspect of development, namely the accumulation of human and physical capital. The accumulation of human and physical capital is a necessary and pretty close to sufficient condition for development even if such accumulation is not the master key to, or sole driver of, development.

Development clearly involves the accumulation of both physical and human capital. Put simply, the former is largely about extensive growth while the latter is largely about intensive growth. True development requires both – extensive growth brings the maximum number of people into the modern economy, boosting overall GDP, while intensive growth improves people's per capita income and quality of life. Infrastructure obviously matters for development. People cannot be integrated into the market if goods cannot flow to and from them, if they cannot get to and from work and if they spend excessive amounts of time simply organizing their daily subsistence. Similarly, firms need to move people and goods back and forth, have access to energy and expend as little time as possible organizing throughput. Transportation networks, utilities and urbanization all enable expansion of the market and a decline in the time and monetary cost of living and producing.

Yet it is important not to fetishize physical capital à la 1960s modernization theory. Modernization theory suggested that simply providing infrastructure and physical capital for manufacturing would produce development. World Bank and other aid agency thinking informed by this theory produced many misguided and unsuccessful aid projects. Local populations could not use the physical objects these projects created in any remunerative way. For example, the World Bank helped finance steel mills in Nigeria that have yet to produce any steel. Similarly, geo-politics and ideology motivated the Soviet Union to finance the equally derelict Ajaokuta Steel Complex in Nigeria. All actors in the Nigerian fiasco were convinced that these steel plants – the means of production – mattered more than the people and the relations of production.

The Nigerian steel debacle shows that development also involves considerable investment in the human capital needed to make things work. Human capital encompasses not only obvious and important things like literacy and numeracy, but also massive changes in human mentality and behavior. Human capital involves the elaboration of three different routines. The first is what Weber (1978) understood as a strong form of means-end rationality, in which traditional values gave way to an emphasis on systematically trying new ways to organize production, as well as an attention to calculating how efficiently capital was used. The second is what de Vries (1994) called the Industrious Revolution, a sharp increase in individual work effort in Europe beginning in the 1500s. The third is what Gorski (2003) called the disciplinary revolution, a strong orientation to the future and the development of norms justifying greater work effort. Development also encompasses a weakening of ascription and of social ties. These in turn allow the two-sided process that generates individuals as self-governing, self-moving entities on the one side and the modern unmediated state directly interacting with those citizen–individuals on the other side. So development involves changes in mental states as well as in physical infrastructure. It involves routines at the personal level, as well as in a bureaucratic infrastructure for managing complicated public and private transactions. Moreover, this means that development is an ongoing process. Countries can regress, which is to say, they can experience declines in the accumulation of physical and human capital, in the routinization of behavior and in the application of Weberian rationality.

What typically blocks accumulation of physical and human capital in poor countries is the fact that they are poor. As noted above, that sounds like a tautology. But the essential truth that it captures is that investment capital is strongly attracted to demand/purchasing power (Amin 1974). In turn, inflows of investment capital increase demand for labor and human capital. This leads to higher wages – which in turn also increase the level of aggregate demand in a given region. Because poor places are poor – lacking in aggregate demand – no one invests in those poor places. Because no one invests, poor places stay poor. The occasional resources boom produces transient wealth, usually expressed as rapidly rising imported consumption. The money that flows in flows out just as rapidly. Even when capital accumulates in poor places it tends to expatriate itself towards rich places rather than investing in immobile local production. We can see this in the outflow of capital from rich people in developing countries to banks in Switzerland and various sunny islands.

Regional capital flight and deficient purchasing power is a generic problem in capitalism and not solely a problem of developing countries. Capitalism generates uneven and unequal development. Rich OECD countries both historically and currently have experienced these problems. For example, rural areas typically were absolutely and relatively much poorer than metropolitan areas before the elaboration of post-World War II welfare states, with their massive, government-planned extension of telecommunications, transportation and power generation infrastructure. In the United States for example, the pre-World War II South had a per capita income level that was 70 percent of the American average and only 50 percent of the income level prevailing in the Northeast. These averages conceal the even greater disparity in the US South between the average person and relatively well-to-do Southern landowners.[2] By itself, the market did not draw in much investment to those poorer areas. American industrialization up until the Second World War was largely confined to a rectangle defined by Portland, Maine, Baltimore, St. Louis, and Milwaukee.

The obvious exceptions, such as the US Steel furnace in Birmingham, Alabama, or lumber mills in the Pacific Northwest, are precisely that — exceptions. Industrialization in the American South, Southwest and Northwest occurred because of massive government-sponsored investment in infrastructure. The most important were the Tennessee Valley, Colorado River and Columbia River hydroelectric projects. The electricity they supplied initially went to factories built during the Second World War to produce military equipment. Boeing in the Pacific Northwest, Douglas and Kaiser in California and shipyards in Alabama all expanded or were built at the behest of the US government. Each then became the nucleus of a new industrial complex as subcontractors flourished around them. Meanwhile, the post-World War II flight of textile and garment production from the Northeast to the newly electrified South left behind regional unemployment and empty factories.

These processes play out even more harshly in developing countries, as rational investors and rational firms face strong incentives to consolidate production close to their largest markets. In the absence of state intervention in the market, domestic and foreign investors have little incentive to build factories to satisfy the limited demand that exists in most developing countries. In the 1960s, for example, the threshold for building a car factory was a national market of 20 million people with a per capita income over $1000 (i.e. about $7200 in 2013 dollars).

The Krugman/Venables (1995) model for the geographic location of production captures this as a tension between economies of scale and transportation costs. Put simply, firms consolidate production when the economies of scale they gain from locating production close to their suppliers of inputs, and in a production facility that is able to maximize output based on the given technology, exceeds the cost of shipping final products to end markets. In other words, low transport costs to end markets and large economies of scale result in concentrated production. But where transportation costs are higher than the gains from consolidating production, firms will rationally disperse production closer to their end markets. In short, where transport costs are high, firms gain little by centralizing production in a place located far from their customers.

Obviously, economies of scale and transportation costs are not the only components of production costs. Labor costs also matter. Consolidation of production in one area can hit limits set by the availability of local labor. If consolidation of production drives up local wages, it can create incentives to relocate production to areas with cheaper labor. These incentives are felt most strongly in production processes that are both labor-intensive and easy to divide into separate segments (technically: production processes that are not strongly coupled). The archetypical example of such an industrial sector is the textile and garment industry. Garment production is extremely labor-intense and is very loosely coupled: One production step does not have to be followed immediately by another production step. Thus, it is possible to weave fabric in one place, ship it to another place to be cut and then, in principle, ship it to a third place to be sewn together.

Krugman and Venables (1995) and Baldwin (2011) have created stylized models for the concentration and then dispersal of global manufacturing. The nineteenth century saw a massive fall in transportation costs and a massive increase in economies of scale in manufacturing. Consequently, global manufacturing centralized into a small number of locations, primarily northwest Europe and northeast North America. This centralization drove up wages in those manufacturing areas and aided unionization. Rising wages and labor militancy eventually swamped the gains from economies of scale in lower value-added industries. This then induced a dispersal of production in search of cheaper labor, as transportation costs fell continuously in the twentieth century.

Consider the twentieth-century American textile and garment industry. Economies of scale were low, transportation costs were relatively high and the industry concentrated itself close to its major markets in the Northeast. Most of the industry was located in New England, New York and Pennsylvania. These areas also were where the bulk of consumer demand was located (recall the differences in per capita income noted above). Concentrated industry created high demand for labor, enabling unionization and high wages. After 1956, when the federal highway system began to connect Southern states cheaply to the main markets in the Northeast, it became rational for garment assembly firms to shift production into the low-wage, un-unionized South. Those firms then attracted producers of textiles and other inputs to garment assembly (Johnson 1985). As these suppliers of inputs clustered around final producers in those Southern states, they created a new industrial complex oriented towards "exports" to the north. They also helped increase incomes in the South, producing a convergence of incomes between

Northern and Southern states. Roughly speaking, the 2 to 1 average prewar income gap between the Northeast and the South shrank to something closer to a ratio of 110:90. This reduction required both huge streams of "exports" of clothing from the South to the North, as well as efforts by Southern state governments to use tax incentives and labor repression to induce northern clothing firms to relocate to the South. Still later, falling transport costs enabled the garment industry to move from the American South to the even cheaper Global South in the Caribbean and Asia.

All the successful developing countries of the nineteenth and twentieth century replicated this process. Falling transportation costs made it possible for more and more countries to export raw materials and low value-added goods to the European core and, in particular, Britain. During much of the nineteenth century, surging exports to rich northwest Europe powered growth in the European periphery (including Prussia), as well as in British colonies/former colonies in North America and Australia. By the end of the nineteenth century, many tropical countries also were spurring their own growth by exporting to the rich countries. Raw material exporters had varying degrees of success in translating export revenue into modern bureaucracies and education systems and the rudiments of an industrial base. But raw material exports alone did not prove sufficient to generate sustained growth. They had to be supplemented with exports of the nineteenth-century equivalent of cheap junk. Thus, the Rhineland area of Germany generated a huge stream of low value-added cuckoo clocks and toys that they exported to Britain (just as later, Korea and Taiwan generated huge streams of toys and cheap furnishings that they exported to the United States). Rhineland toys were not produced with sophisticated machinery or production processes. They were a classic labor-intensive good. The combination of food and junk exports generated enough local growth that the nascent Imperial German state could create a more modern industrial base. Similarly, the US state forced upgrading of American agriculture via the US Department of Agriculture's research programs, the land-grant college research programs and their associated extension services to farmers. In both the German and US cases, exports helped increase local incomes and thus local demand.

Modern-day successful developers have all succeeded by exporting cheap clothing, household goods and other labor-intensive low-value goods. Starting with Japan in the late nineteenth century and again in the post-World War II period, then transiting through Korea and Taiwan to Southeast Asia and on to China and finally to Vietnam, Asian industrialization has rested on exports of the same kinds of goods to rich countries. In the most successful developers, states were able to capture the income from those export streams and redirect it to investment in higher quality, more capital-intense sectors of the economy (Amsden 1989). They also were able to fund creation of human capital through the building of basic schooling and university systems.

Less successful developers, such as Brazil in the 1940–1980 era, had relatively smaller export streams and thus could not supplement domestic demand with external demand. This is not to blame Brazil, as the most intensive period of Brazilian industrialization occurred while world markets were closed because of the Depression, World War II and then during the slow unwinding of trade controls in the 1950s and 1960s. In addition, the stagnant countries largely depend on exports of raw materials whose prices and volumes experience considerable volatility – which deters long-term investment in local industrial capacity – and whose overall long-term growth is much slower than growth of industrial exports.

The absence of industrial export streams has secondary effects that further inhibit industrialization. Exports require a level of quality and productivity that can force local producers to upgrade production. Upgrading production creates demand for additional human and physical capital. Upgrading production also leads to learning by doing, which increases managerial capacity to run industrial operations (Amsden 1989). The most rapid and successful learning by doing typically occurs when growth of output is rising rapidly.

In sum, successful economic development historically has required a surge in exports, preferably industrial exports, to supplement local demand. Increased aggregate demand then helps induce investment in human and physical capital – that, in turn, can lead to a self-sustaining process of growth. By making poor areas less poor, exports induce market actors to invest in the local market. State efforts to accelerate development require export revenues to fund imports of capital goods that cannot be made locally.

Towards a post-scarcity world

Capitalist economies are about scarcity, whether real or manufactured via restriction of output. Moreover, as Hobbes once noted, the satisfaction of human desires for a given set of goods and services only serves to excite the desire for a new set of goods and services. So in some sense, we will never be in a true post-scarcity world. What then do I mean by post-scarcity, and what are its implications for export-led development?

Post-scarcity has three elements. These are: (1) the aging of the rich country populations; (2) increasingly volatile and, generally, more expensive transportation fuels; and (3) technological changes that dramatically decrease the overall need for both capital and unskilled labor inputs in the production of physical objects. These three trends are shifting rich country consumption away from the kinds of physical goods that developing countries tend to export. They also reduce the developing countries' cost advantage from combining low transportation costs with relatively cheap labor. These changes mean that rich country populations will be consuming fewer physical goods per capita and that the composition of those physical goods will shift towards much more customized and locally produced goods. Both trends make it harder to use exports as an engine of growth for developing countries.

First, the average age in rich countries will climb continuously for the next 30 years. In 1990, the average American was 33 years old and only one in eight Americans was over the age of 65. But by 2030 the average American will probably be 40 years old and one in five Americans will be over 65 years old. Aging is even faster in Europe, where roughly 30 percent of the population of Germany and Italy will be over 65 by 2030. Aging causes a substitution away from physical consumption towards non-tradable (non-exportable) services. Generally speaking, older populations typically have most of the physical goods they need and on a net basis are usually replacing, rather than expanding their supply of goods. By contrast, older people tend to buy human intensive services, especially medical services; these services are difficult to export. In principle, some human intensive service production can be done offshore, as when Indian doctors read medical imaging files in India. Practically though, there are limits to this offshoring. Even with medical imaging, however, the combination of regulation, a limited labor supply and time-zone differences tend to offset a huge disparity in labor costs. By the same token, developing countries can export people to do services. Ten percent of the Filipino population is currently offshore. And their remittances are the Philippines' biggest export. But anti-immigrant sentiment has been rising for the past decade, particularly in Europe, limiting revenues from the export of human labor.

Second, volatile but usually rising transportation fuel prices and declining economies of scale also limit Global South exports of goods. Recall the simple Krugman/Venables model whose key dynamic was the degree to which economies of scale offset the cost of transportation to final markets. Rising fuel prices increase the size of the gains from economies of scale that are needed to induce industrial concentration. Similarly, rising fuel prices increase the level of wage savings needed to induce "offshore production" as a way to escape high wages in developed countries. Expensive transportation fuels thus induce firms to locate production closer to their major markets. Oil averaged $23.50 per barrel from 1991 through 2005, but $73.10 from 2005 through 2012. Fuel oil is the major component of the cost of transporting goods from low-wage producers in Asia to major markets in the United States and Europe. At present, there is no obvious substitute for fuel oil to propel ships and trains.

During the 1990s, extremely low transportation costs and the relatively large gap in wages between rich countries and China made it rational to relocate production in China despite the extra costs incurred in production at a distance. But wages in China have been rising, and while Vietnamese and Bangladeshi labor is cheap, their skill and thus productivity levels make them relatively unattractive except for the most labor-intense production processes, such as shoes and clothing. Consequently, offshore production is decreasingly attractive. Some numbers on the relative cost of producing in China illustrate this process: In 2006, for example, the difference in wages between China and the United States amounted to roughly 6.75 percent of final production costs while the extra transportation costs from China to the United States amounted to only a bit over 3 percent of final production costs, creating a roughly 3 to 4 percent cost advantage for production in China (PWC 2012). Given that the typical manufacturing firm has a profit margin of 20 percent of the final cost of its goods, this 4 percent cost advantage was substantial motivation to shift production to China. But rising Chinese wages and oil costs in the mid-2000s have reversed this equation. Manufacturing labor costs in China rose 80 percent from 2008 to 2011 (*The Economist* 2013). By 2010, China's wage advantage only amounted to 6 percent of final costs, while the additional cost of transportation from China had risen to 8 percent of total costs, implying a 2 percent cost *disadvantage* for production in China. And this is before considering any other factors, such as excess inventory, quality or coordination costs that significantly raise overall costs for production at a distance. Production at a distance also limits the ability to customize goods and make and implement design changes quickly.

Current wage and oil price trends disfavor offshore production in China. Concerning wages, they are likely to continue rising in China. This is partly because China's future cohorts of young workers will be smaller, due to the one-child policy adopted about 35 years ago. As a result, China's fertility has long been well below the 2.1 children per woman needed for replacement-level fertility, so each new cohort is smaller than the last. At the same time, the manual labor slice of the new, smaller cohorts is turning out to be relatively less well-educated and less healthy than earlier ones. What made China productive was a combination of extremely low wage levels and adequately educated workers. Now, however, education is rising more rapidly in urban than poor rural areas. This has led to a relatively less-educated unskilled manual workforce just when China is rising in the global value chain and could use better-educated labor. Moreover, high levels of pollution in key industrial cities seem to be making today's workers less healthy and likely to be less productive.

Concerning oil price trends, while peak oil is a matter of dispute, oil prices are likely to remain higher than they were in the 1990s and exhibit considerable volatility. Importantly, oil price volatility discourages the creation of elaborate international production chains.[3]

The third big change limiting the growth of future exports from developing countries is the rise of new manufacturing technologies. These include additive manufacturing techniques such as 3-D printing. But more generally, they reflect the application of information technologies to all phases of manufacturing: this is the third manufacturing revolution. In the 1700s the physiocrats argued that the only source of value in the economy was agriculture and that manufacturing simply reworked that value. At that time, roughly 80 percent of the population of France, Britain and China was involved in agricultural production. The application of water and steam power to manufacturing – part of the first industrial revolution – followed by the production of oil-powered tractors in the second industrial revolution, gradually mechanized agricultural production. As late as the 1930s, one-third of the US population was still involved in direct agricultural production. But the replacement of animal-powered machinery by petroleum-based farming reduced the farming labor force to roughly 2 percent of the population. Equally important, this process shrank the food share of the typical rich country family budget from about 40 percent to 20 percent or less of total spending.

Meanwhile, manufacturing employment increased to roughly one-third of employment in the 1950s and 1960s in most developed economies. Manufacturing replaced agriculture as the heart of the economy – and indeed became the dominant input into agriculture. Deindustrialization in developed countries after 1960 inspired a new version of physiocracy that claimed that only manufacturing, rather than agriculture, created value – and that the offshoring of low-wage, low-skill, labor-intensive manufacturing was destroying developed country economies (see, e.g. Cohen and Zysman 1987). As in agriculture, output rose while the share of the population directly involved in manufacturing shrank continuously.

What petroleum- and electricity-based manufacturing did to agriculture, information technologies are doing to manufacturing. Manufacturing's share of employment will continue to shrink, probably to around 5 percent of the workforce in developed economies, as digitized information and automation replace human labor. Digitalization permits best design and best practices to diffuse almost instantaneously. It permits the application of flexible, cheap automation to production. Just as the absolute levels of agricultural production and agricultural value-added have grown continuously, manufacturing production and value-added will grow. But the share of direct manufacturing value-added in total value-added will fall, just as direct agricultural value-added has fallen continuously in developed economies. Furthermore, just as agricultural exports failed to generate enough revenue to sustain developing country industrialization in the twentieth century, manufactured exports may not generate enough revenue to sustain the creation of developed country levels of human capital. Consider just one new manufacturing technology, 3-D printing:

Department of Defense funding initially developed 3-D printing as a way to rapidly produce spare parts in the rear area of a battlefield. The basic 3-D printing technology is like an inkjet printer that sprays molten plastic or metal, building up a solid object from that spray. Similar systems use lasers to sinter powdered metal. Computer-assisted design and manufacturing systems (CAD-CAM) drive 3-D manufacturing systems. Objects can be designed digitally and directly produced with minimal waste and without equipment dedicated to producing only that object. This dramatically reduces production costs, especially for shorter production runs.

3-D printing thus strips capital and unskilled labor out of the production process. In non-digital production, a prototype would normally be made by hand, often from materials different from the intended final object. 3-D printing allows the rapid manufacture of multiple prototypes from the same final material. 3-D printing also allows production of as many or as few units as the customer desires. Unlike traditional custom production, or traditional mass production, 3-D printing does not require much in the way of general purpose or specialized machinery beyond the printer. Printer prices range from $1300 for a consumer desktop unit all the way to $1 million for large industrial units. But because 3-D printers can produce complex, multidimensional shapes, they substitute for the usual collection of general-purpose machines found in custom machine shops: lathes, milling machines, drills and metal presses. Unlike mass production, which uses highly specialized tools but can only re-coup its cost of investment through long production runs, 3-D printing allows for the production of single items of infinite variety without the need to use any tool beyond the 3-D printer. The biggest cost in 3-D printing is on the design side.

A surprisingly wide range of components for consumer use can be made with 3-D printing. Many of these objects are the traditional fodder for low-wage developing country producers. Imagine designing Christmas ornaments using cloud-based CAD software and transferring the resulting file to a storefront factory in your nearby mall for next-day delivery. The tremendous savings in transportation costs and in the time cost of search and delivery to the consumer are obvious, as is the pleasure from a personally customized ornament. Amazon has already demonstrated that developed country consumers have a strong preference for saving search time costs. In effect, consumers can bypass the large box stores that traditionally have organized flows of low-end junk from Asia to American markets.

What about more complicated products? 3-D printing is not yet sophisticated enough to produce something like a basic electric drill. But if that drill is redesigned for easy manufacturing and assembly (DFMA), then 3-D printed components can replace many of its parts. The lower parts count also lowers the amount of labor needed to assemble the drill, reducing the cost advantage of production offshore. Moreover, the use of 3-D printing eliminates the need to stockpile components, reducing inventory costs and the risks of a disruption to production created by interruptions in a long-distance supply chain. The Boeing 787 production line was repeatedly slowed by a shortage of simple plastic fasteners that were sourced from Italy. Boeing could have avoided this problem with on-site 3-D printing of fasteners.

The general point here is that the manufacturing revolution eliminates the traditional sources for economies of scale, shifting the location equation in favor of (re-)locating production close to major markets. Traditional economies of scale came from the application of highly specialized machinery to long production runs of standardized goods. Economies of scale also came from the co-location of parts suppliers with assemblers (because the now nearby clusters of parts suppliers could also get economies of scale by servicing multiple assemblers). 3-D printing, etc. remove the diseconomies of scale involved in producing unique items, as well as the diseconomies of scale generated by the need to frequently change tooling when producing different components on the same production line. By reducing the benefits from economies of scale, these new forms of manufacturing raise the relative cost of transportation in final product cost. The huge new incentives to produce near major markets, which are mostly near rich markets, come at the expense of export growth for developing countries. These new forms of manufacture eliminate both unconditional convergence (as discussed above) and the aggregate demand boost from net exports.

The collapse of twentieth-century agricultural export markets

What will reduced export growth imply for developing economies? Here, historical experience guides this otherwise speculative analysis. From the late 1920s until the early 1980s, rich countries protected their domestic farmers from international competition using various forms of border protection, phyto-sanitary regulation and producer subsidies. This sharply constricted the opportunities for agricultural export-led growth by developing countries, relative to the nineteenth-century international agricultural market.

Nineteenth-century developing countries used food and nonfood raw materials exports to generate infrastructure, pay for the expansion of state bureaucracies and support substantial inflows of immigrants (Schwartz 2010). Commodity exports from tropical areas rose about 6 percent per year on average from 1900 to 1913 (Lewis 1970). Obviously, some countries did better than others from this export boom. Equally obviously, colonial governments often captured much of the gain from those exports. Nevertheless, in Brazil, Colombia and Mexico, as well as in Australia, Canada and Argentina, exports led not only to an extensive expansion of the economy, but also to rising per capita income and the beginnings of industrialization. By 1914, for example, both Brazil and Mexico produced roughly half of their textile and garment consumption. This period of economic growth ended when agricultural prices began dropping in the mid–late1920s, followed by the imposition of import quotas and prohibitive tariffs in the 1930s after the Depression hit. Some countries – think Brazil and Mexico – responded to the end of agricultural export-led growth with state-directed import substitution industrialization.[4] But most independent developing countries saw increased social chaos and two decades of lost growth, through the end of World War II. Most colonies saw increased repression and the same two decades of lost growth. Similar state collapse and civil disorder occurred in post-independence Africa when rich countries replaced imports of commodities such as natural fibers and palm oil with industrially-generated artificial fibers and (subsidized) vegetable oils.

After the Depression, the volume of developing country agricultural exports rarely shrank, but nearly all faced trade restrictions and weak prices. To give a current example, no one grows bananas in Europe; even so, the European Union's banana import regime dealt out quotas to specific countries. In general, however, where Global South countries produced and tried to export the same commodity as some rich countries – as with sugar, for example – their export opportunities were sharply limited. And where tropical and semitropical exporters tried to produce what were traditionally temperate zone products, they often faced insuperable barriers to exports.

These barriers reduced the growth rates for developing countries that had been dependent on agricultural exports as the major engine of growth. The shifts described above will not be as debilitating for developing country exporters as the Depression era shutdown of global markets. First, obviously, the Depression saw absolute declines in trade, rather than decreases in the rate of growth. Second, less obviously, some of the poorest countries export goods that cannot be made using additive manufacturing. In particular, clothing and shoes are likely to remain labor-intensive products produced with traditional methods. CAD/CAM has intruded into the textile and garment sector, but largely in the form of design and cutting technologies. Yet, garment assembly itself remains a labor-intensive, hard to automate production step. Additionally, middle-income developing countries can themselves use additive manufacturing to substitute local production for imported parts and components. Although this will not generate extra demand, it will reduce their vulnerability to balance of payments crises by reducing their reliance on imported goods.

Conclusion

This chapter extrapolates from a small number of trends to argue that poor countries have traditionally relied on the extra income generated by exports to rich countries to help stimulate growth in their own economies. Agricultural exports provided that extra growth in the nineteenth century. Low-end labor-intensive manufactured exports helped to stimulate growth in a new set of primarily Asian economies in the late twentieth century. By contrast, the closure of international markets led to state collapse and the unraveling of development in many countries during the Great Depression.

Yet, three trends potentially could close the window for this kind of export-led growth. First, the aging of rich country populations will shift consumption away from goods and toward mostly non-traded services, such as medical/health care. Second, rising wage costs in the most successful developing country exporters – think China, for example – and volatile but generally rising transportation fuel costs will reduce the incentives to offshore rich country production to developing countries. Third, the emergence and diffusion of new manufacturing technologies such as 3-D printing will strip out some of the need for low-wage labor. All three trends, taken together, suggest a limit to the growth potential from exports of the low quality, labor-intensive goods that characterize developing economies.

Because the chapter extrapolates from a small number of trends, two cautions are in order. First, aside from the generic dangers of making predictions about the future, it is generally unwise to make linear projections in anything having to do with economic behavior. Even if additive manufacturing such as 3-D printing and other new manufacturing technologies allow for the redesign of products in ways that simplify assembly and thus reduce the labor input, it will take a long time for rich country firms to redesign their production processes and adopt these new technologies. Most organizational practices are very "sticky." Furthermore, because some developing country economies are so large – think China or Brazil – firms may continue to locate production there not only to take advantage of a large domestic market, but also to service nearby markets. So not all developing countries will be losers from this new kind of production. Similarly, periods of high oil prices may stimulate enough new drilling and research into substitutes that oil prices weaken over the next decade. The current boom in drilling for shale natural gas in the United States ("fracking") combines both the availability of new technologies and high demand for oil into a response that reduces US imports of oil from developing countries. 3-D printing will have similar "on-shoring" effects.

Second, development is not purely an economic process and therefore not purely a matter of increasing aggregate demand. Development is "a state of mind" (Harrison 2000). Information and social movements have essentially zero transportation costs and the mentality that we associate with modernity will continue spreading. States' ability to fund local education sets a limit on this. But the combination of modern communications technology and the large diasporas from – and back to – developing nations mean that large-scale transmission of developed country orientations towards the state and the routine practices that underpin modern society and modern production will continue. These also will cause development to continue and they may independently boost income levels, too.

References

Amin, Samir. 1974. *Accumulation on a World Scale: A Critique of the Theory of Underdevelopment.* New York: Monthly Review Press.

Amsden, Alice. 1989. *Asia's Next Giant: South Korea and Late Industrialization.* New York: Oxford University Press.

Baldwin, Richard. 2011. "Trade and Industrialisation after Globalisation's 2nd Unbundling: How Building and Joining a Supply Chain are Different and Why It Matters." National Bureau of Economic Research Working Paper, No. w17716.

Cohen, Stephen and John Zysman. 1987. *Manufacturing Matters: The Myth of the Post-Industrial Economy.* New York: Basic Books.

De Vries, Jan. 1994. "The Industrial Revolution and the Industrious Revolution." *Journal of Economic History* 54(2): 249–70.

The Economist. 2013. "Re-shoring Manufacturing: Coming Home." *The Economist*, 19 January.

Gorski, Philip. 2003. *The Disciplinary Revolution: Calvinism and The Rise of the State in Early Modern Europe.* Chicago, IL: University of Chicago Press.

Harrison, Lawrence. 2000. *Underdevelopment is a State of Mind: The Latin American Case.* Lanham: Rowman & Littlefield.

Johnson, Merrill. 1985. "Postwar Industrial Development in the Southeast and the Pioneer Role of Labor-Intensive Industry." *Economic Geography* 61(1): 46–65.

Krugman, Paul and Anthony Venables. 1995. "Globalization and the Inequality of Nations." *The Quarterly Journal of Economics*, 110(4): 857–880.

Lewis, William Arthur (ed.). 1970. *Tropical Development, 1880-1913: Studies in Economic Progress.* Evanston, IL: Northwestern University Press.

Price Waterhouse Coopers (PWC). 2012. "A Homecoming for US Manufacturing? Why a Resurgence in US Manufacturing may be the Next Big Bet." Available at: www.pwc.com/us/en/industrial-products/publications/us-manufacturing-resurgence.jhtml

Robinson, Joan. 1962. *Economic Philosophy.* New York: Doubleday.

Rodrik, Dani. 2013. "The Past, Present, and Future of Economic Growth." Towards a Better Global Economy Project. Available at: www.gcf.ch/wp-content/uploads/2013/06/GCF_Rodrik-working-paper-1_-6.24.13.pdf

Schwartz, Herman. 2010. *States Versus Markets: The Emergence of a Global Economy.* Basingstoke: Palgrave Macmillan.

Weber, Max. 1978. *Economy and Society: An Outline of Interpretive Sociology*, edited by Guenther Roth and Claus Wittich. Berkeley, CA: University of California Press.

Notes

1 Thanks to John Echeverri-Gent for comment and criticism; all errors remain mine.
2 And these Southern disparities are smaller than the 4 to 1 difference in per capita income between the rich state of Nuevo León and the poor state of Chiapas in Mexico; they're also smaller than the gap between the US average and the Mexican average.
3 Oil prices are very volatile because both supply and demand are highly inelastic, that is, unresponsive to price changes in the short and medium term. Price increases do not reduce demand much because roughly half of oil output is used for transportation, and transport equipment – planes, trains, ships and vehicles – are expensive capital goods with long lifetimes. Price declines do not reduce production much because oil wells are in essence "use it or lose it" investments. Once drilled, the pressure that causes oil to rise to the surface dissipates over time.
4 Import substitution industrialization (ISI) was a popular development policy from about 1930 until the end of the 1970s for Global South countries that wanted to industrialize and not spend much of their limited supply of foreign exchange to import basic products they could make themselves, such as low-cost apparel, shoes, matches, cement, etc. These countries put up high tariff walls so this domestic production could be profitable, thus inducing further domestic investment and growth.

6
(PRO)CREATING A CRISIS?

Gender discrimination, sex ratios and their implications for the developing world

Abigail Weitzman

Introduction

Recent estimates of sex ratios – the ratio of male persons to female persons in a given population – suggest a potential impending crisis for international and domestic policymakers. In China and India, as much as 25 percent of women use antenatal sex selection practices before bearing their first son (UNFPA 2012). In both countries, up to 120 male births for every 100 female births have been recorded in recent years – a proportion that is 15 percent above what is believed to be naturally occurring (UNFPA 2012). Likewise, population estimates from Vietnam, Pakistan, Azerbaijan, Armenia, Georgia, Albania and Montenegro suggest an increasing masculinization of sex ratios (Ibid.; Guilmoto 2012a;), while sex ratios in South Korea also continue to be distorted, though now slowly declining (Chung and Das Gupta 2007; Edlund and Lee 2013). Moreover, future masculinization resulting in high sex ratios (an above-average proportion of male persons) is projected to occur in northwestern sub-Saharan African countries, such as Mali, Niger and Nigeria, where parents express a stronger desirer for sons than for daughters but currently lack access to reproductive technologies needed to implement antenatal sex preferences (Bongaarts 2013).

Across various regions of the world, one of the strongest determinants of imbalanced sex ratios is household-level discrimination against female family members. This discrimination can take place even before birth and extend all the way into adulthood. For example, in many parts of South and East Asia, the Middle East and North Africa, parents express a strong preference for sons (though variation within these regions does occur). Parents who desire sons may manifest their preference through sex-selective abortion, female infanticide, neglect and maltreatment of daughters (Bongaarts 2013; Das Gupta 2005; Klasen and Wink 2003). They may also use contraception to prevent future children after the birth of a son (Bongaarts 2013).

Parents strongly desiring sons but without the means or access to antenatal sex technologies may indirectly affect the adult sex ratio by engaging in risky reproductive practices, such as unsafe abortions or inadvisably short intervals between births (Milazzo 2014a; Rahman and DaVanzo 1993; Weitzman 2013). These behaviors heighten maternal mortality, which when widely practiced, can reduce the number of women surviving into old age.

Additional excess adult female mortality may stem from more direct forms of gender discrimination, particularly against women of reproductive age or older. These include gender-based violence, restricted physical mobility, reduced access to health care and the withholding of essential resources from female family members (Anderson and Ray 2010).

What are the consequences of extreme sex imbalances? With fewer women and girls surviving into adulthood, more men should be left without wives to marry and population growth should eventually diminish. In the case of India and other densely populated countries, this unintended reduction in growth may be welcome. In the case of China, where population growth has already declined dramatically, any additional drop may be undesirable and its unintended impacts may be more difficult to predict.

Beyond changes in population growth, sex ratios present indirect implications for crime, human trafficking, political stability and the division of household labor (Edlund et al. 2007; Messner and Sampson 1991; Zhan 2005). While less discussed, these unintended consequences may exacerbate existing gender inequalities or strain public infrastructures. It is thus important for policymakers and social scientists alike to understand how the social structural environment is linked to gender discrimination in the home; how such discrimination is manifested in ways that affect sex ratios; and finally, the potential impacts of distortions in sex ratios on population processes.

Underlying causes of household gender discrimination

The root causes of household gender discrimination are many. Most often, they include a combination of economic incentives, marriage practices, kinship and property systems, household structure and belief systems. While each individual factor is discussed in detail below, it is important to note that the underlying causes of household discrimination may vary both within and across geocultural regions. They may be exacerbated by the presence of chronic poverty, which can limit parents' choices and influence their survival strategies.

Economic incentives and marriage practices

One of the most commonly cited explanations for household-level gender discrimination in the developing world is household economics and gender bias in the labor force. In many countries where sex ratios are abnormally masculine, men have substantially greater labor force opportunities than women and masculine-typed labor is seen as much more valuable than feminine-typed labor. For example, in North Africa and South Asia, women are respectively only 27 percent and 40 percent as likely as men to be employed (World Bank 2014). Large gender disparities in employment are important because they affect parents' perceptions of boys' and girls' earning potential, both with regard to the present and the future (Koolwal 2007; Qian 2008). When parents rely on children's income (in full or in part), or anticipate relying on their children's income in old age, they are incentivized to invest more resources in the child with the highest income potential. In this way, macrostructural gender imbalances outside the home can become manifested as gender imbalances within the home.

In regions such as South Asia and North Africa, women's restricted labor force participation dates back to agrarian times (Alesina, Giuliano and Nunn 2013; Blumberg 2009; Boserup 1970). Many scholars speculate that gender disparities in these regions emerged with the development of agricultural technologies, namely the plow, which required men's upper body strength for the production of food. Cultivation was especially male-dominated in areas where plow agriculture was "dry", dependent on rainfall rather than irrigation (Boserup 1970). The smaller farming tasks that women did, such as weeding, were seen as non-essential to food production; women's agricultural labor became undervalued (Alesina, Giuliano and Nunn 2013). Under the gender division of labor in "dry" plow agriculture, men's labor came to be viewed as indispensable to the cultivation of the main food source (wheat, rye and non-irrigated rice), while women's became associated with care work and domestic labor (ibid.). Irrigated rice, however, is so labor-intensive that "everybody works" – men, women, girls and boys (Blumberg 2004). Moreover, few people realize that because irrigated rice can support very dense populations, there are more paddy rice farmers than those raising dry crops: taking this into account, not all plow farming systems are male dominated.

Over time, the division of labor in many plow societies influenced the development of broader, institutionalized gender regimes in the Middle East, North Africa and South Asia. Women's low involvement in food production, combined with patrilocal marriage practices, led to the perception of women as a financial drain (Anderson 2007; Boserup 1970). This contributed to the use of dowry as a form of financial compensation to grooms and their families (Anderson 2007; Boserup 1970).

The need to pay dowry in order to marry off a daughter can be an additional gender-related stressor for families, increasing daughter aversion. An abundance of research suggests that in the presence of dowries, parents tend to discriminate more against their daughters in a number of ways, resulting in girls' diminished access to nutritious food, education and inoculations (Anderson 2007; Arnold 1992; Lahiri and Self 2007; Pande 2003).

While the dowry was once prevalent in parts of the Mediterranean (namely Tuscany and Athens), today it most strongly persists in South Asia, where sex ratios among live births are unusually masculine (Anderson 2007). In India in particular, dowry payments have risen dramatically over the last fifty years and continue to be a near-universal practice (Anderson 2003).

In contrast to most of South Asia, the Middle East and North Africa, where child sex ratios are skewed and women's extra-household labor is limited, the sex ratio of children appears much more balanced in sub-Saharan Africa, where women cultivate up to 70 percent of locally grown food crops (Saito and Weidemann 1990). Women in sub-Saharan Africa have been involved in horticultural production for many generations and have long been seen as economically valuable members of their families (Alesina, Giuliano and Nunn 2013). This is reflected in ongoing marriage practices such as bride price and polygyny. Because women in rural, horticultural areas of sub-Saharan Africa often bring in household resources, they are more likely to be seen as economically valuable family members, which increases the demand (or desire) for more women in the household and simultaneously decreases gender-based discrimination in the home (though again, variation exists within the region) (Alesina, Giuliano and Nunn 2013; Boserup 1970). Where the kin/property system is patri-oriented, it is feasible and profitable for men to add extra wives, who are extra producers. Since 75 percent of ethnic groups in the region are patri-oriented (Elondou-Enyegye and Calves 2006), not surprisingly, polygyny remains common in the region (United Nations 1987; Blumberg 1988).

Household structure

Another reason why household-level gender discrimination may be less intense in sub-Saharan Africa than in other developing regions is that when women earn or cultivate their own resources, they tend to have a greater say over how resources are invested. Whereas male earners often direct resources toward other male members and are more likely to spend their earnings on non-essential items (Blumberg 1988, 2005), female earners are much more likely to invest in the household and to direct these earnings and income toward other female members, including children (Thomas 1990). In this way, traditional female labor force participation (including participation in agricultural activities, especially if it facilitates women generating resources under their control) may allow mothers to bolster or protect the well-being of their daughters.

Religion and kinship

Apart from labor force participation rates, religious beliefs and rituals may also influence the status of women and girls. Numerous religions valorize men through patrilineal inheritance systems and traditions that place men or male figures at their center (Donaldson 1981; Dube 1988; Guilmoto 2012a). For example, Confucian traditions place a strong emphasis on patriarchal family structure and patrilineal kinship. These values have been attributed as some of the leading causes for sex-selective abortion in South Korea and Vietnam (Chung 2007; Park and Cho 1995).

In South Korea, however, women's improved economic status has been associated with a rise in female births in recent years, indicating that at least some of this bias is mediated by the macrostructural gender environment (Chung and Das Gupta 2007), especially women's rising income potential.

In Indo-Aryan Hindu regions of Nepal, many parents believe that only sons can usher their deceased parents into heaven (Karki 1988). Similarly, in Hinduism, it is believed that only sons can perform funeral rituals or maintain spiritual connections with their deceased ancestors (Sineath 2004). This is often cited as one of the main reasons why sex ratios have historically been more distorted among Hindus than among Muslims – especially in the (Hindu-dominated) northern regions of India (Freed and Freed 1989; Kaur 2008; Mayer 1999).

Gender discrimination in practice and its implications for sex ratios

Historically, the average society has had a sex ratio of 105 or 106 male births per every 100 female births (Arnold, Kishor and Roy 2002). But owing to higher rates of neonatal and infant mortality among boys, by about age 1 the biological sex ratio is approximately 100 males to 100 females when no distortions are introduced (Guttentag and Secord 1983). In some countries, the female population share could plausibly be even greater. This is because male fetuses are more sensitive to prenatal stress and more likely to be miscarried than female fetuses (Hamoudi and Nobles 2014). In countries that have a recent history of violent conflict, recurring natural disasters or famine, the share of male fetuses surviving is likely to be slightly lower than elsewhere, while inversely, the share of female fetuses is likely to be larger (Catalano et al. 2006; Torche and Kleinhaus 2012).

Despite these projections, today we find an overrepresentation of male births in various parts of the developing world, including South and East Asia (Das Gupta, Chung and Shuzhuo 2009; Guilmoto 2009), the Middle East (Yount 2001) and, increasingly, in Eastern Europe (Bongaarts 2013). Imbalanced sex ratios among live births are also forecasted for regions that are amidst their fertility transition, such as Central Asia and northwestern sub-Saharan Africa (Bongaarts 2013). Masculine sex ratios in these regions are most likely to reflect gender discrimination that is manifested in ways that either prevent female births, heighten female mortality rates or both.

Preventing female births

One way female births are prevented is through "stopping rules" in which parents stop bearing children after they have achieved their desired number of sons (Bongaarts 2013; Park and Nam-Hoon 1995; Yamaguchi 1989). A second but less common way female births are prevented is through sex-selective abortion. Such procedures are contingent on the availability and affordability of neonatal sex determination technologies (Arnold, Kishor and Roy 2002; Patel et al. 2013).

Female infant and child mortality

When parents strongly prefer sons but lack the means or reproductive health care services to prevent daughters, they may carry female fetuses to term and then resort to female infanticide shortly after birth (Bongaarts 2013; Das Gupta 2005). Because of the greater psychic burden of female infanticide than of antenatal sex selection, the former is more likely to occur when either the household or national economic situation prevents access to the latter (Edlund and Lee 2013).

Alternatively, parents may neglect daughters and withhold essential resources from them. For example, in many (relatively more patriarchal) countries sons are provided with better nutrition, more vaccines and greater access to health care than daughters (Blumberg, Dewhurst and Sen 2013; Chen, Huq and D'Souza 1981; Hill and Upchurch 1995; Klasen 1996). These material disadvantages that girls face mean that they are also more likely to die in early childhood than are boys (Arokiasami 2002; Yount 2001).

Maternal mortality

Adult women may also face early mortality as a result of gender discrimination. For example, several studies indicate that in Bangladesh and India, daughters are often followed by another birth much more quickly than are sons (Milazzo 2014b; Rahman and DaVanzo 1993). This, in turn, may heighten maternal mortality (Trussell and Pebley 1984). These shortened intervals between births may be owing to the fact that women breastfeed daughters for shorter amounts of time, or because women with daughters begin trying for a son shortly after bearing their previous child.

Violence against women

In South Asia, fathers' preference for male children may also increase the prevalence of domestic violence (Weitzman 2013). Such violence can jeopardize women's safety, be used to coerce women into having a higher number of pregnancies and contribute to the risk of pregnancy complications, all of which are associated with early mortality. Moreover, domestic violence is not limited to women who have children, nor to women who are married. In fact, one study finds that intentional injuries inflicted upon women 15–59 years old are responsible for at least 10 percent of all deaths among women of this age in India, and 40 percent of all deaths among women of this age in China (Anderson and Ray 2010). Female injury-related deaths may be the result of spousal violence or other forms of gender based violence (such as honor killings and sexual crimes, among many others). In this way, gender-based violence among adults may be a direct contributor to imbalanced sex ratios (Anderson and Ray 2010).

The unintended consequences of imbalanced sex ratios

When widespread and severe enough, gender discrimination occurring at the household or family level can result in a distortion of the overall population sex ratio such that men are overrepresented, or women are purported to be "missing" (Sen 2010). The consequences of such imbalances are multifaceted, ranging from an effect on population growth and age distributions, to marriage markets, marital stability, gender inequality, crime and migration. These unintended outcomes quietly impact the daily lives of billions of individuals.

Population growth and population age structures

The longer a population endures a skewed sex ratio, and the more skewed a population's sex ratio becomes, the smaller that population's growth will be. Intuitively, this reflects the reality that as the number of childbearing women wanes, so too does the number of live births (Guilmoto 2010). The only way this decline could be counteracted is if women's fertility suddenly and starkly rises.

Although the decline in population growth may be welcome in countries with currently booming growth, such as India, it also presents a set of problems. Namely, as the number of live births declines, there may come an eventual time when the elderly outnumber their successors. As the case of China exemplifies, the expanding proportion of the population that needs special care strains institutional support networks and social insurance programs. For families, this may mean that younger generations will have to assume responsibility for a greater share of care-work and costs (Jadhav et al. 2013; Lei et al. 2011). Considering that in most countries, women continue to be responsible for the majority of domestic care, a lopsided age distribution resulting from imbalanced sex ratios is likely to impact women's time spent on household labor far more than men's (Liu et al. 2013). In turn, the rise in care-work may also become a source of cumulative disadvantage for women in the labor force by reducing their hours, flexibility and opportunities for promotion (similar to the ways in which Budig and England [2001] find that childrearing undermines women's employment stability and earnings in the United States).

Marriage squeezes

Imbalanced sex ratios also directly decrease the number of marriageable women – a phenomenon commonly referred to as a "marriage squeeze" (Bhat and Halli 1999; Muhsam 1974). This shrinking of the marriage market occurs in two ways. First, the number of women is decreased through a reduction in the number of girls surviving into adolescence. Second, in many societies, men typically marry women who are several years their junior. In countries with declining fertility rates, each successive cohort should be slightly smaller than the preceding. Thus, even without sex-selective practices or postnatal discrimination against girls, the number of women in younger cohorts will be less than the number of men in older cohorts. As a result, the supply of brides will be inadequate to meet the demand (Guilmoto 2010).

In the cases of China and India, it has been projected that over the next few decades, the number of eligible men will exceed the number of eligible women by more than 50 percent (Guilmoto 2012b). This dearth of marriageable women could be further exacerbated if women begin to delay their first birth or marriage (Caldwell, Reddy and Caldwell 1983; Guilmoto 2012b).

For women, a hidden benefit of marriage squeezes is that they can facilitate upward social mobility, allowing poorer women to marry into families with greater socioeconomic means (Abramitzky, Delavande and Vasconcelos 2011). For men, however, marriage squeezes can lead to exclusion from the marriage market. In particular, lower-class or less-educated men, especially if rural, are the most likely to be overlooked, as they cannot compete with their wealthier competitors (Hesketh and Xing 2006). Marginalization of such lower-class men may, as a result, contribute to the forced or voluntary migration of women. In recent years, for example, rural China has seen an influx of trafficked women from neighboring countries (Lee 2005), while urban China has received an influx of rural women into urban marriage markets (Liu et al. 2013b; Zhao 2003). These possibilities are further discussed in the paragraphs that follow.

Responses to marriage squeeze

If, compared to their wealthier competitors, lower-class men are unable to find a suitable spouse, then they may resort to marrying a wife from outside their community. For example, during the 1990s, as the number of sex-selective abortions rose in East Asia (Das Gupta 2005; Hesketh and Xing 2006), Taiwanese men's proportion of marriages to foreign-born women more than doubled (Belanger, Lee and Wang 2010). In the 2000s, the proportion of marriages to foreign-born women in South Korea almost tripled (ibid.) In both countries, the majority of foreign-born brides came from Indonesia, Vietnam and the Philippines (ibid.; Kim 2012). The recent surge in trafficked women to rural China, noted above, potentially heightens violent and organized crime as well.

In addition to a rise in ethnically and geographically heterogamous marriages, distorted sex ratios and marriage squeezes may also be one factor that creates demand for sex work. That is, while prostitution has been documented in diverse contexts throughout history, it currently may serve as a way to meet an unmet demand for wives (or at least sexual companions) where there is a dearth of women. This is most obvious in the extreme cases of mining towns in South Africa and Chile (Jochelson, Mothibeli and Leger 1991; Laite 2009). There, prostitution became more common after the development of economies that were not only male-dominated but also geographically isolated – in other words, where the sex ratio was unusually masculine. If unregulated, or coupled with an unmet need for STD prevention and reproductive health care services, prostitution may affect the spread of disease. As such, imbalanced sex ratios contributing to the demand for prostitution may indirectly affect the reproductive health of certain populations.

Crime

In most parts of the world, men are responsible for the majority of violent crimes, with unmarried men being the most likely to commit such acts. Implicitly then, when marriage markets leave large segments of the male population unpartnered, the potential for violent crime should increase (Blau and Golden 1986; Messner and Blau 1987; Messner and Sampson 1991). For example, research from China suggests that a 0.01 increase in the sex ratio of male to female births is associated with as much as a 3 percent increase in local crime (Edlund et al. 2007).

The relationship between sex ratios and male-perpetrated crime, however, is disputed. Some argue that no relationship between the two exists (Barber 2000; Messner 1986; South and Messner 1987), while others suggest that although high ratios of men increase violent crime, this crime is offset by an effect of high sex ratios on family stability (Carroll and Jackson 1983; Messner and Sampson 1991). In other words, because the likelihood that a man will find a replacement spouse is low when there is a relative shortage of women, divorce and family dissolution should decrease (Guttentag and Secord 1983). Thus, in societies with higher male sex ratios, the *percentage* of men who are unpartnered and therefore more likely to participate in organized or violent crime should remain low (Hesketh and Xing 2006; Messner and Sampson 1991).

Gender shifts in dyadic and structural power

A related consequence of the relative scarcity of women is an improvement in women's dyadic power. This is because a scarcity of women allows women to have their pick of men (although, according to Gutentag and Secord [1983], some class stratification or assortative coupling is still likely to occur). As a result, women in societies with masculine sex ratios are able to use their good position on the (re)marriage market as a form of leverage when bargaining with their spouse (McElroy and Horney 1981; South and Lloyd 1995). At a macro level, this can be seen by comparing countries with skewed sex ratios to countries with relatively even ratios. In countries where males are overrepresented (and where women usually have substantially fewer economic alternatives outside of marriage), a greater percentage of women marry and a lower percentage divorce (South and Trent 1988).

Although high sex ratios improve relationship stability among heterosexual couples, this improvement in women's dyadic power does not necessarily transfer to their structural power, or control over macro-level resources and institutions. In fact, the opposite is likely true – high sex ratios are negatively correlated with female literacy and labor force participation rates. The exception is the case of contemporary China, under the one-child policy (Amuedo-Dorantes and Grossbard

2007; Angrist 2002; South 1988; South and Trent 1988; Zhang 2007). This may be because masculine sex ratios are most prevalent where women's educational and employment opportunities are low. Alternatively, it could be that the time women spend on family formation and care-giving detracts from the time they spend in the public or civic realm (Hochschild and Machung 1989).

Effects on children and their mothers

Several studies from the United States suggest that compared to sons, daughters decrease the likelihood of marriage for unwed mothers and increase relationship instability and divorce (Dahl and Moretti 2008; Lundberg, McLanahan and Rose 2007). Other studies have found a similarly destabilizing effect of daughters in India (Bose and South 2003), as well as in a number of other developing countries, including Nigeria (Milazzo 2014a; Weitzman 2013). Additional studies from India and the developing world have also found that daughters decrease mothers' nutritional intake, which is often interpreted as evidence of household discrimination against mothers with daughters (Sabarwal et al. 2012; Weitzman 2013). Furthermore, one study finds that women in South Asia (including India and Bangladesh) are more likely to report domestic violence if they bear female children at first-birth (Weitzman 2013). This suggests that when fathers have a strong preference for sons, sex-selective practices that help women secure a son may actually have a protective effect for mothers. To the extent that the sex ratio among live births or young children indicates a society's preference for sons, policies aimed at improving the number of females born and surviving into adolescence may have unintended, detrimental impacts on mothers.

Conclusion

The ratio of male to female individuals presents implications for marriage markets, household labor, crime, human trafficking and political stability.

These are just some of the many reasons why governments and international aid agencies have made recent attempts to curb the growing masculinization of sex ratios in East, Central and South Asia, as well as in the Middle East. Understanding what heightens such strong sex preferences among parents, particularly in the developing world, is an important first step to reducing sex imbalances.

The determinants of household gender discrimination are numerous. First, macroeconomic incentives, such as gender-unequal labor opportunities, make sons more profitable in the long run, creating a desire for sons. At the same time, if girls face particularly low odds of participating in the labor force, then they may be seen as economically burdensome, thereby leading to daughter aversion. Second, gender-specific costs such as the dowry (which is most prevalent in India and other societies where women have historically low agricultural and labor force participation rates), often strain family resources and diminish parents' desire for girls. If the dowry allows husbands' families to extort profit from brides' families, then this may also incentivize parents to prefer sons. Third, both the effects of low female labor force participation and the dowry may be exacerbated by patrilocal marriage customs. This is because when brides move away from their families of origin, their ability to physically care for their parents is undermined. Fourth, kinship structures, patrilineal inheritance systems and religious beliefs may further influence parents' sex preferences by symbolically and materially reinforcing the higher status of men and boys. Finally, mothers may be coerced into preferring sons when they experience household-level backlash for producing daughters.

Given the wide number of reasons parents have to prefer sons, it is not surprising that most laws aimed at reducing prenatal sex selection have had little success in achieving their aim in countries where these traits coincide. In order to avoid impending crises stemming from lopsided sex ratios, a longer-term strategy should focus on the root causes of son preference, rather than on limiting women's reproductive choices. Some changes may be harder to manifest than others, particularly changes to cultural institutions and kin/property systems. However, local and national governments could begin to equalize women's political and economic standing by expanding predominantly female employment sectors; introducing more women into traditional male employment sectors; reducing wage inequality between women and men; and ensuring that women are just as likely as men to not only complete primary school, but secondary school as well.

Refences

Abramitzky, Ran, Adeline Delavande and Luis Vasconcelos. 2011. "Marrying Up: The Role of Sex Ratio in Assortative Matching." *American Economic Journal: Applied Economics* 3(3): 124–157.

Alesina, Alberto, Paola Giuliano and Nathan Nunn. 2013. "On the Origins of Gender Roles: Women and the Plough." *The Quarterly Journal of Economics* 128(2): 469–530.

Amuedo-Dorantes, Catalina and Shoshana Grossbard. 2007. "Cohort-level Sex Ratio Effects on Women's Labor Force Participation." *Review of Economics of the Household* 5(3): 249–278.

Anderson, Siwan. 2007. "The Economics of Dowry and Brideprice." *The Journal of Economic Perspectives* 21(4): 151–174.

——2003. "Why Dowry Payments Declined with Modernization in Europe but Are Rising in India." *Journal of Political Economy* 111(2): 269–310.

Anderson, Siwan and Debraj Ray. 2010. "Missing Women: Age and Disease." *The Review of Economic Studies* 77: 1262.

Angrist, Josh. 2002. "How Do Sex Ratios Affect Marriage and Labor Markets? Evidence from America's Second Generation." *The Quarterly Journal of Economics* 117(3): 997–1038.

Arnold, Fred. 1992. "Sex Preference and Its Demographic and Health Implications." *International Family Planning Perspectives* 18(3): 93–101.

Arnold, Fred, Sunita Kishor and T. K. Roy. 2002. "Sex-Selective Abortions in India." *Population and Development Review* 28(4): 759–785.

Arokiasami, Perianayagam. 2002. "Regional Patterns of Sex Bias and Excess Female Child Mortality." *Population (English Edition)* 59(6): 833–863.

Barber, Nigel. 2000. "The Sex Ratio as a Predictor of Cross-National Variation in Violent Crime." *Cross-Cultural Research* 34(3): 264–282.

Belanger, Daniele, Hye-Kyung Lee and Hong-zen Wang. 2010. "Ethnic Diversity and Statistics in East Asia: 'Foreign Brides' Surveys in Taiwan and South Korea." *Ethnic and Racial Studies* 33(6): 1108–1130.

Bhat, P. N. Mari and Shiva S. Halli. 1999. "Demography of Brideprice and Dowry: Causes and Consequences of the Indian Marriage Squeeze." *Population Studies* 53(2): 129–148.

Blau, Judith R. and Reid M. Golden. 1986. "Metropolitan Structure and Criminal Violence." *Sociological Quarterly* 27: 15–26.

Blumberg, Rae Lesser. 2009. "Mothers of Invention? The Myth-Breaking History and Planetary Promise of Women's Key Roles in Subsistence Technology." Pp. 227–259, in *Technology and Psychological Well-being*, edited by Yair Amichai-Hamburger. Cambridge: Cambridge University Press.

———2005. "Women's Economic Empowerment as the 'Magic Potion' of Development." *100th Annual Meeting of the American Sociological Association*. Philadelphia.

———1988. "Income Under Female Versus Male Control: Hypotheses from a Theory of Gender Stratification and Data from the Third World." *Journal of Family Issues* 9(1): 51–84.

Blumberg, Rae Lesser, Kara Dewhurst and Soham G. Sen. 2013. *Gender-inclusive Nutrition Activities in South Asia: Volume 2. Lessons from Global Experiences*. Washington, DC: World Bank.

Bongaarts, John. 2013. "The Implementation of Preferences for Male Offspring." *Population and Development Review* 39(2): 185–208.

Bose, Sunita and Scott J. South. 2003. "Sex Composition of Children and Marital Disruption in India." *Journal of Marriage and Family* 65(4): 996–1006.

Boserup, Ester. 1970. *Woman's Role in Economic Development*. London: George Allen and Unwin Ltd.

Budig, Michelle J. and Paula England. 2001. "The Wage Penalty for Motherhood." *American Sociological Review* 66(2): 204–225.

Caldwell, J. C., P. H. Reddy and Pat Caldwell. 1983. "The Causes of Marriage Change in South India." *Population Studies* 37(3): 343–361.

Carroll, Lee and Pamela I. Jackson. 1983. "Inequality, Opportunity and Crime Rates in Central Cities." *Criminology* 21: 178–194.

Catalano, R., T. Bruckner, A. R. Marks and B. Eskenazi. 2006. "Exogenous Shocks to the Human Sex Ratio: The Case of September 11, 2001 in New York City." *Human Reproduction* 21(12): 3127–3131.

Chen, Lincoln C., Emdadul Huq and Stan D'Souza. 1981. "Sex Bias in the Family Allocation of Food and Health Care in Rural Bangladesh." *Population and Development Review* 7(1): 55–70.

Chung, Woojin. 2007. "The Relation of Son Preference and Religion to Induced Abortion: The Case of South Korea." *Journal of Biosocial Science* 39: 707–719.

Chung, Woojin and Monica Das Gupta. 2007. "The Decline of Son Preference in South Korea: The Roles of Development and Public Policy." *Population and Development Review* 33(4): 757–83.

Dahl, Gordon B. and Enrico Moretti. 2008. "The Demand for Sons." *The Review of Economic Studies* 75(4):1085–1120.

Das Gupta, Monica. 2005. "Explaining Asia's 'Missing Women': A New Look at the Data." *Population and Development Review* 31(3):529–535.

Das Gupta, Monica, Woojin Chung and Li Shuzhuo. 2009. "Evidence for an Incipient Decline in Numbers of Missing Girls in China and India." *Population and Development Review* 35(2): 401–16.

Donaldson, Mara E. 1981. "Kinship Theory in the Patriarchal Narratives: The Case of the Barren Wife." *Journal of the American Academy of Religion* 49(1): 77–87.

Dube, Leela. 1988. "On the Construction of Gender: Hindu Girls in Patrilineal India." *Economic and Political Weekly* 23(18): WS11–WS19.

Edlund, Lena and Chulhee Lee. 2013. "Son Preference, Sex Selection and Economic Development: The Case of South Korea." Cambridge, MA: National Bureau of Economic Research.

Edlund, Lena, Hongbin Li, Junhian Yi and Junsen Zhang. 2007. "Sex Ratios and Crime: Evidence from China's One-Child Policy." in *IZA Discussion Papers*. Bonn: Institute for the Study of Labor.

Eloundou Enyegue, Parfait M. and Anne Emmanuèle Calvès. 2006. "Till Marriage do us Part: Education and Remittances from Married Women in Africa." *Comparative Education Review* 50(1): 1-20.

Freed, Ruth S. and Stanley A. Freed. 1989. "Beliefs and Practices Resulting in Female Deaths and Fewer Females than Males in India." *Population and Environment* 10(3): 144–161.

Guilmoto, Christophe Z. 2012a. "Son Preference, Sex Selection and Kinship in Vietnam." *Population and Development Review* 38(1): 31–54.

——2012b. "Skewed Sex Ratios at Birth and Future Marriage Squeeze in China and India, 2005–2100." *Demography* 49(1): 77–100.

——2010. "Longer-Term Disruptions to Demographic Structures in China and India Resulting from Skewed Sex Ratios at Birth." *Asian Population Studies* 6(1): 3–24.

——2009. "The Sex Ratio Transition in Asia." *Population and Development Review* 35(3): 519–549. Guttentag, Marcia and Paul Secord. 1983. *Too Many Women: Demography, Sex and Family*. Beverley Hills, CA: Sage.

Hamoudi, Amar and Jenna Nobles. 2014. "Do Daughters Really Cause Divorce? Stress, Pregnancy, and Family Composition." *Demography* 51(4): 1423–1449.

Hesketh, Therese and Zhu Wei Xing. 2006. "Abnormal Sex Ratios in Human Populations: Causes and Consequences." *Proceedings of the National Academy of Science of the United States of America* 103(36): 13271–13275.

Hill, Kenneth and Dawn M. Upchurch. 1995. "Gender Differences in Child Health: Evidence from the Demographic and Health Surveys." *Population and Development Review* 21(1): 127–151.

Hochschild, Arlie Russell and Anne Machung. 1989. *The Second Shift*. New York: Penguin Books.

Jadhav, Apoorva, K. M. Sathyanarayana, Sanjay Kumar and K. S. James. 2013. "Living Arrangements of the Elderly in India: Who Lives Alone and What are the Patterns of Familial Support?" in *Annual Conference of the Population Association of America*. New Orleans.

Jochelson, Karen, Monyaola Mothibeli and Jean-Patrick Leger. 1991. "Human Immunodeficiency Virus and Migrant Labor in South Africa." *International Journal of Health Services* 21(1).

Karki, Yagya B. 1988. "Sex Preference and the Value of Sons and Daughters in Nepal." *Studies in Family Planning* 19(3): 169–78.

Kaur, Ravinder. 2008. "Dispensable Daughters and Bachelor Sons: Sex Discrimination in North India." *Economic and Political Weekly* 43(30):109–114.

Kim, Hee-Kang. 2012. "Marriage Migration Between South Korea and Vietnam: A Gender Perspective." *Asian Perspectives* 36: 531–563.

Klasen, Stephan. 1996. "Nutrition, Health and Mortality in sub-Saharan Africa: Is There a Gender Bias?" *Journal of Development Studies* 32(6): 913–932.

Klasen, Stephan and Claudia Wink. 2003. ""Missing Women: Revisiting the Debate". *Feminist Economics* 9(2/3): 263.

Koolwal, Gayatri B. 2007. "Son Preference and Child Labor in Nepal: The Household Impact of Sending Girls to Work." *World Development* 35(5):881–903.

Lahiri, Sajal and Sharmistha Self. 2007. "Gender Bias in Education: the Role of Inter-household Externality, Dowry and other Social Institutions." *Review of Development Economics* 11(4): 591–606.

Laite, Julia Ann. 2009. "Historical Perspectives on Industrial Development, Mining and Prostitution." *The Historical Journal* 52(3): 739–761.

Lee, June J. H. 2005. "Human Trafficking in East Asia: Current Trends, Data Collection, and Knowledge Gaps." *International Migration* 43(1-2): 165–201.

Lei, Xiaoyan, John Strauss, Meng Tian and Yaohui Zhao. 2011. "Living Arrangements of the Elderly in China: Evidence from CHARLS." in *Labor and Population*. Working paper series. Los Angeles: RAND. Available at: www.rand.org/content/dam/rand/pubs/working_papers/2011/RAND_WR866.pdf

Liu, Lan, Xiaoyuan Dong, Qiqing Chen and Xiaoying Zheng. 2013. "Parental Care and Self-reported Health of Married Women: Evidence from Urban China." *Annual Proceedings of the Population Association of America*. New Orleans.

Liu, Lige, Xiaoyi Jin, Melissa J. Brown, and Marcus W. Feldman. 2013b. "Male Marriage Squeeze and Inter-provincial Marriage in Central China: Evidence from Anhui." *Journal of Contemporary China*: 1-21.

Lundberg, Shelly, Sara McLanahan and Elaina Rose. 2007. "Child Gender and Father Involvement in Fragile Families." *Demography* 44(1): 79–92.

Mayer, Peter. 1999. "India's Falling Sex Ratios." *Population and Development Review* 25(2): 323–343.

McElroy, Marjorie B. and Mary Jean Horney. 1981. "Nash-Bargained Household Decisions: Toward a Generalization of the Theory of Demand." *International Economic Review* 22(2): 333–349.

Messner, Steven F. 1986. "Geographical Mobility, Governmental Assistance to the Poor and Rates of Urban Crime." *Journal of Crime and Justic* 9: 1–18.

Messner, Steven F. and Judith R. Blau. 1987. "Routine Leisure Activities and Rates of Crime: A Macro-Level Analysis." *Social Forces* 65: 1035–1052.

Messner, Steven F. and Robert J. Sampson. 1991. "The Sex Ratio, Family Disruption and Rates of Violent Crime: The Paradox of Demographic Structure." *Social Forces* 69(3): 693–713.

Milazzo, Annamaria. 2014a. "Son Preference, Fertility and Family Structure: Evidence from Reproductive Behavior Among Nigerian Women," *Policy Research Working Paper*. Washington, DC: World Bank. Available at: http://documents.worldbank.org/curated/en/2014/03/19238584/adult-women-missing-son-preference-maternal-survival-india

——2014b. *Why Are Adult Women Missing? Son Preference and Maternal Survival in India*. Washington, DC: World Bank.

Muhsam, H.V. 1974. "The Marriage Squeeze." *Demography* 11(2): 291–299.

Pande, Rohini. 2003. "Selective Gender Differences in Childhood Nutrition and Immunization in Rural India: The Role of Siblings." *Demography* 40(3): 395–418.

Park, Chai Bin and Cho Nam-Hoon. 1995. "Consequences of Son Preference in a Low-Fertility Society: Imbalance of the Sex Ratio at Birth in Korea." *Population and Development Review* 21(1): 59–84.

Park, Insook Han and Lee-Jay Cho. 1995. "Confucianism and the Korean Family." *Journal of Comparative Family Studies* 26(1): 117–134.

Patel, Archana, Neetu Badhoniya, Manju Mamtani and Hemant Kulkarni. 2013. "Skewed Sex Ratios in India: 'Physician, Heal Thyself'." *Demography* 50(3): 1129–1134.

Qian, Nancy. 2008. "Missing Women and the Price of Tea in China: The Effect of Sex-Specific Earnings on Sex Imbalance." *The Quarterly Journal of Economics* 123(3): 1251–1285.

Rahman, Mizanur and Julie DaVanzo. 1993. "Gender Preference and Birth Spacing in Matlab, Bangladesh." *Demography* 30(3): 315–332.

Sabarwal, Shagun, S. V. Subramanian, Marie C. McCormick and Jay G. Silverman. 2012. "Husband's Preference for a Son and Women's Nutrition: Examining the Role of Actual and Desired Family Composition on Women's Anaemia and Body Mass Index in India." *Paediatric and Perinatal Epidemiology* 26(1): 77–88.

Saito, Katrine and C. Jean Weidemann. 1990. "Agricultural Extension for Women Farmers in Africa." *Policy, Research, and External Affairs Working Papers*. Washington, DC: World Bank.

Sen, Amartya. 2010. "More than 100 Million Women Are Missing." Pp. 99–112, in *Women's Global Health and Human Rights*, edited by Padmini Murthy and Clyde Lanford Smith. London: Jones and Bartlett Publishers.

Sineath, Sherry Aldrich. 2004. "Son Preference and Sex Selection Among Hindus in India." MA Dissertation. Florida State University.

South, Scott J. 1988. "Sex Ratios, Economic Power and Women's Roles: A Theoretical Extension and Empirical Test." *Journal of Marriage and Family* 50(1): 19–31.

South, Scott J. and Kim M. Lloyd. 1995. "Spousal Alternatives and Marital Dissolution." *American Sociological Review* 60(1): 21–35.

South, Scott J. and Steven F. Messner. 1987. "The Sex Ratio and Women's Involvement in Crime: A Cross-National Analysis." *The Sociological Quarterly* 28(2): 171–188.

South, Scott J. and Katherine Trent. 1988. "Sex Ratios and Women's Roles: A Cross-National Analysis." *American Journal of Sociology* 93(5): 1096–115.

Thomas, Duncan. 1990. "Intra-Household Resource Allocation: An Inferential Approach." *The Journal of Human Resources* 25(4): 635–664.

Torche, Florencia and Karine Kleinhaus. 2012. "Prenatal Stress, Gestational Age and Secondary Sex Ratio: The Sex-specific Effects of Exposure to a Natural Disaster in Early Pregnancy." *Human Reproduction* 27(2): 558–567.

Trussell, James and Anne R. Pebley. 1984. "The Potential Impact of Changes in Fertility on Infant, Child and Maternal Mortality." *Studies in Family Planning* 15(6): 267–280.

UNFPA. 2012. *Sex Imbalances at Birth: Current Trends, Consequences and Policy Implications*. Bangkok: UNFPA.

United Nations. 1987. *Fertility Behaviours in the Context of Development*. New York: United Nations, Department of International Economic and Social Affairs.

Weitzman, Abigail. 2013. "The Daughter Tax: The Effects of Daughters on Maternal Outcomes in the Developing World." *108th Annual Meeting of the American Sociological Association*. New York.

World Bank. 2014. "Labor Participation Rate, Female (% of Female Population Ages 15+)." Available at: http://data.worldbank.org/indicator.

Yamaguchi, Kazuo. 1989. "A Formal Theory for Male-Preferring Stopping Rules of Childbearing: Sex Differences in Birth Order and in the Number of Siblings." *Demography* 26(3): 451–465.

Yount, Kathryn M. 2001. "Excess Mortality of Girls in the Middle East in the 1970s and 1980s: Patterns, Correlates and Gaps in Research." *Population Studies* 55(3): 291–308.

Zhan, Heying Jenny. 2005. "Aging, Health Care and Elder Care: Perpetuation of Gender Inequalities in China." *Health Care for Women International* 26(8): 693–712.

Zhang, Hong. 2007. "China's New Rural Daughters Coming of Age: Downsizing the Family and Firing Up Cash Earning Power in the New Economy." *Signs* 32(3): 671–698.

Zhao, Gracie Ming. 2003. "Trafficking of Women for Marriage in China: Policy and Practice." *Criminology and Criminal Justice* 3(1): 83–102.

7
GENDER, DEVELOPMENT AND THE ENVIRONMENT

Female empowerment and the creation of sustainable societies

Stephen J. Scanlan

Building sustainable societies has become an important focus of our time.[1] Climate change, epidemics, hunger and famine, population pressure, resource scarcity, poverty and other inequalities associated with how the global citizenry experiences environmental health and ecological well-being have given urgency to understanding how to protect the planet. One approach to that understanding is addressing gender inequality and contributions women make towards sustainability. The United Nations Environmental Program argues at the outset of a *Women and the Environment* policy paper that women around the world play distinct roles: in managing plants and animals in forests, drylands, wetlands and agriculture; in collecting water, fuel and fodder and in overseeing land and water resources. By so doing, they contribute time, energy, skills and personal visions to family and community development. Women's extensive experience makes them essential to environmental management (UNEP 2014: 11).

Yet women's voices often go unheard or are suppressed when it comes to environmental issues and the intersections these have with poverty and inequality. A patriarchal world denies women the economic, political and social recognition, fostering gender inequality while reinforcing barriers to women's empowerment and achievement.

Empowered women are important agents of social change and when they take hold of the reins they positively affect development (Blumberg et al. 1995). Women throughout the world have taken it upon themselves to seek empowerment and justice, not merely for their own sake and their families but also for the planet with which they are so intimately involved: "Mama" Aleta Baun, an indigenous Molo woman in Timor challenging marble mining companies in her homeland; Sofia Gatico of Argentina leading the charge of concerned mothers fighting health threats from the indiscriminate use of pesticides by global agribusiness; or Ikal Angelei of Kenya fighting the construction of the Gibe 3 Dam on the Omo River and the economic, environmental and social impacts of the declining water levels of Lake Turkana on the border of Kenya and Ethiopia (Goldman Environmental Prize 2014). Although these names are likely not commonly recognized, they speak volumes to the significant place of women's voices in seeking sustainability.

This chapter thus addresses two primary research questions: (1) What is the connection between women's empowerment and environmental well-being? and (2) How does improving women's lives on economic, political and social fronts contribute to sustainability?

Theoretical considerations

Through globalization and the political economy of the world system, ecological change becomes intertwined with inequality in many forms, particularly gender. Negative impacts on sustainability in one corner of the world affect the quality of life in another and women have an important place in these dynamics.

Bernard defines sustainability as "To live richly, equitably and peaceably with each other and with our natural surroundings so that our 'home' may offer itself to the imaginations and tables of generations to come" (2010: 39). Bernard introduces notions of equity and peace to discussions of sustainability, for no society can be sustainable without such foundations. Furthermore, there is a notion of community and "place attachment" in his approach. Such ideas are essential to considering the connections women have to development and related inequalities and achieving sustainability.

The goal of achieving "sustainable societies" reflects the intersection of three systems that simultaneously affect this: Economic, environmental and social systems (Edwards 2005). One may argue that economic and social systems are irrelevant if environmental degradation continues to a point where the planet is no longer inhabitable, thus making it most fundamental. Griggs et al. propose that instead of looking at these intersecting systems as "pillars of sustainable development" as the United Nations has done, they should instead be viewed as a nested concept in which "the global economy services society, which lies within Earth's life support systems" (2013: 306). Analyzing development in this way seeks to protect the planet while creating a viable and just economy with equitable social rewards and outcomes for all.

Sustainable development as a concept is not without its critiques, particularly with regard to whether such a concept is even possible given the contradictions between ecological well-being and the mass consumption dynamics of modernity (Mies and Shiva 1993). Gender and development perspectives are often the source of such criticisms. However, many want "to make development work" and therefore approach the issue in a way that emphasizes justice, sustainability and empowerment from below.

The study of gender and development (GAD) focuses on gender and the cultural, economic, political and social inequalities women experience relative to men (Moffat, Geadah and Stuart 1991; Tinker 1990). GAD has evolved from origins in the women in development (WID) perspective rooted in Boserup's (1970) ground-breaking work. The classic WID perspective argued by Boserup addresses: (1) How women affect development; and (2) how development affects women.

These concerns play out in analyzing women's roles in achieving sustainable societies. There is a valuable body of work examining the gendered impacts of climate change and inequality associated with environmental politics and climate justice (Newell 2005; Roberts and Parks 2006; Strachan and Roberts 2003; Terry 2009). This research focuses primarily on how women are *affected by* development. The present analysis focuses more in how *women affect development* and how empowered women contribute to sustainability (Moraes and Perkins 2007; Sharma 1998; Vázquez Garcia 2001).

The GAD perspective helps understand the barriers to protecting the planet and the ecological, economic and social challenges to environmental health and sustainability (Littig 2002). A women, environment and development (WED) perspective and a variety of ecofeminist ideas including liberal, cultural, spiritual and Marxist-socialist forms emerged from this (Leach 2007; Merchant 2005; Mesina 2009; Mies and Shiva 1993; Moore 2008; Sydee and Beder 2001; Vazquez Garcia 2001). Cutting across these approaches are concerns regarding the contradictions between development versus ecology and capitalist exploitation of women and the environment in parallel fashion via production and reproduction.

The work of Blumberg (1984, 1989, 2004, 2008, 2015) provides a foundation for connecting female empowerment with environmental well-being. As Blumberg (2015) notes, economic power is the most important factor affecting gender equality and has spillover effects for improving the environment. Women in the world's poorest countries often spend countless hours gathering water and hauling firewood (Blumberg 2008, 2015) for the home while also contributing greatly to agriculture and food security (Scanlan 2004). Women are more acutely aware of the harms done from economic practices such as clear-cut-deforestation and slash-and-burn horticulture that abuse the environment.

Not only are women intricately involved with the land but they have also borne the brunt of environmental crises resulting from colonial marginalization, economic growth and unsustainable development projects (Mies and Shiva 1993; Nixon 2011; UNDP 2011), hence the key roles played by women in environmental activism. With roots in ecofeminism the study of women, the environment, and development (WED) assumes that women have a close connection with nature and the environment that makes them particularly suited to the nurturing and management of ecological well-being (Jackson 1993). Reinforcing this, Item 20 of the Earth Summit's Rio Declaration notes that: (1) women have a vital role in both development and environmental sustainability; and (2) their full participation is essential to achieve sustainable development which is central to ecofeminist and WED perspectives. There are many examples of women's actions on these fronts in the research literature. For example, Devasia (1998) reveals the roles women have played in water management programs and the acquisition of safe drinking water in India while Moraes and Perkins (2007) indicate similar findings pertaining to water in Brazil. Sharma (1998) examines women's sustainability efforts across Africa while Walker (2001) looks specifically at fisheries management and conservation in Ghana. These studies are important examples of women's contributions to sustainability when granted a partnership in development policy and programs – empowerment à la Blumberg (2008, 2015) that has positive ecological benefits.

Data and methods

This analysis uses ordinary least squares regression to examine the impact of GAD considerations on a country's environmental well-being net of controls. Data come from multiple sources including the Cingranelli and Richards Human Rights Data Project, the Polity IV Project, the Walk Free Foundation, the World Bank, the World Resources Institute and the Yale Center for Environmental Law and Policy/Center for International Earth Science Information Network (YCELP/CIESIN).

The dependent variable

Table 7.1 summarizes the measures and their sources, beginning with the dependent variable, progress toward achieving sustainable societies as captured by the Environmental Performance Index (EPI) averaged over the years 2000–2010. Averaging the values over time prevents any single year from artificially influencing the findings. The higher the score on this measure the closer proximity to being a sustainable society. The measure indicates a country's performance across policy categories that include both environmental health and ecosystem vitality, thus capturing a broad range of key components of sustainability (YCELP/CIESIN 2013). Table 7.2 summarizes the EPI and its components, breaking down the index by objective, policy category and indicator. The EPI captures sustainability in the comprehensive way desired for this analysis.

The independent variables

In keeping with other research on gender and development, the analysis uses multiple measures that tap into whether women are able to fully participate in society relative to men.

First, is the *prevalence of women's risk of discrimination* captured by the Walk Free Foundation's (2013) index for this. This measure is a country's score with regard to gender discrimination and inequality as constructed using a gini coefficient for inequality from the World Bank and scores for discrimination against women on economic and political rights from the Cingranelli and Richards database (see Cingranelli and Richards 2010). The measure therefore considers the treatment of women and their inclusion in society's institutions and processes. The Walk Free Foundation uses this in its human trafficking work, thus taking into account the potential for harms attributed to gender.

TABLE 7.1 Variable descriptions and sources

Variable	Description
Sustainable societies*	The creation of sustainable societies as indicated by a country's score on the Environmental Performance Index measuring performance across policy categories that include both environmental public health and ecosystem vitality, averaged over the years 2000–2010 (YCELP/CIESIN)
Economic development	The logged gross domestic product per capita in US$ to indicate a country's "level of income" (World Bank World Development Indicators)
Population pressure	The total fertility rate measured as the number of children that would be born to a woman if she were to live to the end of her childbearing years and bear children in accordance with current age-specific fertility rates for her country (World Bank World Development Indicators)
Democratization	A country's level of democracy based on its polity score as derived from the combination of an autocracy and democracy index combining political competition and political participation (Polity IV Project)
Presence of war	Measured as a dummy variable for the simple presence versus absence of war in a country between 2005 and 2010, 1=yes and 0=no (UCDP/PRIO Armed Conflict Dataset)
Oil economy GDP	This is measured as oil rents as a percentage of a country's GDP, which are a reflection of the difference in the cost of producing oil and selling it on the global market at world prices. The higher the difference, the greater the profitability and importance of oil to a country's economy (World Bank World Development Indicators)
Prevalence of women's risk of discrimination	A country's score with regard to gender discrimination and inequality as constructed using a gini coefficient for inequality from the World Bank and scores for discrimination against women with regard to economic and political rights from the Cingranelli and Richards database (Walk Free Foundation)
Prevalence of women's social rights	A country's score with regard to the prevalence of women's social rights as indicated by a number of internationally recognized rights including the right to equal inheritance; the right to enter into marriage on a basis of equality with men; the right to travel abroad; the right to obtain a passport; the right to confer citizenship to children or a husband; the right to initiate a divorce; the right to own; acquire, manage and retain property brought into marriage; the right to participate in social, cultural and community activities; the right to an education; the freedom to choose a residence/domicile; freedom from female genital mutilation of children and of adults without their consent and freedom from forced sterilization (Cingranelli and Richards Database)

TABLE 7.1 Continued

Variable	Description
Women's economic rights	A country's score with regard to the prevalence of women's economic rights as indicated by a number of internationally recognized rights including equal pay for equal work; free choice of profession or employment; the right of gainful employment; equality in hiring and promotion practices; job security (including maternity leave, unemployment benefits, safety from arbitrary firing etc.); freedom from sexual harassment and the right to work at night, in dangerous occupations or in a country's military or police force (Cingranelli and Richards Database)
Women's political rights	A country's score with regard to the prevalence of women's political rights as indicated by a number of internationally recognized rights including the right to vote; the right to run for political office; the right to hold elected and appointed government positions; the right to join political parties and the right to petition government officials (Cingranelli and Richards Database)
Level of gender equality in income	The ratio of female income to that of men's in the non-agricultural sector (industry and services) of a country's economy (World Resources Institute)

Notes: Independent variables are measured circa 2005 unless otherwise noted. *Dependent variable.

Connected to this, the analysis next uses three indicators from the Cingranelli and Richards Database (2013): *Women's economic rights, women's political rights* and *women's social rights*. In using these singular indicators apart from the Walk Free Foundation index, one can examine whether the economic, political and social elements of that indicator have different effects. It is useful to understand whether women's risk of discrimination is more economic, political or social in nature from both a theoretical and a policy-related perspective. Table 7.1 summarizes the specific internationally recognized rights comprising each of the three indicators and their meanings for gender inequality.

Fourth, the analysis includes the level of gender income equality measured as the ratio of women's non-agricultural income to men's. The more income that women derive from employment outside of the home and in non-traditional sectors of the economy such as services and industry, the greater likelihood there is for tendencies toward gender equality. Women's access to income in new ways and greater amounts is a form of empowerment with potential for trickle over into household and societal well-being, including spillover for achieving sustainable societies.

Control variables

Five variables are in the analysis because of their theoretical relevance to gender, sustainability and development as well as to strengthen the findings.

TABLE 7.2 Components of sustainable societies as indicated by the Environmental Performance Index, 2014

Objective	Policy category		Indicator
Environmental health	1	Health impacts	Child mortality
	2	Air quality	Household air quality
			Air pollution
	3	Water and sanitation	Access to sanitation
			Access to drinking water
Ecosystem vitality	1	Water resources	Access to wastewater treatment
	2	Agriculture	Access to subsidies (intensive agriculture)
			Pesticide Regulation
	3	Forests	Forest cover
	4	Fisheries	Coastal shelf fishing pressure
			Fish stocks overexploited
	5	Biodiversity and habitat	Terrestrial protected areas
			Critical habitat protection
			Marine protected areas
	6	Climate Change and Energy	CO_2 emissions per GDP
			CO_2 emissions per electricity generation
			Access to electricity

First, is the logged gross domestic product per capita in US purchasing power parity dollars to indicate a country's *level of economic development* in 2005. This measure ensures that any harmful effects of the independent variables on sustainability are due not solely to a country's limited wealth.

Second, is a control for Neo-Malthusian concerns regarding the impacts of overpopulation on sustainable development (see Brown, Gardner and Halweil 1999). I use *population pressure* indicated by the total fertility rate (TFR) in 2005. This is measured as the number of children that would be born to a woman if she were to live to the end of her childbearing years and bear children in accordance with current age-specific fertility rates for her country (World Bank 2014). Neo-Malthusian arguments claim unchecked population growth strains a society's resources and threatens ecological well-being – particularly with regard to provision of basic sanitation or access to clean water in addition to pollution in many forms.

Third, is a measure of *democratization* in 2005 as indicated by a country's "polity score" that is derived by combining the democracy and autocracy indices from the Polity IV Project of Marshall and Gurr (2014). This measure accounts for the level of a society's political competition and political participation. Democratization provides a foundation for gender equality and environmental security associated with sustainability, health and environmental protection and regulations. As opposed to authoritarian regimes, states with more transparency and those that value and facilitate political participation by the citizenry are likely to emphasize the basic needs of their populations (see Inglehart, Norris and Welzel 2002) and the protection of discriminated-against groups such as women from ecological harms. In sum, the polity score captures the implementation of democratic principles and the presence or absence of authoritarian threats to democratic freedoms.

Fourth, because of important impacts on climate change and environmental degradation (Clark, Jorgenson and Kentor 2010) the analysis controls for the impacts of militarization and conflict on achieving sustainable societies, using a dummy variable for *the presence versus absence of war* in a country between 2005 and 2010 (UCDP/PRIO 2014). The world's militaries are both large consumers of the earth's resources and large polluters as well. Furthermore, the impacts of war on the environment are highly detrimental, thus revealing the long-term negative impacts on sustainability and well-being that the absence of peace brings, particularly for more vulnerable segments of the population (Nixon 2011). This is especially the case for women who have long suffered the consequences of conflict in the form of sexual violence, trafficking and rape as a weapon of war.

Finally, to account for the impact of an extraction-based economy on sustainable development, the analysis includes a control for the importance of the *oil economy in a nation's GDP* (World Bank 2014). This is captured by including the oil rents as a percentage of a country's GDP. According to the World Bank (2014), this percentage reflects the difference in the cost of producing oil and selling it on the global market at world prices. Thus, oil exporters have larger values on this indicator indicating its importance in their economy but also its likely impact on their environment. The oil industry is one of the most "masculine," polluting and powerful industries on the planet making its gender implications and connection to the creation of sustainable societies essential. According to Ross (2008) and Blaydes and Linzer (2008), oil economies are linked to male economic empowerment and women's economic *disempowerment*. Connecting with arguments presented here, economically disempowered women have less say in decisions on environmentally sustainable or environmentally destructive practices (Blumberg 2008, 2015).

Findings

Table 7.3 presents the results of the regression analysis examining women's contributions to creating sustainable societies. Findings reveal that empowered women help create sustainability. Reducing women's risk for discrimination, granting women greater economic, political and social rights and moving towards female-male income equality not only improves women's well-being but the society and planet as a whole. Ecosystem vitality and environmental health as reflected in the dependent variable benefit from societies recognizing the contributions that women can make when granted equal partnership in addressing challenges confronting the planet.

Gender, development and the environment 123

TABLE 7.3 Regression of sustainability index on gender and development indicators controlling for economic development, population pressure, democratization, war and oil economies

Variable	Model 1 b (S.E.)	Model 2 b (S.E.)	Model 3 b (S.E.)	Model 4 b (S.E.)	Model 5 b (S.E.)	Model 6 b (S.E.)
Economic development	3.062*** (.602)	2.640*** (.611)	2.603*** (.619)	2.890*** (.595)	2.719*** (.623)	3.165*** (.582)
Population pressure	.492 (.708)	.828 (.704)	.969 (.720)	.433 (.695)	.581 (.702)	.691 (.687)
Democratization	.182*** (.054)	.160*** (.054)	.170*** (.054)	.170*** (.053)	.168*** (.054)	.167*** (.052)
The presence of war	-1.956 (1.627)	-1.878 (1.588)	-1.480 (1.604)	-1.543 (1.605)	-1.628 (1.618)	-1.462 (1.579)
Oil economy GDP	-.191*** (.042)	-.166*** (.042)	-.162*** (.042)	-.156*** (.043)	-.172*** (.042)	-.171*** (.041)
Prevalence of women's risk of discrimination		-.110** (.043)				
Prevalence of women's social rights			2.042** (.844)			
Prevalence of women's political rights				2.789** (1.197)		
Prevalence of women's economic rights					2.013* (1.079)	
Level of female-male income equality						.128*** (.043)
Constant	27.057	34.256	29.939	22.759	27.107	26.939
N	114	114	114	114	114	114
Adjusted R²	.492	.526	.514	.512	.504	.527
F-value	22.902	21.112	20.916	20.771	20.104	21.970
(Probability)	(.000)	(.000)	(.000)	(.000)	(.000)	(.000)

Notes: *significant at p=.10. **significant at p=.05. ***significant at p=.01 or greater.

Strengthening the findings, the results are net of controls which Model 1 presents. Each of these predictors significantly affect sustainability on their own: democratic and wealthier societies are associated with the achievement of sustainable societies while population pressure, the presence of war and the importance of the oil industry to a country's GDP have negative effects and thus detract from sustainability. In constructing the combined model, population pressure disappears with the inclusion of economic development while the effect of war disappears when oil economies is added. Using this model as a foundation for the remaining results, findings reveal that empowered women free of the risk of discrimination are able to overcome the barriers associated with poorer, non-democratic societies or others whose economy is dominated by extractive industries unfriendly to the environment and women as well.

Model 2 indicates that the greater the risk of gender discrimination, the less likely it is that a country moves in the direction of achieving sustainability. Unjust treatment of women parallels environmental degradation, reinforcing arguments that patriarchal societies viewing women as second-class citizens are also likely to exploit the environment. In this sense, societies that think nothing of gendered violence or treating women as property will likely also abuse the land with intensive agriculture or overuse of pesticides for example. Societies that discriminate against women are less likely to recognize their potential not only for contributions toward the achievement of sustainable societies but also toward the economy, education and politics among other realms empowering women beyond traditional roles. Such "disempowerment" as described by Blumberg (2015) "is linked not only to subjugated women but also a woeful array of problems, including a widespread worsening of human welfare" of which failing to achieve sustainable societies is certainly a part.

Continuing this theme, Models 3 and 4 conversely indicate that countries granting women greater social and political rights are likely to become more sustainable societies. Speaking to social rights specifically, giving women equal footing with regard to contraceptive decision-making, educational attainment, marital rights and participation in society among other factors reflect a form of empowerment that women may then transfer into environmental protection that is in their best interest (Blumberg 2008) and that of the planet as a whole. This extends further to the political front in that women who can hold office, vote or participate freely in politics in a variety of other ways can make their voices heard. As has often been the case with numerous women in all corners of the world this means fighting for ecosystem vitality and environmental health in many forms, again with spillover from personal interests to the larger society. Empowering women with rights means greater access to water or basic sanitation, for example, or improved child well-being and critical habitat protection that are important reflections of sustainability.

Model 5 and especially Model 6 reinforce Blumberg's (2015) notion that economic power is central to gender equality and its spillover effects for environmental well-being. Income is essential to empowerment that strengthens women's political and social rights and generates opportunities to improve their life chances and those of their families and community. Greater rights in the form of equal access to jobs, equal pay for equal work or income opportunities from non-agricultural sectors of the economy are likely to result in the creation of more sustainable societies.

In addition, Model 6 reflects the extension of women's rights and freedom from discrimination examined in Models 2 through 5 to actual practices or outcomes in society. Granting rights and recognition is different than seeing how this actually comes to fruition with regard to the level of income equality between men and women. In other words, the latter of these implies the acquisition of an actual form of power for women and their level of this relative to men. Connecting this to previous research, generating women's wealth improves development (Blumberg et al. 1995) and the analysis here importantly extends this to sustainability, reinforcing ideas from Blumberg (2008) who notes that "if women ... are to realize their preferences for conservation and sustainability, they need economic clout."

Countries with improved women's lives are thus more likely to be sustainable societies. Global movements for the environment and women's rights can contribute greatly to ecosystem vitality and environmental health on multiple fronts including agriculture, air quality, biodiversity and habitat, climate change and energy, fisheries, forests, health impacts and water resources, as reflected in the indicator for sustainable societies used here.

Discussion

GAD approaches should be increasingly incorporated into the dialogue on creating sustainable societies. This is particularly the case as the world moves from the Millennium Development Goals (MDGs) that have shaped development policy to the Sustainable Development Goals (SDGs) arising from the Rio+20 gathering in 2012 (Griggs et al. 2013; UNDESA 2014). Furthermore, as climate change becomes increasingly pressing it is imperative that reducing strain on global ecology be a priority. It is also important to consider how protecting the environment feeds back into supporting gender equity and the benefits that sustainable societies have for women, thus continuing a cycle of gender and ecological wellbeing reinforcing each other. Finally, there are major policy considerations further connecting women, the environment and development. To frame the discussion that follows it is helpful to revisit the lives of the courageous women fighting for the environment mentioned briefly at the outset of this chapter.

Central to the importance of global conversations on issues of environment and sustainability and the significance of women's role in this dialogue, the 2014 Summit on Women and Climate took place in Bali, Indonesia. Mama Aleta Baun was a participant and featured speaker at this gathering, sharing her story of nonviolent protest and year-long weaving sit-in that challenged mining practices threatening her Molo homeland. With machete scars on her legs from being physically attacked, she eventually won closure of several mines and continues working to protect the environment and the rights to the land of Indonesia's indigenous peoples (Global Greengrants Fund 2014).

Argentina's Sofia Gatica has shown steadfast commitment and strong leadership in the environmental movement. She too is no stranger to violence in carrying out her struggles. For years she and her children have received anonymous threats of violence because of her organizing work on ecological issues. Gatica has long been concerned about health and environmental justice, targeting in particular the indiscriminate spraying of pesticides on the soybean fields (Goldman Environmental Prize 2014) surrounding her hometown where the rates of birth defects, cancer and infant mortality soar much higher than national averages (Graves 2012). A leading advocate for sustainable agriculture, Gatica has expanded her fight to address genetically modified organisms in her country as well. Her movement has spread throughout South America and she is prepared for a long struggle against multinational agrochemical corporations that she and growing numbers of others believe are poisoning people throughout the world (Cernansky 2012).

And then there is Ikal Angelei from Kenya fighting the Gibe 3 Dam in project in Ethiopia –which would be the world's fourth largest dam – because of its impact on water levels in Lake Turkana, which lies mostly in northern Kenya. The issue walks a difficult line between the supply of needed electricity for impoverished regions of these countries versus the consequences and potential for increased violence over water scarcity, the devastation of fish stocks and the lake ecosystem as well as the failure to include indigenous peoples in Ethiopia and Kenya who rely on the lake for their livelihoods in the discussion (Russo 2012). She argues that sustainability and the environment must ultimately take precedence, for "there's absolutely no way that dam can go on and the people in Turkana will survive" (Russo 2012).

Taken together, these stories and the battles fought by women the world over are the epitome of what creating sustainable societies means and the place that women have in this process. Eliminating exposure to toxins, protecting ecosystems and water access or saving forests from destruction are a few among many of the ways that women have challenged economic systems and development practices that operate without consideration of the impacts on the environment and the people whose livelihoods depend on it. Women's intimate involvement with the world's ecological crises have put them in an important position of demanding that sustainability be the priority. Their well-being and that of their families, communities and the entire world demands it. Considering these stories and the many that go untold, the connections between women's contributions to sustainability and important policy considerations moving forward become clear.

Women's contributions to sustainability

Addressing women's rights and empowerment benefits societies as a whole, not just women. The wide-ranging effects have impacts from the household and village level to national and global issues associated with climate change and development policies.

This reflects the "half the sky" idea attributed to Mao Zedong on the importance of gender equality for economic growth. This argument has been picked up as a global movement relating to ideas from Blumberg (2004) and Kristof and WuDunn (2009), including the "girl effect" and its relationship with the economy, education, hunger, population pressure, poverty, violence, war and women's health. Kristoff and WuDunn say very little about the environment or sustainable development, however, and this chapter extends the discussion on this front. Investing in gender equality improves sustainable development and other important ways that women hold up half the sky.

Findings here connect well with discussions of inequality and environmental well-being experienced by various groups in the world. One connection in particular is that women are central in helping to reduce or eliminate what Nixon (2011) thoughtfully addresses as "slow violence" and how the poorest and most disenfranchised segments of the world's population suffer the most from ecological destruction. Because environmental degradation often does not have the "spectacular" quality to it that attracts attention or enables understanding of its significance, it is essential that the "quiet," seemingly passive, though destructive, impacts of unsustainable practices by the nations of the world be given the attention deserved. Supporting Nixon's thesis and reinforcing the need for examining the role that women have in addressing environmental issues, looking at sustainable development through the lens of gender reveals how best to address environmental degradation.

This connects with the role that women have played in the environmental movement, particularly in challenging environmental injustices and threats to environmental health (see Barry 2012; Bell 2013; Buckingham and Rakibe 2009; Gibbs 2010; Merchant 1981; Musil 2014; Sze 2007). Women who are free from discrimination and granted economic, political and social rights and who increasingly earn income are empowered to act in the public sphere and have their interests inserted into the public dialogue. Building sustainable societies comes with women's voices behind them.

The cycle of sustainability

As important as women's contributions to sustainability are, at the same time one should consider how sustainable societies empower women to make the change they wish to see. This implies the importance of feedback cycles akin to circular causal mechanisms. Women indeed have an important role in creating sustainable societies, but in the other direction one must also consider the meaningful impacts that sustainability has on women's well-being as a consequence. This could result in a feedback loop in which women are "freed up" to contribute more to creating sustainable societies. Thinking about various components of the sustainability index used as the dependent variable illustrates this.

Consider environmental health as captured by child mortality, for example. Women with economic resources in particular or more generally recognized rights that free them from discrimination are empowered to reduce child mortality. Thomas (1990, 1997), for example, has found that women's income has up to twenty times the impact on reducing child mortality in Brazil compared to men's. At the same time, reductions in child mortality and improvements in environmental health mean that women will not be forced to have as many children. Lower fertility rates mean fewer demands on child-rearing or less risk of maternal mortality or other complications. Women's well-being could thus result in improvements in societal well-being that allows women and girls to devote more time to education, working outside the home, civic engagement or any number of other endeavors.

Another example is research on gender and climate change (Dankelman 2002; Denton 2002; MacGregor 2010; Terry 2009) and the need to consider economic, political and social inequalities alongside environmental well-being. Similar mutually reinforcing benefits can come from women who are empowered to reduce indoor air pollution with alternative fuel sources and methods for household cooking and/or heating. Considering fuelwood for example, less time having to collect it means more time devoted to other endeavors and reduced impacts on the land, climate change and environmental health. This cycles back to improve women's lives and the health of the planet. Parallel arguments could be made for access to water, sanitation or wastewater treatment as well as protection of biomes of various kinds.

Julekha Begum, a peasant woman from Bangladesh notes "Life is a whole, it is a circle. That which destroys the circle should be stopped. That which maintains the circle should be strengthened and nurtured" (quoted in UNEP 2014: 11). Women are central to that circle and their empowerment reaps great benefits for building sustainable societies — women affect development. When rooted in sound policy and planning in which women with recognized economic, political and social rights and economic resources are empowered to contribute, *sustainable* development can also affect women in positive ways.

Policy considerations and the future

Making this possible means there are important policy implications of this research to consider as well. Women's impacts regarding how best to protect the planet are significant for ongoing climate change discussions such as the 2012 Rio+20 meetings and other gatherings, as well as agricultural policy, education, food security and health. Recognizing the value that women have in contributing to these discussions reveals how their part in holding up half the sky creates sustainable societies. The more women are granted a seat at the table or the greater their voices of protest outside closed doors are heard, the better-off the planet will be. Policy must reflect that.

This is also clear when considering MDG 3, which promotes gender equality and the empowerment of women as a key component of achieving development, poverty alleviation and sustainability (see Abu-Ghaida and Klasen 2004; Heyzer 2005). However, with the 2015 deadline for the MDGs upon us, despite progress on some fronts they have achieved only limited success regarding women and MDG 3 (Friis 2013). Many lingering and interconnected issues remain, including employment, environmental health, food security, gendered violence and poverty among others that detract from achieving sustainable societies.

Implementation of the Sustainable Development Goals as a central part of the post-2015 agenda is an ideal way to move forward. UN Secretary-General Ban Ki-Moon's 2012 High-Level Panel on Global Sustainability has noted that "any serious shift towards sustainable development requires gender equality" (quoted in Menon 2012 and Friis 2013). Similarly, the Eighth Session of the Open Working Group on the Sustainable Development Goals that took place in New York in

February 2014 discussed the SDGs and the post-2015 development framework. They conclude that "promoting equality, including social equity, gender equality and women's empowerment" (Scampini 2014) is a key issue to be addressed. Achieving sustainable societies comes both in recognizing the role that women have had in helping societies achieve these ends while at the same time understanding the need to give voice to women's perspectives through greater empowerment and equality.

Conclusions

Women have a critically important role in building sustainable societies. The empowerment of women has powerful effects on environmental well-being and the health of societies around the world. Development planning and implementation demands a GAD perspective – especially as the world falls more deeply into the current climate crisis. As the world's proportion of women in the labor force increases (see World Bank 2014) as well as their roles in other areas such as agriculture and food systems, conflict/war, domestic violence, education, family planning and health, population and politics, women have claimed an increasingly influential place in shaping policy and program implementation. Sustainable development can be included as also benefitting from the contributions that women make.

As Menon (2012) notes, "when women have equal access to resources and opportunities to participate in decision-making processes they become drivers of sustainable development by taking environmental, economic and social action." GAD perspectives can produce results on multiple fronts, making the achievement of sustainable societies at the core of the post-2015 development agenda and the Sustainable Development Goals.

References

Abu-Ghaida, Dina and Stephan Klasen. 2004. "The Costs of Missing the Millennium Development Goal on Gender Equity." *World Development* 32: 1075–1107.

Banerjee, Damayanti and Michael Mayerfeld Bell. 2007. "Ecogender: Locating Gender in Environmental Social Science." *Society and Natural Resources* 30: 3–19.

Barry, Joyce M. 2012. *Standing Our Ground: Women, Environmental Justice and the Fight to End Mountaintop Removal.* Athens, OH: Ohio University Press.

Bell, Shannon Elizabeth. 2013. *Our Roots Run Deep as Ironweed: Appalachian Women and the Fight for Environmental Justice.* Champaign, IL: University of Illinois Press.

Bernard, Ted. 2010. *Hope and Hard Times: Communities, Collaboration and Sustainability.* Gabriola Island, Canada: New Society Publishers.

Blaydes, Lisa and Drew A. Linzer. 2008. "The Political Economy of Women's Support for Fundamentalist Islam." *World Politics* 60(4): 576–609.

Blumberg, Rae Lesser. 2015. "The Magic Money Tree? Women, Economic Power and Development in a Globalized World." In *Sociology of Development Handbook*, edited by Gregory Hooks. Berkeley, CA: The University of California Press.

———2008. "Gender, Environment and Environmental Ethics: Exploring the Critical Role of Economic Power in Thailand, Ecuador and Malawi." Presentation at the UNESCO

Conference on Ethics of Energy Technologies: Ethical Views of Nature. Seoul, South Korea.
——2004. "Extending Lenski's Schema to Hold Up Both Halves of the Sky: A Theory-Guided Way of Conceptualizing Agrarian Societies that Illuminates a Puzzle about Gender Stratification." *Sociological Theory* 22(2): 278–291.
——1989. "Toward a Feminist Theory of Development." Pp. 161–199 in *Feminism and Sociological Theory*, edited by Ruth A. Wallace. Newbury Park, CA: Sage.
——1984. "A General Theory of Gender Stratification." *Sociological Theory* 2: 23–101.
Blumberg, Rae Lesser, Cathy A. Rakowski, Irene Tinker and Michael Monteon (eds). 1995. *Engendering Wealth and Well-being: Empowerment for Global Change*. Boulder, CO: Westview Press.
Boserup, Esther. 1970. *Women and Economic Development*. New York: St. Martin's Press.
Brown, Lester R., Gary Gardner and Brian Halweil. 1999. "16 Impacts of Population Growth." *Futurist* 33(2): 36–41.
Buckingham, Susan and Kulcur Rakibe. 2009. "Gendered Geographies of Environmental Injustice." *Antipode* 41(4): 659–683.
Cernansky, Rachel. 2012. "The Mother who Stood up to Monsanto in Argentina." *Grist*, April 17. Available at: http://grist.org/industrial-agriculture/the-mother-who-stood-up-to-monsanto-in-argentina/
Cingranelli, David L. and David L. Richards. 2010. "The Cingranelli and Richards (CIRI) Human Rights Data Project." *Human Rights Quarterly* 32: 395–418.
Clark, Brett, Andrew K. Jorgenson and Jeffrey Kentor. 2010. "Militarization and Energy Consumption." *International Journal of Sociology* 40: 23–43.
Dankelman, Irene. 2002. "Climate Change: Learning from Gender Analysis and Women's Experiences of Organising for Sustainable Development." *Gender and Development* 10: 21–29.
Denton, Fatma. 2002 "Climate Change Vulnerability, Impacts and Adaptation: Why Does Gender Matter?" *Gender and Development* 10: 10–20.
Edwards, Andres R. 2005. *The Sustainability Revolution: Portrait of a Paradigm Shift*. Gabriola Island, Canada: New Society Publishers.
Friis, Anette Engelund. 2013. "Time for Recognition: Building on the Progress at CSW57 to Empower Women in Agriculture." *The World Post*, May 25. Available at: www.huffingtonpost.com/anette-engelund-friis/time-for-recognition_b_2926266.html
Gibbs, Lois. 2010. *Love Canal: and the Birth of the Environmental Health Movement*, 3rd edn. Washington, DC: Island Press.
Global Greengrants Fund. 2014. "Mama Aleta: One Woman's Struggle to save Indonesia's Forests from Mining." July 20. Available at: www.greengrants.org/2014/07/20/mama-aleta-one-womans-struggle-to-save-indonesias-forests-from-mining/
Goldman Environmental Prize, The. 2014. "Recipients by Year." Goldman Environmental Foundation. Available at: www.goldmanprize.org/recipients/year
Graves, Lucia. 2012. "Sofia Gatica, Argentine Activist, Faced Anonymous Death Threats for Fighting Monsanto Herbicide." *The Huffington Post*, May 3. Available at: www.huffingtonpost.com/2012/05/03/argentine-activist-sofia-gatica-monsanto_n_1475659.html)
Griggs, David, Mark Stafford-Smith, Owen Gaffney, Johan Rockström et al. 2013. "Policy: Sustainable Development Goals for People and Planet." *Nature* 495: 305–307.
Harcourt, Wendy. 1994. *Feminist Perspectives on Sustainable Development*. London: Zed Books.
Heyzer, Noeleen. 2005. "Making the Links: Women's Rights and Empowerment Are Key to Achieving the Millennium Development Goals." *Gender and Development* 13: 9–12.
Inglehart, Ronald, Pippa Norris and Christian Welzel. 2002. "Gender Equality and Democracy." *Comparative Sociology* 1: 321–345.

Klasen, Stephan. 2002. "Low Schooling for Girls, Slower Growth for All? Cross-country Evidence on the Effect of Gender Inequality in Education on Economic Development." *World Bank Economic Review* 16: 345–373.

Kristof, Nicholas D. and Sheryl WuDunn. 2009. *Half the Sky: Turning Oppression into Opportunity for Women Worldwide.* New York: Vintage Books.

Leach, Melissa. 2007. "Earth Mother Myths and Other Ecofeminist Fables: How a Strategic Notion Rose and Fell." *Development & Change* 38: 67–85.

Littig, Beate. 2002. "The Case for Gender-sensitive Socio-ecological Research." *Work, Employment and Society* 16: 111–132.

MacGregor, Sherilyn. 2010. "'Gender and Climate Change': From Impacts to Discourses." *Journal of the Indian Ocean Region* 6: 223–238.

Marshall, Monty G. and Ted Robert Gurr. 2014. "Polity IV Project: Political Regime Characteristics and Transitions, 1800–2013." College Park, MD: Integrated Network for Societal Conflict Research Program. Available at: www.systemicpeace.org/polity/polity4.htm

Menon, Saraswathi. 2012. "The Sustainable Development Goals and the Post-2015 Development Agenda: The Gender Dimensions." New York: United Nations Entity for Gender Equality and the Empowerment of Women. Available at: www.unwomen.org/en/news/stories/2012/3/the-sustainable-development-goals-and-the-post-2015-development-agenda-the-gender-dimensions

Merchant, Carolyn. 2005. *Radical Ecology: The Search for a Livable World*, 2nd edn. New York: Routledge.

——1981. "Women and the Environmental Movement." *Environment* 23(5): 6–16.

Mesina, Rita Marie L. 2009. "A Take on Ecofeminism: Putting an Emphasis on the Relationship between Women and the Environment." *Ateneo Law Journal* 53: 1120–1146.

Mies, Maria and Vandana Shiva. 1993. *Ecofeminism*. London: Zed Books.

Moffat, Linda, Yolande Geadah and Rieky Stuart. 1991. *Two Halves Make a Whole: Balancing Gender Relationships in Development*. Ottawa: Canadian Council for International Co-operation.

Moore, Niamh. 2008. "The Rise and Rise of Ecofeminism as a Development Fable: A Response to Melissa Leach's 'Earth Mothers and Other Ecofeminist Fables: How a Strategic Notion Rose and Fell'." *Development & Change* 39: 461–475.

Moraes, Andrea and Patricia E. Perkins. 2007. "Women, Equity and Participatory Water Management in Brazil." *International Feminist Journal of Politics* 9: 485–493.

Musil, Robert K. 2014. *Rachel Carson and Her Sisters: Extraordinary Women Who Have Shaped America's Environment*. New Brunswick, NJ: Rutgers University Press.

Newell, Peter. 2005. "Race, Class and the Global Politics of Environmental Inequality." *Global Environmental Politics* 5: 70–94.

Nixon, Rob. 2011. *Slow Violence and the Environmentalism of the Poor.* Cambridge, MA: Harvard University Press.

Roberts, J. Timmons and Bradley Parks. 2006. *A Climate of Injustice: Global Inequality, North-South Politics and Climate Policy*. Cambridge, MA: MIT Press.

Ross, Michael L. 2008. "Oil, Islam and Women." *American Political Science Review* 102(1): 107–123.

Russo, Christina M. 2012. "A Kenyan Woman Stands Up Against Massive Dam Project." *Yale Environment 360*, April 25. Available at: http://e360.yale.edu/feature/kenyan_ikal_angelei_stands_up_to_ethiopia_gibe_iii_dam/2520/

Scampini, Alejandra. 2014. "Sustainable Development Goals: Where Do Gender Equality and Women's Rights Stand?" Toronto: Association for Women's Rights in Development. Available at: www.awid.org/News-Analysis/Friday-Files/Sustainable-Development-Goals-Where-do-Gender-Equality-and-Women-s-Rights-Stand

Scanlan, Stephen J. 2004. "Women, Development and Food Security in Less Industrialized Societies: Contributions and Challenges for the New Century." *World Development* 32: 1807–1829.

Sharma, Anjali. 1998. "Contribution of Rural Women to Environmentally Sustainable Economic Development: An African Experience." *Journal of Rural Development* 17: 681–701.

Strachan, Janet and Maryse Roberts. 2003. "Poverty, Environment and Sustainable Development." *The Round Table* 92: 541–559.

Sydee, Jasmin and Sharon Beder. 2001. "Ecofeminism and Globalisation: A Critical Appraisal." *Democracy & Nature* 7:1085–5661.

Sze, Julie. 2007. "Boundaries of Violence: Water, Gender and Globalization at the US Borders." *International Feminist Journal of Politics* 9(4): 475–484.

Terry, Geraldine. 2009. "No Climate Justice without Gender Justice: An Overview of the Issues." *Gender and Development* 17:5–18.

Thomas, Duncan. 1997. "Incomes, Expenditures and Health Outcomes: Evidence on Intrahousehold Resource Allocation." In *Intrahousehold Resource Allocation in Developing Countries: Models, Methods and Policy*, edited by Laurence Haddad, John Hoddinott and Harold Alderman. Baltimore, MD: The Johns Hopkins University Press.

——1990. "Intrahousehold Resource Allocation: An Inferential Approach." *Journal of Human Resources* 25: 635–664.

Tinker, Irene (ed.). 1990. *Persistent Inequalities: Women and World Development*. New York: Oxford University Press.

Uppsala University Department of Peace and Conflict Research/The Peace Research Institute Oslo. UCDP/PRIO 2014. "Armed Conflict Dataset." Available at: www.pcr.uu.se/research/ucdp/datasets/ucdp_prio_armed_conflict_dataset/

United Nations Department of Economic and Social Affairs, Division for Sustainable Development (UNDESA). 2014. "Sustainable Development Goals." New York: UN. Available at: http://sustainabledevelopment.un.org/?menu=1300)

United Nations Development Programme (UNDP). 2011. *Human Development Report 2011*. New York: Oxford University Press.

——2006. *Human Development Report 2006*. New York: Oxford University Press.

United Nations Environment Program. 2014. "Women and the Environment." Nairobi: UNEP. Available at: www.unep.org/Documents.Multilingual/Default.asp?Document ID=468&ArticleID=4488

Vazquez Garcia, Veronica. 2001. "Taking Gender into Account: Women and Sustainable Development Projects in Rural Mexico." *Women's Studies Quarterly* 29: 85–98.

Walker, Barbara Louise Endama o. 2001. "Sisterhood and Seine-Nets: Engendering Development and Conservation in Ghana's Marine Fishery." *Professional Geographer* 53: 160–177.

World Bank. 2014. "World Development Indicators." Washington, DC: The World Bank. Available at: http://data.worldbank.org/data-catalog/world-development-indicators

——2012. *World Development Report 2012: Gender Equality and Development*. Washington, DC: World Bank Publications.

World Commission on Environment and Development. 1987. *Our Common Future*. New York: Oxford University Press.

World Resources Institute. 2009. "Earth Trends Database." Washington, DC: World Resources Institute. Available at: www.wri.org/

Yale Center for Environmental Law & Policy/The Center for International Earth Science Information Network. 2013. "Environmental Performance Index." New Haven, CT: Yale University. Available at: http://epi.yale.edu/

Note

1 This research was made possible by a 2013 Fulbright Scholar Award. I benefited greatly from the advice of colleagues in the School of Political Science and Sociology at the National University of Ireland Galway and participants in the Research Cluster on Environment, Development and Sustainability. Drafts of this work benefited from the feedback of Rae Blumberg, Sam Cohn, Andrew Dawson, Andrew Jorgenson and Liam Swiss.

8
A WALK ON THE WILD SIDE OF GENDER, WAR AND DEVELOPMENT IN AFGHANISTAN AND NORTHERN UGANDA

Rae Lesser Blumberg

First, I'll tell you about my actual walk on the wild side of gender stratification: in July–August 2011, I was in Afghanistan doing two final evaluations for UNDP.[1] One hot, August day during Ramadan, a new UNDP driver didn't know that the main entrance to the Green Zone of international development agencies, embassies and ISAF (the allies' military HQ) was almost around the corner from our building. Instead, he drove me to the far side, on busy Massoud Square. He left me near a long, deserted sidewalk that led to a turnstile – a little-used pedestrian entrance. Afghanistan was the thirteenth conflict country I've worked in, of 45 since Peace Corps, but it was scary. I wasn't in full hijab, wearing only a narrow, flowered headscarf and a hip-length blouse with ¾ sleeves, not a long tunic. The only other woman I could see was a beggar in a burqa, cadging change from drivers stopped at a light a block away. I walked alone along a metal fence. Behind it I saw the steel superstructure for a building of about 12 stories. Later I learned it was to be a hotel, maybe a Marriott, but it seemed deserted. Still, I had a strong feeling that someone was aiming at the center of my back. The walk to the turnstile and the bored guard took forever. A few weeks later, on September 13, five members of the Haqqani terrorist network, armed with rocket launchers, military assault rifles, grenades, you name it, climbed that superstructure and laid siege to the Green Zone for 20 hours – a first. So they probably *were* there as I walked past and something probably *was* aimed at my back. Later, I asked Randy Collins why so many security forces in the Green Zone permitted a structure that looked down on every building to be completely unguarded – certainly a violation of rule no.1 about war: never let your enemy have the high ground. He said that each security force probably was sure someone else was doing it. But my tale is about gender stratification, not a military blunder: My point is that oppressing women is linked to armed conflict and lousy development, a trifecta of misery.

Introduction

Although this article is linked to theory – specifically, a general theory of gender stratification and theory of gender and development[2] – it's unlike anything I ever wrote for a sociological publication. This time it's personal. Accordingly, I'll use first person when writing about some of what I encountered in war-torn Afghanistan (in South Asia) and among the Acholi in Northern Uganda (in East Africa) after the ceasefire that ended 23 years of terror, war and atrocities by the horrific Lord's Resistance Army (LRA).

Both gender theories focus on the importance of economic empowerment – or economic *dis*empowerment – for women's equality and well-being, and the ripple effects these have on the woman's family, community and nation, as well as for development. Afghan and Acholi women differ greatly in their access to economic power.

The "walk on the wild side" took place in Afghanistan where women have almost *zero* economic power and their overall position is arguably about the most unequal on earth. The fact that the overwhelming majority are almost wholly without economic power – neither earning income nor owning/controlling land or other assets – has had strong repercussions. The introductory chapter characterizes women's economic empowerment as a "magic potion for development" and women's economic *dis*empowerment as a "poison potion for development." Afghanistan, as discussed later, embodies what happens where economically powerless women, a long history of war (the most recent series of wars began in 1978) and distorted development come together.

The picture is less grim among the Acholi in Northern Uganda after the government ceasefire with Joseph Kony, LRA founder and supreme leader (he claims that he'll rule by the Ten Commandments – apparently he hasn't heard about the one stating, "Thou shalt not kill"). We'll see what a difference the modest amount of economic power Acholi women acquired in the refugee camps has been making in their people's recovery, healing and nascent development.

Background

In Afghanistan, I conducted final evaluations of two major UNDP projects (Blumberg 2011a; 2011b). There were few gender angles, although the government's participatory process to formulate the Afghanistan National Development Strategy (ANDS) was the first time in the country's history that people from all 34 provinces had been consulted on their country's development and future: urban and rural, well-off and poor, males and – an absolute first – females. It was Ramadan and very hot. The Muslims abstained from water and food during the day. I never saw a foreigner drinking or eating. My work took me to various ministries (especially Finance) and development entities around Kabul. But UNDP travel elsewhere was on hold because of intelligence about possible attacks. Travel was in armored UNDP SUVs. I lived in the heavily fortified Green Village; up to that point, it had never been attacked (it has been since; we did, however, have one major security alert for an attack in Kabul that necessitated donning our light blue UN flak jackets and helmets and activating our field radios). Aside from some UN people, almost everyone else living there did work requiring arms; about 90 percent were men.

I also worked in Northern Uganda in March–April 2010, after the ceasefire. I did baseline research (as in Afghanistan, using my version of Rapid Appraisal, Blumberg 2002; see below) and created a monitoring and evaluation system for the first *development* project that was *not* humanitarian aid after 23 years of war (Blumberg 2010). The USAID/Winrock project aimed to rehabilitate 5,000 km of unusable roads and deepen village bore wells that had run dry. The roads had become overgrown over the years of conflict; the water problem, however, was man-made. During the war, government soldiers (when unpaid) and the LRA chopped down and sold the trees. Cutting down the trees led to much less rainfall, causing the water table to drop far below the depth of the village wells. Launching the project quickly was essential: the government was trying to empty the Internally Displaced Persons (IDP) camps as fast as possible. They sent people home to villages without working wells, reachable only on foot over nearly impassible roads. Their promises of tools and seeds for their crops had yet to be fulfilled. When I arrived, I was told that only 10–15 percent of the "worst cases" remained in the IDP camps.[3]

Some reasons why Afghanistan is so patriarchal

Ahmed-Ghosh (2003) provides the first key to Afghanistan's history: this has been a tribal society – multilingual and multiethnic – never fully governed by a weak state. Moghadam (2002: 19) provides the second: almost nowhere on Earth do men dominate women so absolutely, with "a particularly entrenched form of patriarchy and a tribal-based social structure in which only men have rights, equality, and unlimited access to public space." A third strand, I suggest, comes from the dominant Pashtuns' traditional and extraordinarily masculinist tribal code, *Pashtunwali*. Moghadam quotes Nancy Tapper (1984: 304), an anthropologist who studied the Durrani Pashtuns of North-Central Afghanistan in the 1970s: "The members of the community discuss control of all resources – especially labor, land, and women – in terms of 'honor'." Moghadam adds: "Note that 'community' is the community of men and that 'women' are assimilated in the concept of 'resources'" (ibid.: 20). Men view women (and children) as property, period. Moghadam also cites Veronica Doubleday (1988), who studied women in seclusion (*purdah*) in the Pashtun-majority western city of Herat in the 1970s and learned that *purdah* was not just almost unending seclusion – it meant men had complete control over their women's mobility. Moghadam concludes that this "gave men ultimate power" (ibid.: 22). I argue that these women lacked all "power of the purse." So, in terms of the "gendered economic power" theory of gender stratification discussed later in this chapter, the women had nothing to counter men's monopoly of power and were forced to accept seclusion and complete subordination.

A note about methods

I've worked in almost every sector of development (except for big dam projects) in 45 countries since my Peace Corps years in Venezuela. This includes 13 countries each in Asia and the Pacific, and in Latin America and the Caribbean, as well as 10 in sub-Saharan Africa; the rest are scattered worldwide. I frequently use my version of Rapid Appraisal (RA) for development research (Beebe 2001; Blumberg 2002). RA's validity principle is "triangulation": For each of a tightly honed list of variables and issues, one collects at least two data sources, if possible via different techniques. These include key informant interviews, focus groups, observation,[4] secondary analysis of existing data sets, content analysis of written or videotaped sources and documents ranging from project reports to scholarly literature. In addition, given my geographic experience and prior work with quantitative methods and ethnographic sources and databases, I can "triangulate" from my own personal experience too. So I don't enter a new country (Afghanistan) with a tabula rasa – and I'd worked in Uganda in 2000 and 2002.[5] Still, the material on Afghanistan is more my impressions than well-triangulated: gender was only a marginal topic in my "terms of reference" and I wasn't able to properly double-check what I observed or heard. In Northern Uganda, gender became a salient topic when we realized that most men were drunk by early afternoon – while the women continued with their work. This affected focus groups, group meetings and individual interviews and showed that some of the project assumptions about men working on the road rehabilitation near their village needed rethinking. So I was able to delve deeper into gender issues.

A first look at Afghan and Acholi women's economic situation through a theoretical lens

This section introduces two gender theories and applies them to Afghan and Acholi women. The main variable in both theories is *relative economic power of women vs. men*, defined as control of key economic resources, including income and assets (e.g. land, livestock, credit).

Again, Afghan women have virtually no economic power: Only 8 percent have non-agricultural employment and only 5.6 per cent owned businesses (Government of the Islamic Republic of Afghanistan 2010: 10). Worse, in a nation over three-quarters rural, only 1.87 percent of women owned – or had rights to – land (Grace 2005: 16). But the report notes that the "dominant and traditionally more conservative ethnic group (Pashtuns) were not heavily represented" in Grace's sample of mainly "minority ethnic groups" (ibid.: 18). This is striking: If less than 2 percent of women from ethnic groups considered less patriarchal than the Pashtuns owned or used land, what might be the proportion among the Pashtuns?

Moreover, women have more rights in Islam than they're given in Afghanistan: Islamic law permits them to own property and entitles them to half-share inheritance; additionally, brides are entitled to a property or money gift (*maher*).

Nevertheless, "Women's rights to property and inheritance are not upheld, and the bride's *maher* is given to the bride's family even if it rightfully belongs to the bride according to law and Islam" (Government of the Islamic Republic of Afghanistan 2009: 22).

Acholi women have no effective land rights because the group is patrilineal with male inheritance of land. The bride moves to the husband's village, where she arrives without allies and is expected to farm land she doesn't own. But years of living in the IDP camps caused some positive changes in women's economic position: they could leave the camps to earn income through day labor, trading or selling craft goods they learned to make from humanitarian aid groups' female income-generation training. People in the camps were mostly rural; they were there because the LRA rampaged and kidnapped child soldiers in the countryside. Most men spent their time drinking home-brew; many became hard-core alcoholics; meanwhile, women increasingly provided extra income (food rations were provided and camps had their own water pumps).

More propositions about the importance and outcomes of women's economic power

Here are a few more hypotheses from the theories. Of the five main types of power – economic, force (ranging from military might to individual violence), political, ideology and information/education – it is argued that for women, *economic power* is both (a) the most achievable empirically, and (b) the most important.

Most achievable power

Imagine a scale from near-0 to near-100 percent for both genders. Let's apply it to each form of power. Women's power is lowest with force/violence. Politically, currently Rwanda, Bolivia and Andorra have 50 percent or more women in parliament – but women haven't reached 50-50 political power in any country (e.g. president plus major ministers). Ideologically, 136 countries proclaim male-female equality in their constitutions (World Bank 2012: 2) but many groups have an ideology of male supremacy (e.g. the Pashtuns) and none say that women are superior. The only type of power that varies from near-zero to near-100 percent for men and women is economic power. In Afghanistan, men approach 100 percent of economic power. In colonial America, Iroquois women controlled virtually 100 percent of their economy, growing, storing and controlling the food supply. This also gave them influence in male-controlled political and some military matters (Brown 1975).

Where women have economic power, it is posited that it tends to soften hostile, negative uses of the other forms of power against them (Blumberg 1984, 2004b): Women with well-established economic power are less likely to be beaten, negative political and legal restrictions are less likely, the ideology is less male supremacist and a large gender gap in education is unlikely (but where women previously low in economic power begin gaining it, the more that men view this as a threat or zero-sum game, the more likely is a short-term spike in violence against the women).

Most important power

Economic power has consequences that range from the micro level of the woman and her family to the macro level of the state. When women have economic power, good things result; when they don't, nasty consequences often ensue. First the good news:

At the *micro* level, a large number of empirical studies (see, e.g. Blumberg forthcoming, 2015) support the following: (1) Increased economic power is causally linked to increased self-confidence, as well as (2) increased say in household decision-making power. (3) This includes decisions about (a) domestic well-being, e.g. which children are taken to the doctor when sick and how this differs for boys and girls; (b) economic issues (e.g. acquisition, allocation or sale of assets); and (c) fertility. Increased control of *fertility* is, perhaps, most important for a woman's life chances. Studies since 1968 (Weller) often find it's often the first thing a woman does for herself, after focusing on improving her children's diet, education and health needs, when she starts controlling income. Moreover, most women able to control their fertility opt for fewer children spaced farther apart and a later age of first birth. With greater economic power, most choose not to be baby-making machines – resulting in important benefits at the macro level.

At the *macro* level, fertility is inversely related to national income growth (Hess 1988; Das Gupta et al. 2011; Nolan and Lenski 2015). So, developing nations where women control their own fertility are likely to have a lower birthrate – and higher economic growth.

Also, education, health and nutrition make up "human capital" in social development. At the micro level, women and men with provider responsibilities tend to spend income under their control differently, with women spending disproportionately on precisely their children's education, health and nutrition. This is a hypothesis from the gender and development theory that now has considerable empirical support (see references in Blumberg 2015, forthcoming). And at the macro level, it is well-established that human capital increases both national income growth and national well-being.

Women's economic empowerment also is linked to other positive development outcomes, including: (a) increased environmental conservation (Blumberg 2008, forthcoming), hence more sustainable development; (b) less corruption (Mason and King 2001: 95), hence stronger economic growth; and (c) lower HIV/AIDS prevalence (Copeland 2006), which can affect a multiplicity of well-being and income growth outcomes. Furthermore, it doesn't take much female economic power to make a difference.

For example, modest female economic empowerment already has had impact in Bangladesh, which has the world's greatest saturation of microcredit: between the

Grameen Bank and BRAC (the world's largest NGO), programs exist in almost every village; clients overwhelmingly are women. When microcredit began its meteoric rise around 1982 (the year the Grameen Bank was chartered), almost all women lived in *purdah,* except for a few elites and the poorest (who did day labor in agriculture, including backbreaking toil in the rice paddies). Now, *purdah* is less strict – most women are permitted to spend some hours at the weekly or bi-weekly meetings of their microfinance group. With their income, these women are more likely to send their children to school – girls as well as boys – so the gender gap in primary and secondary education has vanished (UNESCO 2013/14). And some of their educated daughters are likely to be employed in the country's $20 billion export textile industry that is second only to China (Motlagh 2014).[6] Additionally, women's fertility has nose-dived to 2.2 children (World Bank 2015).

The "poison potion" for development: where women are economically disempowered

All you have to do is flip those positive "magic potion" relationships just enumerated and you find economically *dis*empowered women and a veritable "poison potion" for development: nations with development-sapping high fertility; ignorant, unhealthy, malnourished children; more avoidable diseases and deaths; and, quite likely, a more degraded environment and more corruption. There's even more bad news about women's economic disempowerment, including very high correlations with armed conflict. Although the authors don't (yet) claim causality (Caprioli 2000, 2005; Hudson et al. 2009), it's a dramatic picture.

Mary Caprioli's work (e.g. 2000, 2005) finds a strong inverse correlation between women's labor force participation (LFP) and armed conflict both internationally and within a nation: every 5 percent drop in women's LFP is correlated with an approximately 500 percent increase in international and internal armed conflict. Currently, the average of the world's nations for women in the labor force is 53 percent (World Bank 2014, my calculations). The countries with the lowest average female labor force participation are in the Middle East–North Africa (MENA) or South Asia. There, the seven lowest female LFP countries average only 13–18 percent: they are Afghanistan, Algeria, Iran, Iraq, Jordan, Saudi Arabia and Syria (ibid.). This means that a nation with only 15 percent (on average) of its women in the labor force is around 3,500 percent – seven times – more likely to have armed conflict than one with 50 percent of women in the labor force, i.e. just below the world average. Indeed, *all* of the "low LFP seven" recently have been or currently are involved in conflict.

Gender and three other types of power: political, force/violence and information/education

Here, we examine all but one of the remaining types of power affecting the level of gender stratification (the final type, ideological, is discussed later).

With respect to *political* power, there's an irony: Under pressure from the United States and its allies in ISAF (International Security Assistance Force), Afghanistan adopted gender quotas in both the upper and lower houses of parliament. Women make up 27.7 percent of the lower house and 27.5 percent of the upper chamber, ranking 40th of 190 countries, well above the world average of 22.3 percent for the lower house (Inter-Parliamentary Union 2015).[7] But though some incredibly brave, smart women legislators risk being murdered by extremists for speaking out, other women have proven more prudent or less passionately committed. Regardless, women have almost no clout in parliament and their political position doesn't seem to extend beyond the legislative chambers.

Concerning the power of *force/violence*, women are subject to mind-boggling levels of physical mistreatment. Although the *Afghanistan Country Report 2008–2010* (Government of the Islamic Republic of Afghanistan 2010: 10) notes that incidents of violence against women (VAW) are deliberately concealed in the name of family honor, "UNIFEM [has estimated] that 87% of women face abuse and violence in Afghanistan" (Khan 2012: 2; UNIFEM 2006). In 2009, President Karzai signed the Elimination of Violence against Women (EVAW) law by presidential proclamation, criminalizing 22 acts of VAW, including domestic violence, rape and underage and forced marriages (UNIFEM 2006 found that child and forced marriages comprise 60–80 percent of all marriages; Morgan 2008). Conservative lawmakers keep trying to abolish or gut EVAW; in February 2014, President Karzai rejected such an attempt passed by parliament (Amnesty International 2014). So it remains on the books – for now.[8]

Finally, let's consider the education aspect of the power of information/ education. The situation is grim: Only 6 percent of women aged 26 and over have ever been to school and about 88 percent are illiterate (Government of the Islamic Republic of Afghanistan 2009: 13).[9] The situation among females 18–24 years old is only slightly better: 82 percent are illiterate, vs. 50 percent of males (ibid.). Few Afghans enter and graduate from higher education. But for many women, finding a job after graduation may be tough.

More independent variables from the gender stratification theory: 1. The kin/property system

First, the most important kin/property variable is inheritance, followed by marital residence, with descent the weakest of the three.

Inheritance

The strictest rules tend to be about land and other zero-sum variables. You can't (easily) make more land. So if land previously went only to males and a new law says that rural land has to be divided among both male and female heirs, rural men are likely to contest or ignore it. For example, 75 percent of sub-Saharan African ethnic groups are patrilineal/patrilocal with male-dominated inheritance (Elondou-

Enyegye and Calves 2006; Murdock 1967). Women cultivate up to 70 percent of food crops in sub-Saharan Africa (Saito and Weidemann 1990) but most farm on land belonging to their husband or his patri-kin. Even when new laws give women inheritance rights, customary law remains embedded in much of the legal code and constitution; in practice, this means that only a minority of African women farmers can claim the land they cultivate, or inherit land (Blumberg 2004c).

Patrilocal residence

The bridal couple lives with/near the husband's male kin; a bride typically arrives without friends or relatives.

Descent

This tends to be the weakest of the kin/property variables vis-à-vis gender stratification. Nonetheless, history shows that it's often a difficult, prolonged process to impose a new kin/property system, even one backed by force (Blumberg 2015; Eisler 1987).

Geographically, MENA has 100 percent patri-oriented kin/property systems and, with several exceptions, so does South Asia (it's not just Afghanistan).

2. "Discount factors"

Second, the theory introduces cultural variables in the form of "discount factors" (Blumberg 1991 provides the most detailed discussion). These can be macro or micro. If macro, they're always negative for women, though to varying degrees. They include the legal, religious and ideological systems (as well as economic and other structural barriers). But levels vary (1) over time, and (2) between groups/nations. We can compare levels of gender stratification over time in, for example, the United States in the 1950s vs. today, or between countries, for example America vs. Afghanistan.

In Afghanistan, almost all the macro-level discount factors are extremely negative for females: all the major forms of power are lined up against them. This includes not only women's relative economic position, as discussed above, but also their legal, religious and ideological status.

Legal status: Women traditionally have been unable to register cases themselves so they're often denied equal and fair access to justice; also, only 3 percent of judges are women (Morgan 2008: 3).[10]

Religious status: It's now subject to strict Wahaabi interpretation of Islam, since Saudi Arabia has been pouring billions into Afghan madrassas promulgating this hardline doctrine.

Power of ideology: Women are widely held to be weak and inferior; Pashtun ideology typically treats them as property. The single most memorable (and shocking) statement I heard in Kabul came from the No. 3 person in the Ministry of Women's Affairs, who said: "Most Afghan men don't think that women are quite human beings." The UNDP Afghan woman program officer who accompanied me to the meeting locked eyes first with her, then with me and slowly nodded agreement.

Among the Acholi, the macro-level discount factors are negative but not as negative as in Afghanistan. The Acholi are patrilineal/patrilocal, with male-dominated inheritance. The main sticking point is men's unwillingness to give land – the main source of wealth in a farming society – to women. But during and since the LRA insurgency, women have become more involved in earning their own income, as discussed later in this chapter.

Returning to the discount factors, let's consider the *micro* level – where discount factors can be negative or positive in a couple. The person who is less committed to the relationship has more power. The person who is more dependent on the partner's income has less power. Attractiveness may briefly raise a woman's micro position and assertiveness may count, too (if it doesn't lead to a beating). But most Afghan women, even those at the peak of their attractiveness, tend to be completely dependent on their husband's income. They're underdogs with respect to micro-level discount factors, just as they are with respect to macro-level discount factors.

Compared to Afghan women, the micro-level discount situation for Acholi women is not as negative, especially in households where the husband needs the income she brings into the home.

3. War close to home

Third, both Randall Collins (1971) and I (2011) posit that war fought close to home negatively affects women's relative position, although our gender stratification theories differ on a few other variables. Even though Afghan women may be largely confined to their homes, bombs and fighting can destroy those too. Most deaths and injuries are of civilians. So, Afghan women feel the full impact of war close to home. In contrast, rural Acholi villagers in Uganda often were pushed into IDP refugee camps, where they were safe from the horrors of the LRA but camp rules gave women much more freedom of movement – and opportunities to earn income – than the men. On the one hand, they were much less affected by the patriarchal impact of war close to home. On the other, the camps had their collateral dangers, e.g. women were exposed to the risk of rape by combatants once they left the camp.

The dependent variables of women's economic power: greater control of "life options"

The main dependent variables in the general theory of gender stratification are "life options": aspects of one's destiny found in all human societies, including marriage, divorce, sexuality/control of one's body, fertility, freedom of movement and household power (Blumberg 1984). It is posited that with greater economic power, a woman gains in the extent she can control life options, even though some also are regulated by the State (e.g. marriage, divorce; in China, fertility; in Saudi Arabia, freedom of movement, etc.) With greater economic power, women are less likely to be disadvantaged by an extreme double standard.[11] In general, Afghan women have far less control over their destiny – i.e. fare much worse with respect to life options – than their Acholi counterparts

A closer look at Afghanistan

Turning to the dependent variables, life options, most women have no say in marriage; their rights to divorce are far less than men's; even the merest suspicion of sexual misconduct can get a woman killed. Few women have any control over their fertility – which is one of the world's highest: the Total Fertility Rate (TFR) is estimated at 5.43 children per woman and Afghanistan is the only non-sub-Saharan African nation in the "fertility top 10" (it is 9th; CIA 2015). Half the population is under 18.

Despite opportunities for profiteering from corruption, war and the opium trade, most young men are very poor; they're also under-educated, under- or unemployed and well armed. Still, their life options are not constrained compared to women's. For space reasons, I discuss only women's lack of control of (1) their body's health and risk of maternal mortality, and (2) freedom of movement (especially in comparison with Acholi women).

Health and maternal mortality risks

Housebound women viewed as economically useless (e.g. those studied by Doubleday 1988) complained of sickness and that "sometimes their husbands would not allow them to visit a doctor" (Moghadam 2002: 22). That's only part of the story: "the culture does not favor women being treated by male health practitioners" (Government of the Islamic Republic of Afghanistan 2009: 14). Yet, as of June 2007, women comprised only 21.9 percent of all doctors and 17.1 percent of all nurses in government (ibid.) – a major factor that contributes to high maternal mortality. The report states state: "The health situation of Afghan women is one of the worst in the world" (ibid.). Until recently, the Afghan maternal maternity rate (MMR) was the world's second-highest, after Sierra Leone (Ministry of Women's Affairs 2008: 37); it was estimated at 1,600 per 100,000 live births (ibid.; based on Government of the Islamic Republic of Afghanistan 2005; UNICEF estimate).[12] This MMR affected life expectancy for women. The Asian Development Bank (2006) indicators for 2002 show women living one year *less* than men, 44 vs. 45 years (in Ministry of Women's Affairs 2008: 35). This is a rare reversal of the greater female longevity found nearly worldwide.[13]

Freedom of movement constraints

From my field notes: Except around the Ministries, men were around 90 percent of the people on the street. Even near the Ministries, approximately half the women wore burqas. Afghan burqas are almost always blue and seemingly never personalized with embroidery or decorations (unlike the black abayas worn by Persian Gulf Emirates women) – the ideal is to be anonymous because many men don't think a woman should be out in the street to begin with. Anonymous burqas reduce the danger women feel in public space. But they restrict and blur a woman's sight: The rectangular eye slit is very narrow, allowing no peripheral vision. The cross-hatched fibers covering the rectangle are very thick, making things fuzzy. Each year, an unknown number of women are hit by drivers who can't see them at dawn, dusk or in rain (Blumberg 2011c).

One Friday, mid-morning, I had reason to consider how the wartime-exacerbated constraints on and dangers of women's freedom of movement affect their possibilities of earning income; I finally got to Kabul's famed Chicken Street, its commercial center. It's the safest time: most men go to the week's main mosque service. A UNDP woman from East Asia and I were accompanied by the UNDP security chief. His voluminous Hawaiian shirt could have concealed an arsenal – but since none of us spoke Dari or Pashto, we relied on shopkeepers' English. I asked of the one whose English was best who made the embroidered clothing, velvet evening purses, cell phone covers etc. that filled his shop. Local women, he said. But I couldn't ascertain if intermediaries who brought goods included any women. Would they be safe collecting money even if accompanied by an armed male, I wondered?

A closer look at the Acholi of Northern Uganda

Before the 23-year horror story of the LRA, the Acholi were an agrarian people practicing rain-fed (non-irrigated) cultivation. This system, which spread under colonialism, meant they relied on animal-drawn plows and men became the primary farmers. During the conflict years, the draft animals were stolen and sold or eaten by both LRA insurgents and government troops – and the plows also disappeared. People went back to the original farming system of hoe horticulture, involving small, garden-sized plots; it is much more reliant on women farmers.[14]

Before the war, women had little economic power. But in the camps, as noted, international NGOs promoted women's income-generating projects. They taught women how to make products they could sell in the market and helped them to become petty entrepreneurs. As men increasingly fell victim to alcoholism in the camps, women gained autonomy due to their greater income and freedom of movement. They often became the main providers. Meanwhile, in the IDP camps, the men's land ownership was irrelevant. Also, there was another advantage for women: camps contained bore wells with (theoretically) clean water located close to people's huts. This meant that they didn't have to spend hours every day hauling water, one of women's worst burdens in the rural areas.

Back in the villages, we found that water was the most acute problem. But fixing the roads had to come first; otherwise, it was impossible to get the needed equipment into the villages so they could deepen the bore wells enough to reach the much-lowered water table. This meant most women could be stuck for years with an enormous amount of work fetching water. Since the old bore wells were dry, women had to go much farther – twice a day – to reach generally filthy, contaminated creeks in order to haul water. From my interviews, the average woman carried a 20-liter jerry-can of water on her head. It weighed 44 pounds because a liter weighs a kilogram, which is 2.2 pounds. She also carried a 5-liter can in one hand, another 11 pounds, for a total of 55 pounds per trip. This doesn't count the weight of the child or burdens she carried on her back or hip. The round trip averaged several kilometers to several miles. And the amount of water she provided twice daily from all her efforts barely covered the household's most urgent needs.

Some were forced to pull their older daughters out of school to help. But since most of the village schools had long before been trashed and looted, and the project wouldn't start rehabilitating schools and health clinics until after the roads and water points had been fixed, few of their children would be going to school in the immediate future. This was in contrast to the camps, where schools were provided. But despite the hardships, none of the men or the women said they'd rather be back in the camps. All stated they preferred to be free, even if living precariously, to staying in the refugee camps.[15]

Will the ceasefire hold? The LRA agreed not to fight on Ugandan soil but continues to terrorize neighboring countries, carrying out large-scale massacres in the Democratic Republic of Congo and smaller actions in other adjacent nations. Still, a return to the LRA's reign of horror in Northern Uganda looks unlikely.[16]

Assuming that peace prevails, will the Acholi women hang on to their economic autonomy? In our baseline research, we learned that the women continued to do day labor and bring in a significant proportion of the income. Because the government had not (yet) provided the promised farming tools, seeds and other inputs, very little had been planted. But, we were told, some of the most alcohol-addicted men had taken to slipping out of the village very early in the morning to get day labor jobs – before the women could leave: They first had to take care of the hard work of morning chores (including fetching water and cooking). Those men, however, worked only long enough to get money for liquor and the employers (better-off farmers) found the women more reliable and capable horticulturalists. The women were in no danger of being displaced. Additionally, we found that the women recognized and valued their economic autonomy and, based on our meetings and focus groups, the men didn't seem jealous or threatened by it.[17]

The long years in the camps may not have changed the patrilineal/patrilocal kin and property basis of Acholi society, but they tempered the previous level of patriarchy by offering women a way to earn income and help themselves and their families. As the expression goes, "if life gives you lemons, make lemonade." That's what the Acholi women are doing. So far, they're continuing to build an economic base and their children are likely to benefit once more schools are rehabilitated and reopened. Also, I suspect, if the Afghan women were offered the level of increased income, autonomy and freedom of movement that war brought to the Acholi women, they'd think that lemonade was ambrosia.

What next for Afghanistan and its women?

But the Afghan women won't be offered any such benefits. The "transition" – i.e. the withdrawal of US and other foreign troops – is far advanced and may be nearly total by the end of 2015. The women I spoke with were terrified that the small gains they enjoyed since the United States and its allies defeated the Taliban government will vanish with the departing troops. They fear that there will be a deal that will bring the Taliban into the government and that the Taliban will again ban schooling for girls, work for women, and those US-promoted quotas that has made the Afghan parliament more than a quarter female – even if they don't have power to match their numbers. They are not alone in their fears. Khan (2012: 2) cites an Asia Foundation 2011 survey conducted in six provinces (including highly conservative Helmand). It found that "women from different social classes believe that they are experiencing a slow but steady improvement in their lives. However, they also showed fear that the return of the Taliban to power might undo women's recent gains."

I personally observed very little freedom for women in Afghanistan.[18] But of the educated, urban women I interviewed, the ones who were most scared about what happens when the last US troops leave were those who had tasted one or more of the three brief intervals of reduced gender repression: during the late 1960s/early 1970s, during the years of the Soviet-installed government, and since the United States and its ISAF partners invaded in the wake of 9/11. They feared that what came after the withdrawal would be even worse because it would snatch away the few crumbs of opportunity and progress they had found in the rubble of war and the development efforts of the United States and its allies.[19]

The big picture and conclusions

First, today, almost 100 percent of high-conflict states are in South Asia, the Middle East–North Africa (MENA) or sub-Saharan Africa. They're in societies with patrilineal inheritance and patrilocal residence systems such as those of Afghanistan and the Acholi, where women are structurally disadvantaged in ways that limit their economic power and their country's development. Actually, almost all of the world's "fragile" or "failing" states also are high in patriarchy.

Second, very high conflict states are often like Afghanistan, both patriarchal and poor – with high fertility, low education, violent youth and too few urban jobs for those youths' aspirations. The lure – and pay – of a jihadist movement can seem quite attractive to youth in such a situation. And the brazen vision of a jihadist group such as the Islamic State – they aim to revive the ancient caliphate – can appeal, too, to those from more auspicious circumstances, e.g. coming from a Western European nation they consider slow and reluctant to assimilate them.

Third, such groups of (overwhelmingly male) youth tend to have highly traditional ideas of masculinity and men and women's place (public sphere vs. home and hearth). As Bahri (2014) found, the views among the young men he interviewed in his qualitative, non-random sample in/near Kabul were unanimous: His sample included many professionals working for development entities. But he found 100 percent agreement among the nearly 50 men about the importance and correctness of traditional gender roles. They – including those who worked for international development agencies or their local partners – intensely disliked what the women's rights activists and gender programs were trying to introduce. All opposed even the idea of gender equality (ibid.: 177). Here are two quotes: "Now, when they become equal, women don't need men's permission, this is against our customs and religion." And "when it says that men and women's rights are equal, it contradicts Islam." Bahri says they believe "approval of freedom for women is equivalent to accepting a diminished role for men, one where they are no longer in control" (ibid.: 179). And they don't believe that women are equal to men on religious grounds – but feel that if women accept their "Islamic duties as chaste wives and mothers, they are being given their rights" (ibid.). They also feel disdain for Western culture and democracy, as well as for the international organizations operating in Afghanistan that have such a "negative" influence on women. Bahri ends with two recommendations: (1) That gender initiatives must include men; and, more controversially (2) that gender issues should be addressed from their Islamic perspective.

Fourth, consider that Afghanistan's neighbor, Pakistan, has about 100 nuclear weapons and a shaky government. Its least stable, most patriarchal tribal areas are adjacent to the high-conflict areas of eastern and southern Afghanistan, and on both sides of the border, most share the same Pashtun ethnicity and customs. In fact, almost all the Afghan and Pakistani Taliban are Pashtun.[20]

Fifth, the price of high patriarchy/high-conflict is dampened and distorted development. War, like oil (Ross 2008; Moghadam 1995), pulls economies in counter-productive and patriarchal directions, even if GDP growth looks healthy. Both lead to increased luxury imports, while depressing production of local manufactures and established export industries. This happened in Afghanistan, where "there was considerable decline in exports, especially in dried fruits and carpets … [which] may have affected women considerably since they predominate in these areas of production" (Government of the Islamic Republic of Afghanistan 2010: 9). Donor inflows may cushion a war economy from such export downtrends. Now, they're leaving. And male-dominated construction booms are over, with prices plunging on palatial quarters for development or military entities and luxurious private homes for speculation or owner-occupancy (some Kabul neighborhoods make US "McMansions" look puny).[21]

Sixth, the level of distorted development and high violence that often accompanies intense patriarchy is not just a problem for them; in today's globalized world it's a problem for all of us. Consider the Islamic State, trying to impose a new caliphate and attracting so many disaffected youth. So does that mean that our future also will be grim because of this group of poor, bellicose, patriarchal nations?

Seventh and fortunately, there are other trends in the world economy that point in the opposite direction: (a) increased income for women is a near-global trend that is far more common than war and armed conflict worldwide; and (b) according to an analysis by *The Economist* in 2006 before the Great Recession, the biggest single driver of growth in the world economy from 1985–2005 was the increase in women's paid labor force participation in the rich advanced industrial countries – exceeding the rise of computers and the Internet as well as that of China and India. In sum, in most of the world, the sun of women's economic power seems to be rising, putting us on the right side of history and development.

References

Ahmed-Ghosh, Huma. 2003. "A History of Women in Afghanistan: Lessons Learnt for the Future or Yesterdays and Tomorrow: Women in Afghanistan. *Journal of International Women's Studies* 4(3): 1–14.

Amnesty International. 2014. "Afghanistan: President Karzai Blocks Law Protecting Perpetrators of Domestic Violence." February 17. Available at: www.amnesty.org/en/articles/news/2014/02/Afghanistan-president-karzai-blocks-law-protecting-perpetrators-of-domestic-violence

Asian Development Bank. 2006. *Key Indicators*. Kabul: Asian Development Bank Afghanistan.

Bahri, Javed. 2014. "Western Gender Policies in Afghanistan: Failing Women and Provoking Men." *Gender, Technology and Development* 18(2): 163–185.

Beebe, James. 2001. *Rapid Appraisal Process: An Introduction*. Walnut Creek, CA: Altamira/Rowman & Littlefield.

Blumberg, Rae Lesser. Forthcoming. "The Magic Money Tree? Women, Economic Power and Development in a Globalized World." In *Handbook of Sociology of Development*, edited by Gregory Hooks et al. Berkeley, CA: University of California Press.

——2015. "'Dry' versus 'Wet' Development and Women in Three World Regions." *Sociology of Development* 1(1): 91–122.

——2011a. "Afghanistan National Development Strategy (ANDS) Project: Final Project Evaluation." July-August. Kabul: United Nations Development Program Afghanistan.

——2011b. "Afghanistan National Development Program (ANDP) Support Project: Final Project Evaluation." July-August. Kabul: United Nations Development Program Afghanistan.

——2011c. Fieldnotes, UNDP ANDS/ANDP Research, July-August.

——2010. "Measuring the Rebuilding of Hope in Northern Uganda." Report. Kampala and Washington, DC. Winrock International and USAID.

——2009a. "Mothers of Invention? The Myth-Breaking History and Planetary Promise of Women's Key Roles in Subsistence Technology." Pp. 227–259 in *Techno-Well: Impact of Technology on Psychological Well-Being*, edited by Yair Amichai-Hamburger. Cambridge: Cambridge University Press.

——2009b. "The Consequences of Women's Economic Empowerment vs. Disempowerment: From the 'Magic Potion' for Development to the 'Four Horsemen of the Apocalypse'"? Keynote paper presented at the UNESCO Women's Studies and Gender Research Networking Conference, February, Bangkok.

——2008. "Gender, Environment and Environmental Ethics: Exploring the Critical Role of Economic Power in Thailand, Ecuador and Malawi." Presented at the UNESCO Conference on Ethics of Energy Technologies: Ethical Views of Nature, held in conjunction with the World Congress of Philosophy, Seoul, South Korea, August.

——2004a. "Extending Lenski's Schema to Hold Up Both Halves of the Sky: A Theory-Guided Way of Conceptualizing Agrarian Societies that Illuminates a Puzzle about Gender Stratification." *Sociological Theory* 22(2): 278–91.

——2004b. "Climbing the Pyramids of Power: Alternative Routes to Women's Empowerment and Activism." Pp. 60–87 in *Promises of Empowerment: Women in Asia and Latin America*, edited by Peter H. Smith, Jennifer L. Troutner and Christine Hunefeldt. Lanham, MD: Rowman and Littlefield.

——2004c. "Women's Rights, Land Rights and Human Rights: Dilemmas in East Africa." *Journal of Development Alternatives and Area Studies* 23(3–4): 17–32.

——2002. "Fast, Cheap and Valid? Using Rapid Appraisal for Gender Research: A Guide and Some Cases from the Global South." Presented at the Meetings of the International Sociological Association, Brisbane, Australia, July.

——1995. "Introduction: Engendering Wealth and Well-Being in an Era of Economic Transformation." Pp. 1–14 in *Engendering Wealth and Well-Being: Empowerment for Global Change*, edited by Rae Lesser Blumberg, Cathy A. Rakowski, Irene Tinker and Michael Monteón. Boulder, CO: Westview Press.

——1991. "Introduction: The 'Triple Overlap' of Gender Stratification, Economy and the Family." Pp. 7–32 in *Gender, Economy, and the Family*, edited by Rae Lesser Blumberg. Newbury Park, CA: Sage.

——1989a. *Making the Case for the Gender Variable: Women and the Wealth and Well-Being of Nations*. Washington, DC: US Agency for International Development, Office of Women in Development.

——1989b. "Toward a Feminist Theory of Development." Pp. 161–199 in *Feminism and Sociological Theory*, edited by Ruth A. Wallace. Newbury Park, CA: Sage.

——1988. "Income Under Female vs. Male Control: Hypotheses from a Theory of Gender Stratification and Data from the Third World." *Journal of Family Issues* 9(1): 51–84.

——1984. "A General Theory of Gender Stratification." *Sociological Theory* 2: 23–101.

Boserup, Ester. 1970. *Woman's Role in Economic Development*. New York: St. Martin's Press.

Brown, Judith. 1975. "Iroquois Women: An Ethnohistoric Note." Pp. 235–251 in *Toward an Anthropology of Women*, edited by Rayna R. Reiter. New York: Monthly Review Press.

Caprioli, Mary. 2005. "Primed for Violence: The Role of Gender Inequality in Predicting Internal Conflict." *International Studies Quarterly* 49: 161–178.

——2000. "Gendered Conflict." *Journal of Peace Research* 37(1): 51–68.

CIA. 2015. *Factbook*. Washington, DC: Central Intelligence Agency.

Collins, Randall. 1971. "A Conflict Theory of Sexual Stratification." *Social Problems* 19: 3–21.

Copeland, Curtis. 2006. *Social Determinants of High HIV Prevalence in sub-Saharan Africa*. Honors thesis, Charlottesville, VA: University of Virginia.

Das Gupta, Monica, John Bongaarts and John Cleland. 2011. "Population, Poverty and Sustainable Development: A Review of the Evidence." Working Paper. Washington, DC: World Bank.

Doubleday, Veronica. 1988. *Three Women of Herat*. Austin, TX: University of Texas Press.

Eisler, Riane. 1987. *The Chalice and the Blade*. New York: Harper and Row.

Elondou-Enyegyeh, Parfait M. and Anne Emmanuele Calves. 2006. "Till Marriage Do Us Part: Education and Remittances from Married Women in Africa." *Comparative Education Review* 50(1): 1–20.

Government of the Islamic Republic of Afghanistan. 2010. *Afghanistan Country Report*

2008–2010: India Forward Moving Strategies for Gender Equality 2008. Kabul: Government of the Islamic Republic of Afghanistan.

——2009. *Country Report 2004–2009 on the Implementation of the Beijing Declaration and Platform for Action (1995) and the Outcome of the 23rd Special Session of the General Assembly (2000)*. Kabul: Government of the Islamic Republic of Afghanistan.

——2005. *Afghanistan MDG Report*. Kabul: Government of the Islamic Republic of Afghanistan.

Grace, Jo. 2005. "Who Owns the Farm? Rural Women's Access to Land and Livestock." Working paper. Kabul: Afghanistan Research and Evaluation Unit.

Hess, Peter N. 1988. *Population Growth and Socio-Economic Progress in Less Developed Countries: Determinants of Fertility Transition*. New York: Praeger.

Hudson, Valerie, Mary Caprioli, Bonnie Ballif-Spanvill, Rose McDermott and Chad F. Emmett. 2009. "The Heart of the Matter: The Security of Women and the Security of States." *International Security* 33(3): 7–45.

Inter-Parliamentary Union (IPU). 2015. "Women in National Parliaments: Situation as of 1st January 2015." Available at: www.ipu.org/wmn-e/classif.htm

Khan, Ahmed. 2012. "Women & Gender in Afghanistan." Kabul: Civil-Military Fusion Centre (CFC)/ Afghanistan Resource Desk.

Mason, Andrew D. and Elizabeth M. King. 2001. *Engendering Development: Through Gender Equality in Rights, Resources and Voice*. New York: Oxford University Press.

Ministry of Women's Affairs. 2008. *Women and Men in Afghanistan: Baseline Statistics on Gender*. Kabul: Government of the Islamic Republic of Afghanistan.

Moghadam, Valentine. 2002. "Patriarchy, the Taleban, and Politics of Public Space in Afghanistan." *Women's Studies International Forum* 25(1): 19–31.

——1995. "Gender Dynamics of Restructuring in the Periphery." Pp. 17–37 in *Engendering Wealth and Well-Being: Empowerment for Global Change*, edited by Rae Lesser Blumberg, Cathy A. Rakowski, Irene Tinker and Michael Monteón. Boulder, CO: Westview Press.

Morgan, Clara. 2008. "Afghanistan: The Status of Women." Ottowa: Library of Parliament, InfoSeries, Parliamentary Information and Research Service Publication PRB 07-34E.

Motlagh, Jason. 2014. "What Remains after Rana Plaza." *Washington Post*, April 20: B2.

Murdock, George Peter. 1967. "Ethnographic Atlas: A Summary." *Ethnology* 6(2): 109-236.

NAPWA (National Action Plan for the Women of Afghanistan). 2008. *National Action Plan for the Women of Afghanistan (NAPWA) 2008–2018*. Kabul: Government of the Islamic Republic of Afghanistan.

Nolan, Patarick and Gerhard Lenski. 2015. *Human Societies: An Introduction to Macrosociology*, 12th edn. New York: Oxford University Press.

Ross, Michael. 2008. "Oil, Islam and Women." *American Political Science Review* 102(1): 107–123.

Saito, Katrine and Jean Weidemann. 1990. "Agricultural Extension for Women Farmers in Africa." Women in Development Working Paper. Washington, DC: World Bank.

Tapper, Nancy. 1984. "Causes and Consequences of the Abolition of Brideprice in Afghanistan." Pp. 291–305 in *Revolutions and Rebellions in Afghanistan*, edited by M. Nazif Sharani and Robert L. Canfield. Berkeley, CA: University of California Press.

United Nations Development Program (UNDP). 2005. *Millennium Development Goals, Islamic Republic of Afghanistan, Country Report 2005: Summary Report*. Kabul: UNDP.

UNESCO. 2013/14. *Teaching and Learning: Achieving Quality for All*. Education for All, EFA Global Monitoring Report. Paris: UNESCO.

UNICEF. 2006. *Best Estimates*. Kabul: UNICEF Afghanistan.

UNIFEM. 2006. *Uncounted and Discounted: A Secondary Data Research Project on Violence against Women in Afghanistan*. Kabul: UNIFEM Afghanistan.

Weller, Robert H. 1968. "The Employment of Wives, Dominance and Fertility." *Journal of Marriage and the Family* 30: 437–442.

World Bank. 2015. "Fertility Rate, Total (Births per Woman)." World Bank: World Development Indicators. Available at: http://data.worldbank.org/indicator/SP.DYN.TFRT.IN

——2014. "Labor Force Participation Rate, Female (% of Female Population Ages 15+) (modeled ILO estimate)." Washington, DC: World Bank: World Development Indicators. Available at: http://data.worldbank.org/indicator/SL.TLF.CACT.FE.ZS

——2012. *World Development Report: Gender Equality and Development*. Washington, DC: World Bank.

Notes

1 These were planned to be important projects: the Afghanistan National Development Strategy and the follow-up Afghanistan National Development Program, through which 80 percent of the billions in annual foreign aid for Afghanistan were supposed to be aligned and channeled, although delays in operationalizing the strategy meant that implementation at the time of final evaluation was incomplete.

2 For the general theory of gender stratification, see Blumberg 1984, 1991, 2004a, 2009a, 2015; for the theory of gender and development, see Blumberg 1988, 1989a, 1989b, 1995, 2004b, 2009b, forthcoming.

3 The previous owners of the land were pressuring the government to throw the remaining IDPs out and return the land. Those still in the camps were the proverbial "basket cases." We found the disabled (there were many, often because a major LRA atrocity was the lopping off of limbs with machetes); the elderly whose adult children had died or abandoned them; the teen-aged girls who were child heads of household because they were its oldest surviving member, and worst-off of all, the boys who had been kidnapped to be child soldiers at about 10 or 11 years old and forced to commit a terrible atrocity to their own relatives or neighbors before being marched off – so they would feel they could never return. Psychologically, they were in the sorriest shape.

4 Here's a breakdown of 217 people interviewed for the Northern Uganda RA, village names deleted: 122 men (56%) and 95 women (44%). *Key Informant Interviews*: 36: 21 men (58%); 15 women (42%). *Group Meetings:* N=4. Village 1=2 groups: 29 men (69%), 13 women (31%); Village 2=2 groups of grades 5–7 pupils: 34 boys (49%), 35 girls (51%); Group Meeting Totals=111: 63 males (57%); 48 (43%) females. *Focus Groups*: N=12. (1) Village 3=10 male secondary students, 9 who were 18 or older and a 15-year-old; (2) 8 women villagers in Village 4, (3) 5 urban women from Town 1; (4–7) in IDP Camp 1: (4) 4 male elders; (5) disabled – 2 men, 2 women; (6) 5 male ex-abducted child soldiers; (7) 4 female child household heads. (8–9) Village 5: (8) 5 men; (9) 5 women; (10–12) in Village 6: (10) 6 women; (11) 6 elders: 4 men and 2 women, and (12) 8 men. Totals=70: 38 males (54%), 32 females (46%).

5 I traveled extensively but not in the north due to the war; in 2000, I waited out the 21-day incubation period after possible Ebola exposure in Mbarara.

6 After two major disasters in 2013 (a tragic factory fire that killed 112 and the collapse of an eight-story factory plaza that killed 1,134 and injured 2,515), Bangladesh now has signed agreements with its huge corporate customers to improve worker conditions and safety (Motlagh 2014).

7 Another irony is that the USA has long been below the world average in proportion of women in parliament in both lower and upper houses. After the November 2014

elections, women were 19.3 percent of the House, vs. a 22.3 percent world average for the lower house; women were 20 percent of the Senate, vs. a 20.5 percent world average for the upper house. Not only does the United States remain well below the world's lower house average, it's now below Saudi Arabia(!): Saudi Arabia is tied for 70th place and the United States is tied for 73rd (Inter-Parliamentary Union 2015).

8   EVAW also prohibits setting women on fire or using chemicals [acid] and *baad* (using women to settle a feud). Importantly, it also criminalizes prevention of "women's rights of inheritance" or of "possessing personal property." And it bans deterring women from education, work and access to health services, or seeing their kin (Government of the Islamic Republic of Afghanistan 2010: 5).

9   I showed the education data to the Afghan UNDP program officer who hired me – an Islamist educated in Wahaabi-funded schools – but he refused to believe that 88 percent of women were illiterate and said there was no sizeable gender gap in education.

10 Concerning constitutional rights, Article 22 gives citizens (women or men) equal rights and duties before the law but Article 3 states that "no law can be contrary to … Islam," so Article 3 may trump Article 22 (Morgan 2008).

11 Sometimes there are other actors than the woman and the state, e.g. honor killings are carried out by males from the woman's family; even where these men are punished very lightly or not at all, the honor killings are almost always illegal.

12 Kahn (2012: 5) claims a 2011 "Afghanistan Mortality Survey" paints an incredibly improved picture, including MMR plunging by 80 percent to 327 per 100,00 live births. He doesn't cite the source (I was warned by UN staff to be wary of excessively rosy data).

13 "despite the high level of male casualties during the 25 years of war, men still outnumber women by significant levels in the contemporary era, with an average ratio of 104 men to 100 women for all ages" NAPWA 2008:1

14 Whereas non-irrigated plow agriculture is male-dominated (Boserup 1970), hoe horticulture is considered a "female farming system" (ibid.): women are primary or equal farmers. In sub-Saharan Africa, most farming is horticultural, in part because only a small percentage of the land has soils deep enough to take the plow. And in sub-Saharan Africa, it's not the "farmer and his wife"; it's the "African farmer and her husband." (As noted above, women raise most of the food crops).

15 Since boys and girls wandered around the grassy areas where we interviewed female focus groups, some women might have worried about a child telling the men that the women preferred the camp to their husbands' village; the women's unanimous preference for the village might have been prudent, not wholehearted.

16 If Joseph Kony was eliminated, the danger of a return would surely plummet. Despite campaigns to capture him he remains elusive and in charge.

17 Although men complained about the lack of water in the villages, few seemed to grasp just how much time and labor the women had to expend to provide the little they had; and even fewer said that they sometimes helped the women get water.

18 Overall, I found them to be about the most subjugated women I'd ever encountered, with the possible exception of the women of the bellicose Yanomamo we studied when I led an expedition of Andres Bello University social science students to the jungle headwaters of Venezuela's Orinoco River during my Peace Corps days.

19 As for the Acholi women, as long as Joseph Kony, the LRA's top leader, keeps the ceasefire with Uganda and does his killing in neighboring countries, such as the Democratic Republic of Congo, South Sudan and the Central African Republic, they probably will hold on to their increased economic autonomy and provide important help in the rebuilding and development of their villages, even if the men continue to own the land.

20 Among Pakistani Pashtun tribal people, the women are said to be just as oppressed and as low in economic power as among their Afghan counterparts; their fertility is about as high and prospects of economic growth seem just as low.
21 Every day, UN SUVs drove personnel living in the allegedly attack-proof Green Village (it wasn't but the attack happened after I left) down the Jalalabad Road to the Green Zone and back. We passed forests of construction cranes for rent or sale on scores of unpaved lots lining both sides of the street. There were too many to count accurately, though I tried. How many remain now, I wonder?

9
ZIMBABWE
A case study in bipolar development

Lorna Lueker Zukas

Zimbabwe burst onto the global scene in 1980 after nearly one hundred years of colonial and white-settler rule and after a lengthy liberation war (1966–1979). The nation seemed well-positioned for success with developed agricultural and manufacturing sectors. Women who had actively supported the liberation war were mobilized in politics, education and civil society; an inclusive government seemed to support people-centered development and the common good. Yet, in a not-so-untypical story, thirty-five years after independence Zimbabwe has failed to prosper. A wealthy ruling elite headed by Robert Mugabe, a revolutionary who became President for Life, has risen. The majority of people in Zimbabwe remain mired in poverty. Over-reliance on development aid has led to economic crisis. A neoliberal strategy designed to privatize resources and liberalize markets enriched international financial institutions (IFIs) and transnational corporations while neither producing growth nor reducing poverty. Sadly, development in Zimbabwe is bipolar.

While the state has degenerated into neoliberalism, cronyism and corruption – one pole of development – ordinary people demanded human-centered development and continued the struggle for independence and equity. Since independence, women from all ethnic groups and classes have created organizations to develop their communities' self-reliance and demand social justice, participatory decision-making and equality. They represent the other pole of development. This chapter then addresses two women's groups that attempt to hold the Zimbabwe African National Union-Patriotic Front (ZANU-PF) government accountable for its promises of development and equality made during the liberation struggle.

A feminist reading of women's activism and the organizations they created to focus on gender issues reveals the dynamics of social change and bipolar development in Zimbabwe. This activism, which I am calling "women's development activism," purposefully highlights participants as both women and feminists seeking to challenge patriarchy and traditions that limit female empowerment. Women's development activism occurs on three distinct, but sometimes interrelated levels, including (1) political action, (2) social action and (3) direct action. Political action includes the use of the public sphere to change the structural and legal terrain of women's lives. Social action includes collective women's protests for dignity and daily living needs (housing, health care and municipal services), as well as more – and more gender-equal – education, social justice and human rights. Direct action involves individual women networking to achieve better, more modern and secure lives. Women's development activism is part of the cultural landscape of Zimbabwe: women have long sought decision-making power over quality-of-life choices including where to live; whether or not to marry, as well as to whom and when; whether or not to have children, including how often, how many and age of first and last births; where to work; how long to remain in school, and even what to wear. This activism demonstrates that women regarded having a voice in these life choices as fundamental to their quality of life and the development of the nation. Zimbabwe's bipolar development is articulated below first in the story of the developing crisis and second in women's responses to state actions.

Zimbabwe: a case study in development

An analysis of Zimbabwe's development crisis offers a classic case study in the failure of neoliberal development. "At independence in 1980, Zimbabwe inherited US$700 million of debt from the Rhodesian government" (Jones 2011). The former Prime Minister, Ian Smith, borrowed the money for weapons purchases during the nationalist liberation struggle. Smith declared there would be no black rule in his lifetime, "not within 1,000 years." After independence, Zimbabwe was unable to pay debt obligations on the loan and borrowed more money to make the payments. Additional development funding proffered by IFIs, sometimes for questionable projects, enabled Robert Mugabe and top ZANU-PF supporters to become multi-millionaires. As a result of neoliberal growth strategies associated with development funding, the nation's indebtedness grew to more than US$10 billion by 2013.

In the course of this development for the few, women's equality (previously given verbal support by Mugabe) was denounced, many people lost their livelihoods, more lost access to basic public services and millions became impoverished and now live on US$1–2 per-day. From 2000 to 2008, millions of people fled the country just to survive, as hyperinflation (2008–2009) set in and the Zimbabwean currency became worthless. In 2000, the exchange rate between the US and Zimbabwean dollar (USD/ZWD) was US$1 = ZW$1000; in July 2008 US$1 = ZW$18,700,000,000. By late 2008, the daily inflation rate was 98 percent; prices doubled every twenty-four hours. The nation's "cumulative inflation was nearly 3.8 billion percent and living standards fell by 38 percent (as measured by real gross domestic product [GDP] per capita)" (Hanke 2008: 1). Zimbabwe surpassed the hyperinflation of the German mark during the 1920s and entered the record book in second place, behind 1946 Hungary, for the world's worst hyperinflation. The Zimbabwe government printed billion and trillion dollar notes and people needed armfuls of cash to buy basic provisions – if any could be found. The nation, previously called "the breadbasket of Africa" and a grain exporter, was reduced to relying on humanitarian aid to feed its people. Godfrey Chikowore argues that Zimbabwe's failed development is due to "neocolonial manipulation of development aid, political intolerance by the government of Zimbabwe and ineffective global, continental and regional institutions" (2010: 45). One must add corruption to this list.

Robert Mugabe's new government sufficiently accommodated the international development community so that within months of independence, United Nations' agencies and diplomats from many countries set up operations in Harare. More importantly, a donor conference to raise funds for reconstruction of the country was organized for 1981 (Kachingwe 1994: 55). Zimbabwe desperately needed funds to rebuild the war-torn country and to enable millions of black Zimbabweans to reap the benefits of their labor and the country's resources.

At independence in 1980, Zimbabwe was a nation in a contradictory situation: it had one of the highest average per capita incomes in sub-Saharan Africa while at the same time the majority of the population was poor. To improve economic conditions, the new government restructured the agricultural sector focusing on communal African – rather than white commercial – farmers; credit, extension and marketing services were redirected to this sector as existing producer incentives were kept in place. The government also focused on education and adult literacy campaigns. Educational achievement skyrocketed between 1980 and 1985; concomitantly, the gender gap in education also shrank and parity was reached at primary grade levels (Zukas 1998). These actions in the agricultural and education sectors, coupled with the resumption of normal economic activity, two minimum-wage increases and expanding manufacturing, generated economic gains with minimal changes to existing policy or economic controls. The government relied on donor funding for the development of civil society organizations and poverty alleviation programs.

From 1981 to 1989, billions of dollars in development assistance flowed into Zimbabwe from the United States, Europe and Japan. In addition to the development loans taken by the Zimbabwean government, De Graaf, Moyo and Dietz (1991) estimated that during the 1980s, external donors disbursed more than US$30 million a year to non-governmental organizations (NGOs) alone (Moyo, Makumbe and Raftopoulos 2000: 67). However, people-oriented development based on local socioeconomic needs, including local and indigenous expansion of businesses and industry, was not pursued. For the IFIs, Zimbabwe was simply the latest place to hawk its wares; a potential new debtor nation. The former Rhodesia now was a new nation with resources to tap, including "a relatively well-developed and diverse market economy, albeit highly regulated, and an under-developed peasant-based economy" (Dawson and Kelsall 2013: 51). This view is borne out by subsequent hunger, poverty, high food prices and bureaucratic mismanagement

(Raftopoulos 1996). By 1982, the first sign of Zimbabwe becoming a kleptocracy under Mugabe appeared. Since then, with more than twenty financial scandals recorded, the evidence continues to accrue. These include (Yamamoto 2014):

1. Paweni scandal (1982)
2. National Railways housing scandal (1986)
3. Air Zimbabwe Fokker plane scandal (1987)
4. Zisco Steel blast furnace scandal (1987)
5. Willowgate scandal (1988)
6. ZRP Santana scandal (1989)
7. War victims compensation scandal (1994)
8. GMB grain scandal (1995)
9. VIP housing scandal (1996)
10. Boka banking scandal (1998)
11. ZESA YTL Soltran scandal (1998)
12. Harare City Council refuse tender scandal (1998)
13. Housing loan scandal (1999)
14. Noczim scandal (1999)
15. DRC timber and diamond UN reported scandals (1999)
16. GMB scandal (1999)
17. Ministry of Water and Rural Development Chinese tender scandal (1999)
18. Harare Airport scandal (2001)
19. Pillaging and milking of Ziscosteel (2005–8)
20. Pillaging of diamonds in Chiadzwa (2006–present)
21. Airport Road scandal (2008–14)
22. Pillaging of the Central Bank under Gideon Gono

The local beneficiaries of the neoliberal development assistance increasingly were Mugabe and favored members of ZANU-PF.

By the mid-1980s, when the growth rate of Zimbabwe's GDP stagnated around 2.7 percent, the international development community, particularly the IFIs, demanded Zimbabwe restructure its economy to emphasize growth rates and returns on capital investment and cut social spending. The cuts in government payrolls were particularly hard on black middle-class women who were disproportionately likely to work in the public sector. The theory underlying this demand was that public sector debt needed to be reduced so that private expenditure and investment could grow. Zimbabwe's economy became subject to the "free-market Washington Consensus" ideology. State regulations were weakened and the economy was opened to private investment. These "reforms" required market deregulation, financial liberalization, trade liberalization, adjustments to the foreign exchange allocation system and restrictions on trade union activities. By 1991, Mugabe accepted a full-fledged Structural Adjustment Program (SAP) imposed by the International Monetary Fund (IMF) and the World Bank (WB). Once begun, the liberalization continued within multilateral and regional frameworks superintended by the World Trade Organization (WTO), Southern African Development Community (SADC) and the Common Market for Eastern and Southern Africa (COMESA).

Shortly thereafter, Zimbabwe was in a development crisis and poverty was increasing rather than decreasing. Under international direction, the state had implemented development programs that ultimately left the anticipated beneficiaries poorer and worse off than they were before. The development crisis was intensified by a one-party state that mismanaged funds and distributed resources based on political allegiance rather than national development needs. Mugabe's share of the spoils increased apace. Development aid served to create profits for transnational corporations and wealthy national elites, primarily ZANU-PF allies, who extracted resources and rents for their own and donor nations' gains while the majority of indigenous people suffered worsening poverty and misery. Hindsight shows that Zimbabwe was the victim of the "'lost decade of development' in the 1980s, when aid agencies peddled structural adjustment programmes that deepened poverty and vulnerability" (Ramalingam 2013: 8).

The 1991 market-oriented economic reforms imposed by the SAP were responsible for increasing unemployment and reducing real wages for those who remained in formal employment (UNDP 1998). The SAP austerity policies quickly assailed the public sector, which lost 40,000 jobs and eroded the public safety net. Moreover, the gains women had made since independence were quickly eroded by these policies as "the share of the national budget devoted to health, housing, and transportation decreased by 20, 24, and 40 percent, respectively" (Osirim 2011: 181). According to Patricia Made and Nomasomi Mpofu (2005: 2), the Gender Development Index (GDI) declined steeply from 0.505 to 0.433.

Post-colonial women's struggles for independence and development

Zimbabwean women's struggles for independence and human development include a commingled history of struggle against "tradition" and colonial oppression, as well as women's participation in the liberation war. Estimates of women's participation in the liberation war range from 1,500 to 10,000 depending on how they are being counted (Zukas 1998). At independence, women expected the right to fully participate in civil society, to stand for public office and develop careers in the public sector (ibid.). As citizens, they wanted to direct their own lives, to participate in cooperatives, control their own resources and have access to education and family planning.

When Zimbabwe's first democratically elected government came to power in 1980, its rhetoric was explicitly feminist and socialist. As the new government and the people worked to redress all forms of inequality, the people elected women to parliament at unprecedented rates. Women's presence in parliament went from 8 percent in 1980 to 22 percent in 1995. In the 2000 elections, women only made up 14 percent of parliament due to gender repression and violence, but by 2005 the figure rebounded to 22 percent. Currently, according to Inter-Parliamentary Union data from 2015, Zimbabwe ranks 28th out of 189 countries for women in parliament, at 31.5 percent (South Africa is currently ranked 10th with 41.5 percent of women in parliament and the US ranks 72 out of 189 at 19.4 percent [Inter-Parliamentary Union 2015]). Women's success in political representation despite lack of development in other sectors is indicative of Zimbabwe's bi-polar development. In part, this success can be attributed to an international focus, from the mid-1970s, on gender issues and the availability of donor funding for woman's empowerment and education projects. Additionally, Within five years of independence, girls reached near-parity with boys in education, especially in the lower grades, albeit not at secondary and tertiary levels (Zukas 1998). Various pieces of legislation benefiting women were passed. These included the Legal Age of Majority Act, which eliminated black women's status as minors under the law for the first time; the Sex Disqualification Act allowed women to hold public office; other legislation ensured women equal pay. These pieces of legislation were passed by government as a result of women's political activism, as well as pressure from women elected to parliament and support from the leaders within the ruling party.

As women's position advanced, cultural tensions arose between men who had long benefited from patriarchal privilege and women who asserted independence in the new society. The first signs of strains came in 1980 with incidences of infanticide, euphemistically termed "baby dumping" by the media. At independence, women who had been promised equality started "dumping" infants as the men who impregnated them abandoned paternal responsibility. When women were sentenced to jail for the crime of infanticide, outraged women demanded that the men who fathered these children and abandoned them also be considered culpable. Although authorities conceded that "men who make school-girls pregnant should also be prosecuted when the 'unfortunate' girls are brought before the courts for baby dumping," few prosecutions of men actually took place. (Mugabe 1986).

The public statements of Robert and Sally Mugabe illuminate the continuing struggle for development and empowerment that women faced. In September 1983, amidst increasing cases of infanticide, President Robert Mugabe said: "The ailment here is a breakdown in moral standards produced by the war and misuse of newly-won freedom" (Mugabe 1983). Rather than admitting to systemic social problems that could be solved, Mugabe attempted to blame individuals, primarily women, for moral failings. First Lady Sally Mugabe instead offered a systemic view of the problem: "I think there is ignorance and lack of education behind the dumping. I think that young girls should be taught the dangers of meeting with men from early school so that by the time they grow up they will know what to expect" (Lapchick and Urdang 1982: 101). So, although she too burdened women to "know better," she recognized gender power differentials that needed to be addressed by the state. She supported the position of women's groups that "society should judge both the young girl and the man responsible for the pregnancy" (ibid.). She was a strong advocate for family planning. Perhaps understanding the struggles that Zimbabwean women would face, the First Lady said, "History shows that women have had a specially active role in the fight against injustice" (Kachingwe 1994: 56).

As gender-based confrontations (some initiated by the state) occurred in the mid-1980s (mass arrest of women for alleged prostitution and the public stripping of women wearing pants or short skirts), a number of women's groups formed to resist the revival of male-asserted patriarchal authority. The formation of women's groups coincided with two important events. In the early 1980s, international donors placed an emphasis on funding women's empowerment efforts. By the 1990s, mainly due to UN efforts around the "Decade of the Woman," the proliferation of aid money in Zimbabwe led to over "700 registered ... NGOs ... with more than 100 of them having a program aimed at the advancement of women; at least half of them were designed specifically for women" (Chitiga 1994: 2). By 2008, there were 900 Civil Society Organizations (CSOs) in Zimbabwe and 20 percent of them (180 organizations) dealt with gender and human rights issues (Zimbabwe Institute 2008).

The proliferation of NGOs and CSOs that included a gender portfolio was most likely the result of the United Nations' two-decade-long focus on women, 1975–1995, with its attendant emphasis on donor funding for women's issues. After 2000, additional emphasis on gender came with the adoption of the United Nation's Millennium Development Goals (MDGs). The third of the eight MDGs is to "promote gender equality and empower women" (UN 2014). As significant as aid funding was to women's development programs, equally important was the homecoming of educated diaspora Zimbabweans who returned in 1980 and the influx of foreign diplomats, aid workers from Europe and America to help develop the country. These individuals arrived with new understandings about women's roles in society.

In the 1980s, women utilized political and social activism for norm-busting gendered claims to independence and equality. They began to question patriarchal practices of state administration and traditional authority. Women demanded entitlements as citizens and as active participants in Zimbabwe's liberation struggle. Notions of feminism, imported and indigenous, were critical parts of these debates (Essof 2005). However, by the 1990s, as the Mugabe government moved to create cultural consensus on the meaning of being Zimbabwean, crucial funding for women's social activism became a trap. The state frequently questioned the motivations and activities of groups that successfully obtained donor funds for gender and development and women's empowerment activities. Self-identified feminist groups were targeted as the state's patriotic and patriarchal discourses became openly hostile to feminism as a foreign idea and there was a return to the incessant rhetoric of being a good woman (Chogugudza 2010).

Women activists became targets of state-sponsored violence, subject to beating, rape and arrest. In 1997, NGOs deemed oppositional to ZANU-PF were closed under the Private Voluntary Organizations Act (PVO Act) (Saki and Ketema 2011). The remaining women's rights organizations survived this hostile environment by carefully converting work on women's rights into educational, training and information services. Sometimes it was donors' priorities that changed the nature of projects and dampened the radical orientation of a group or led to its bureaucratization. State repression and the dictates of donors created a bipolar continuum of acceptable development strategies among women's groups. As one group made compromises with the government to avoid repression and continue in existence, new less conciliatory groups arose – to soon face violence and arrests. Government repression did not stop women's development activism nor did it send women scurrying back to their kitchens.

Myriad women's groups have successfully agitated for gender equality and development in Zimbabwe since 1983. The next section presents an analysis of two such groups, Women's Action Group (WAG), Zimbabwe's first successful women's group, and the newer Women of Zimbabwe Arise (WOZA). The development activism of these two groups clearly illuminates the polarizing nature of development aid. Not only are there tensions between the divergent goals of state sponsored, neoliberal development and the more idealized human-centered development, but there is also a continuum within women's groups. At one end of the continuum today is WAG. It began in 1983 as a fire-breathing, socialist feminist organization. To survive, it now does development projects for major donors that provide modest advances for women; it also has been forced to soft-pedal its relations with the government. At the other end of the continuum is WOZA, formed in 2003. It is still breathing fire – and paying the price in government repression and violence against its 75,000 members.

Both women's groups began as firebrands utilizing social action as a means of development activism to enhance opportunities for increased gender-equal education, social justice and human rights. In a period of political repression, WAG abandoned social activism for mainstream development projects. This entailed a reliance on donor funding and close relationships with government entities to accomplish its goals. According to trustee Jonah Gokova, over the years WAG has moved from "critical engagement to co-optation" (Dorman, 2001). WOZA's development activism still remains defiant; the group regularly engages in street protests for dignity and daily living needs around housing, health care and municipal services. These protests subject members to police beatings, jail time and death. These organizations represent two ends of the development continuum; WAG is professionalized, can move money, turn development projects in on time and do some good. WOZA is a feminist group whose revolutionary fire is born of need, neglect and development crises. Both of these organizations have been shaped by the failure of Mugabe's government to generate adequate development for the majority of Zimbabwean people and, especially, women.

Women's Action Group

The formation of Women's Action Group (WAG) marked the beginning of women's development activism in Zimbabwe. The first meeting of WAG, held

October 31, 1983, was in response to Operation Clean-Up, the mass, arbitrary arrest of women that began October 28, 1983, five months after Mugabe publically declared baby dumping the result of "low moral standards produced by the war and misuse of newly-won freedom" (Mugabe 1983). From October 28 to 30, 1983, soldiers and police randomly arrested thousands of women – young, old, school girls – and held them in custody until they provided proof of employment or marriage. The government claimed it was trying to rid the city of prostitutes, vagrants and squatters. Over a five-week period, some 6,316 women were held in custody around Zimbabwe (Watson 2003; Shaw 2007). The purpose of these arrests was to limit women's freedom of movement and to put women on notice that they could be controlled at any time.

Harare-based women were outraged over the blatant disregard for women's rights and such malicious male violence against women. When a Canadian development worker, Rosemary Doughty, called for a meeting at her home to discuss the issue, the 40–50 women and men who attended formed the group (Watson 1998). At a follow-up meeting two days later more than 100 women met at Catholic Hall in Harare (WAG 1984). Shaw (2007) reported that within a few weeks, the multi-ethnic international group encompassed black, white, Indian and mixed-race Zimbabweans from the university, civil service, NGOs and trade unions; two black women from the United States and expatriate white women from the United Kingdom, South Africa and Australia joined.

WAG members used political and social action to stop the mass arrests and get women released from jail. They filed petitions with the government to stop detentions, wrote protest editorials to major newspapers and cataloged agonizing tales of unfair arrests in Operation Clean-Up in a leading news magazine. Delegations of women went to government offices and worked through the Women's Ministry to have their voices heard. They openly criticized government policies and adopted a then-pathbreaking discourse of women's rights as human rights. They showed that without the ability to move about freely, associate with colleagues and determine for themselves where and when women entered the public sphere, women were unable to participate in the development of their country. They successfully established that the government owed its existence to women who supported the liberation struggle and who voted it into power in the 1980 election. They developed *Speak Out/Taurai/Khulumani*, a tri-lingual magazine in English, Shona and Ndebele to mobilize women's anger into protests against the violation of their rights. As a pressure group, WAG was so successful that in 1984, "a directive was issued to staff at the Ministry of Community Development and Women's Affairs that WAG must be discredited and destroyed" (Watson 1998: 21). The group was then put under surveillance by the Central Intelligence Organization (CIO).

Initially the organizational operating costs were borne largely by WAG members. After gaining funding ($15,000) from the Ford Foundation for a workshop and an additional $5,000 from the Friedrich Ebert Foundation for a second, the group sought outside funding to expand its work and pay hired staff. By 1987,

WAG became a fully registered NGO with donor funding (Watson 1998). While funding enabled WAG to launch greater outreach and expanded programming for women's health and education, it also began to change the nature, if not the mission, of the organization. The question of race, which had been the cause of an early rift in the group (Shaw 2001), raised its head once more as did the question of feminism. The original members were clearly feminist, some socialist, politically active and progressive in their push for structural reforms regarding women's rights and development. As a result of many debates on race, feminism(s), socialism(s) and the ongoing cultural tensions in Zimbabwe, many of the founding members of WAG moved on and the organization changed.

By 1998, WAG was fully part of the development machinery in Zimbabwe; the group employed a well-paid full-time staff of 14 plus six fieldworkers (Dorman 2001; Shaw 2001). By 2003, members and staff were overwhelmingly black and included at least one man; the Board of Trustees was racially- and gender-inclusive, but all were Zimbabwean (Shaw 2001). Development funding enabled WAG to mature into an organization capable of engaging multi-sector, issue-based projects that utilized funding from bilateral donors, multilateral agencies and religious and local organizations. The group showed little resemblance to the activist group of women who funded meeting space and paid for printed literature out of their own pockets. In order to survive, WAG began to downplay its early activist history where socialist, feminist women denounced government action and patriarchy, spoke out against gender oppression, political repression and injustice and called for structural change. In a 1999 interview, Selina Mumbengegwi, WAG's Director, noted that:

> when we have our members meeting, I always call for a government official to attend, to show we are not doing anything wrong. I always emphasize that as NGOs we complement the government … If you are allowed to sit at the right table that is where you can have influence.
>
> *Dorman 2001:141*

Extensive donor funding from the international donor community has enabled the professionalization of WAG. In 2014, WAG's publications and its website are glossy; they embody mainstream development rhetoric about women's empowerment, but they make no calls for structural change. An analysis of a 2010 project report on the "Campaign for Social Change," initiated in 2004, highlights the muted nature of the group. Moreover, it gives rise to the question, how has twenty-five years of donor funding helped WAG accomplish its goal of gender equality? The report clearly demonstrates that Zimbabwean women face the same oppressions in 2010 that they faced in 1983.

The 2004–2009 Campaign for Social Change was part of a strategy aimed at reducing the incidence of HIV/AIDS by creating public awareness of the cultural practices that make women more vulnerable than men to the disease. The project goals were to promote women's sexual and reproductive health rights as part of public health in six Morondera districts, about 45 miles outside of Harare. At the outset of the project, WAG personnel informed communities about HIV/AIDS and its transmission with the goal of enabling individuals to adopt behaviors to protect themselves from the disease. The theory was that health and rights education would position the community to value and support women's rights and health. The project "trained a total of eighty traditional leaders on gender, culture and HIV and AIDS as well as laws on inheritance, the Sexual Offences Act and the Domestic Violence Act" (WAG 2010: 15).

Project personnel identified cultural practices of roora (bride wealth), polygyny, wife inheritance and some girl-child pledging that made women more vulnerable to HIV infection than men. A further issue was dry sex – a popular practice in which women dry out their vaginas with herbs, detergents, salt, cotton or shredded newspaper. Dry sex causes vaginal lacerations and suppresses normal bacteria, both of which increase the likelihood of HIV. They found that most people in these communities lacked basic knowledge of HIV/AIDS and its transmission, women's sexual and reproductive health rights, as well as communication skills between partners necessary to reduce incidence of HIV infection. The project strategy was to provide health and rights information only and let communities decide how best to approach their problems. Community-based problem solving was supposed to improve participation and outcomes as well as empower women "with knowledge of sexual and reproductive health and rights and knowledge of personal risk to HIV infection if those rights are denied" (WAG 2010 [emphasis in original]).

The decision of WAG to work through the traditional male authorities is an indication of a loss of feminist fire and the country's declining recognition of women's equality. The project's very modest outcomes show no improvement in HIV-related popular attitudes or behavior. The outcomes are presented as six vignettes from the customary court of Chief Svosve after he underwent WAG training. Svosve presides over bi-monthly community court meetings to settle community disputes; he is assisted by four assessors – always including a woman – and a clerk. Svosve's training resulted in the following six decisions:

Case 1: A 53-year-old widow was asked by her deceased husband's relatives to vacate her home of more than 20 years. Svosve ruled that the house was her home and she could stay. He relieved the family of its customary responsibilities of looking after her by agreeing to help look after her himself if need be.

Case 2: A cohabitating couple broke up because the male formed a new attachment. Svosve ordered the man to pay roora (a type of bride-wealth payments) and compensate the woman for damages resulting from premarital sex.

Case 3: A young widow's brother-in-law demanded she leave her home 15 months after her husband died because she had a lover. Svosve refused to hear the case because the woman's parents were unavailable. Her elopement years earlier had alienated her from them. Svosve ruled they needed to be present according to custom. He then decided that the brother-in-law could not remove the widow from her house but that the young widow could not bring a lover into her home.

Case 4: A woman left her husband after he kicked her out of their home and sent her back to her parents. A month later, he changed his mind and sent for her. She refused to return to him as she was employed and living with another man. One of the court assessors maligned the woman as a prostitute for living in another man's homestead. The court ordered this man to pay damages to the husband. He refused; she did not return.

Case 5: The customary court ordered a man to pay roora for a woman he had lived with and with whom he fathered a child. Because the man did not show up in court, Svosve admonished the man's father for not reprimanding his son. He said that if the son refused to appear, he would send the case to the judicial system and the law would force the son to pay maintenance.

Case 6: This involved overdue roora payments to a deceased wife's family as well as money the husband owed the wife before she died. Svosve ordered the man to pay the family all the money owed; he agreed to pay, but said he expected the family to give him another wife. Svosve suggested that he could approach the family on this matter, but reminded the man that women were free to choose their own spouses.

The project outcomes from the Campaign for Social Change provide an example of the double-edged sword of using development aid for securing human rights for women. The once vociferous demands for women's equality were replaced by participation in development projects in which the capricious decisions of a traditional chief becomes the voice for women. WAG working with traditional male leaders is on the opposite end of the continuum from the firebrand group of women in 1983 who demanded equality for women. This once-mass organization has been co-opted by development funding and compelled by state coercion to move away from social action for development towards more modest direct action in which individual women tapping into networks of opportunity can make their own lives better, more modern and more secure. Thus, WAG's staff members have improved their position but overall their gains for women are miniscule.

The project goal of promoting gender equality by challenging traditional value systems was noble. However, exclusively targeting traditional male leaders was ineffective. There was no attempt to challenge patrilineal restrictions on women's participation in dialogue on crucial questions of reproductive health. Nor could there be discussions of gender equality or women's concerns outside of the HIV/AIDS discourse (WAG 2010). Traditional leaders, mostly male, were urged to promote significant behavior change. They did little more than to preach not having multiple sexual partners (ibid.). The project reinforced the use of customary law as a means to control women's sexuality. Chief Svosve promoted marriage, obedience of women to social norms, extramarital abstinence and curtailing the freedom of unmarried women. The two widows keeping their homes hints at progressive thinking but the decisions were still tempered with gender restrictions.

To bolster this success, the report quotes from a WAG study completed the year before: "there are still challenges regarding attitudes among the project beneficiaries towards gender equality because these have 'remained largely sexist and patriarchal'" (2010: 27). The report addresses gender inequality as the critical driver of HIV/AIDS infections but does not make a direct call for an end to gender discrimination or to the cultural practices that put women at increased risk. The soft recommendations call for: (1) increased coordination between stakeholders working in the project area; (2) material resources for HIV testing, psychological counseling and health centers for treatment; (3) better representation of women and youth in leadership positions; and (4) a need for healing and reconciliation in communities. There are also calls for capacity building, extended training and retraining of community leaders and outreach to religious leaders. There is no challenge to the status quo and little hope for gender equality in these rural communities in the near future (both of Zimbabwe's main ethnic groups, the Shona and Ndebele, are patrilineal-patrilocal, so women are structurally as well as culturally disadvantaged).

The fact that WAG has survived thirty years is a testament to Zimbabwean women, their commitment and their managerial and political skills. Increasingly oppressive political conditions since the 1990s have limited their development activism to that of direct action; these women have been able to use the development industry to their advantage. As Rudo Gaidzanwa (1985) notes, it is liberated women who exercise choice, act creatively, exploit opportunities and maximize options. Donor funding has helped create decent, mostly urban well-paying jobs for a small number of educated women who tackle social problems. However, outside of holding many meetings, writing reports and producing glossy documents, it is difficult to document progressive social change as a result of their development-funded work. Women's problems continue to be severe. Infanticide and child abandonment are endemic. Women are still indiscriminately arrested for not being "good Zimbabwean women." Women still lack the right to wear clothing of their choice (notably mini-skirts) without having it ripped from their bodies.

Women's continued push for human development: WOZA

The repression and donor funding that muted WAG inflamed other women; new groups have arisen to pursue WAG's humanistic and feminist goals. In 2003, the grassroots activist organization WOZA formed to empower women to fight for their communities and livelihoods, as well as to demand social justice and equal rights; in 2006 men joined the organization. The group began protesting chronic food shortages and deteriorating public services in the face of violence and repression associated with the 2000 fast-track land reform program. WOZA street protests for human survival provide a beacon of hope for poor Zimbabweans (Saki and Katema 2011: 56).

WOZA members protest the failure of corrupt, authoritarian and neoliberal development and serve as a reminder of the failed promises of the liberation struggle. In street demonstrations, the group demands public services such as clean water and electricity (for both of which people pay). They demand an end to state-sanctioned violence against lawful citizens and suggest that the money used for repression of the people would be better spent on free primary education. WOZA's development activism has "rejuvenated the notion of governance to include the provision of basics and social safety nets for citizens" (Saki and Katema 2011: 57). Their protests highlight the bipolar continuum amongst women's groups, and the nation's development crisis in the face of continued autocracy and kleptocracy by the Mugabe regime, as well as the failure of the free market and neoliberal development programs to deliver on the promise to end poverty and misery.

WOZA members are frequently subject to violence and repression. Maria Moyo (1950–2007), a freedom fighter who joined the liberation struggle in 1970, traveling to Zambia and Botswana, was among the founding members of the group. She was often on the front lines of protests and frequently the first arrested. From 2003 to 2007, she was arrested ten times and more often subjected to arbitrary police harassment. Her death in 2007 was the result of police violence (WOZA 2007). In a 2013 survey of over 7,000 members the organization found that 81 percent of WOZA Harare and Bulawayo members did not believe that women are respected and did not believe that violence against them has ceased. Eight-nine percent of members did not believe that they would be able to benefit from ZANU-PF's indigenization policies, and 68.2 percent felt that the police harassment and criminalization of women informal traders hurt socioeconomic growth.

> All believed that women were working very hard to create food security for their families, but many noted that this was done against all odds. The vast majority believe the development situation in their communities had deteriorated .
>
> *WOZA 2013*

WOZA has conducted more than 500 street protests since 2003 and over 3,000 women and men have spent time in jail as a result (WOZA 2013). Like WAG before it, WOZA has been targeted by the Mugabe government; members have been gassed at demonstrations, abducted from the streets and their homes, threatened with guns and badly beaten. They are thrown in filthy jail cells without adequate food or water for exercising their constitutional rights and calling for people-centered development. In July 2014, WOZA co-founder Jenni William said she 'had been in jail 38 times and had many scars on her body from the beatings she received." She then stated, "When you hit a woman, you hit a rock; they will never break me" (Jaffer 2014). WOZA has received numerous international awards and recognition for their human rights and development work. These women's struggles in Zimbabwe promote development because "they contribute directly to improvements, both materially and in terms of generating more freedoms, of their lives and of their dependents and communities" (Selwyn 2014: 21).

Conclusion

The future of development in Zimbabwe remains uncertain. Political stability is tenuous. The rebound of 2010 has ended. GDP growth decelerated from 10.5 percent in 2012 to 4.5 percent in 2013 and an estimated 3 percent in 2014 (Mangudya 2013: 1). The country remains mired in debt to the IFIs and is unable to enter into new loan agreements. "Since 1980 Zimbabwe has been lent US$7.7 billion but repaid US$11.4 billion. Yet the Southern African country is still said today to have a debt in excess of US$7 billion" (Jones 2011: 8). Will a new round of development aid from the IFIs improve conditions in Zimbabwe? It is unlikely if it continues on a growth without development trajectory that allows a few to do well but leaves the overwhelming majority in poverty.

Regardless there are some bright spots. In 2013, as a result of pressure from women's groups, international agencies and other stakeholders, Zimbabwe adopted a new constitution that recognizes the rights of men and women to equal opportunities in political, economic, cultural and social spheres. It also guarantees the right to equal pay and voids all laws, customs, traditions and cultural practices that infringe on the rights of women. In addition, it calls for the state to ensure gender balance and fair representation of marginalized groups and to promote women's participation in all spheres of society. It is too soon to see if its provisions will be enforced but prospects look dim under the current regime.

The bipolar nature of Zimbabwe's development is likely to continue, since there presently is "an on-going governance crisis, a result of the ruling ZANU-PF party's internal wars to succeed the party's nonagenarian President, which have not made development any easier" (Moyo 2014). The current in-fighting pits First Lady Grace Mugabe, who recently ascended to head ZANU-PF Women's League, against long-time Vice-President and ex-combatant Joice Mujuru, who was ousted from power in December 2014. Mujuru is fighting back.

While Zimbabwe's elite struggle for succession rights and control of Zimbabwe's wealth, women's groups continue their development activism. NGOs such as WAG, with donor community help, will continue their policy-oriented work for women's rights and gender equality, jobs, education and health care. Concomitantly, civic groups such as WOZA demand women-friendly development in the form of repair of community buildings, roads, clinics and schools; the provision of modern water and electricity systems with metered billing, and an end to violence. For Zimbabwean women, development is less about large-scale projects that bring profits to investors. It is more about protection of public health through provision of adequate sewage treatment facilities, regular garbage collection and public toilets and garbage cans in community locations. They support free primary education and women's rights. They also assert that development entails decent housing for all; jobs in all sectors – public and private, formal and informal – and freedom from corruption, exploitation, tribalism and gender discrimination.

Women's social activism for development, civil rights and independence reaffirms that development is not merely or even primarily about GDP, corporate or private gain; nor about state-business relations or branding to sell; it is about people and their ability to live sustainable, meaningful and productive lives. Many Zimbabwean women are development activists who sometimes work both within and outside of the donor community to agitate for people-orientated development. Women's groups actively opposed and continue to oppose a neoliberal development agenda and growing state-sanctioned violence against women. Their successes, such as the inclusion of explicit equal rights for women in the 2013 Constitution, are tenuous. Implementation or remedies overwhelmingly are at the will and whim of the men who dominate the government and the hierarchy of traditional chiefs.

Nevertheless, a focus on women's responses to neoliberal policies and declining living standards within a failed development framework allows for the articulation of women as active change agents rather than as mere victims – poor, oppressed or dependent. This shift in discourse away from traditional, patriarchal and oppressive ideas about African womanhood to a feminist and equalizing understanding of women's evolving lives shows that some women's groups have successfully engaged the international community – and their own members – for development. This, then, is Zimbabwe's bipolar development today. It shows that when the state fails, some women take matters into their own hands.

References

Chikowore, Godfrey. 2010. "Contradictions in Development Aid: The Case of Zimbabwe." *South-South Cooperation: A Challenge to the Aid System?* Special Report for The Reality of Aid. Quezon City: IBON Books. Available at: www.realityofaid.org/wp-content/uploads/2013/02/ROA-SSDC-Special-Report4.pdf

Chitiga, Rudo M. 1994. *Zimbabwe National Report to the World Conference on the Advancement of Women: Contribution by Zimbabwe NGOs.* Harare.

Chogugudza, Patricia. 2010. "The Good Woman." Pp. 118–130 in *African Women Writing Resistance: An Anthology of Contemporary Voices*, edited by Jennifer Browdy de Hernandez, Pauline Dongala, Omotayo Olaosho and Anne Serafin. Madison, WI: University of Wisconsin Press.

Dawson, Martin and Tim Kelsall. 2013. "Anti-Developmental Patrimonialism in Zimbabwe." Pp. 49–66 in *'Progress' in Zimbabwe?: The Past and Present of a Concept and a Country*, edited by David Moore, Norma Kriger and Brian Raftopoulous. New York: Routledge.

Dorman, Sara R. 2001. Inclusion and Exclusion: NGOs and Politics in Zimbabwe. Unpublished PhD thesis. University of Oxford.

Essof, Shereen. 2005. "She-Murenga: Challenges, Opportunities and Setbacks of the Women's Movement in Zimbabwe." *Feminist Africa: Women Mobilized* 4: 1–13. Available at: http://agi.ac.za/sites/agi.ac.za/files/fa_4_feature_article_2.pdf

Gaidzanwa, Rudo B. 1985. *Images of Women in Zimbabwean Literature.* Harare: College Press.

Graaf, Martin de, Sam Moyo and Ton Dietz. 1991. *Non-Governmental Organisations in Zimbabwe*. Report for the impact study co-financing organisations. Amsterdam/Utrecht: Impactstudie Medefinancieringsprogramma NGO Landenstudie Afrika.
Hanke, Steven H. 2008. "Zimbabwe from Hyperinflation to Growth." *Development Policy Analysis* 6 (June 28). Available at: http://object.cato.org/sites/cato.org/files/pubs/pdf/dpa6.pdf
Inter-Parliamentary Union. 2014. "Women in National Parliaments." Available at: www.ipu.org/wmn-e/classif.htm
Jaffer, Mobina. 2011. "Women of Zimbabwe Arise!" *The Afro News*, July 14. Available at: www.theafronews.com/women-of-zimbabwe-arise
Jones, Tom. 2011. "Uncovering Zimbabwe's Debt: The Case for a Democratic Solution to the Unjust Debt Burden." London: Jubilee Debt Campaign. Available at: http://eurodad.org/uploadedfiles/whats_new/reports/uncovering%20zimbabwe%27s%20debt_final_11.11.pdf
Kachingwe, Sarah. 1994. *Sally Mugabe: A Woman with a Mission*. Harare: ZANU-PF Central Committee.
Lapchick, Richard and Stephanie Urdang. 1982. *Oppression and Resistance: The Struggle of Women in Southern Africa*. Westport, CT: Greenwood Press.
Made, Patricia, and Nomasomi Mpofu. 2005. *Beyond Inequalities 2005: Women in Zimbabwe*. Harare: Zimbabwe Women's Resource Centre and Network and Southern African Research and Documentation Centre.
Mangudya, J. P. 2013. *2013 Annual Report*. Harare: Reserve Bank of Zimbabwe. Available at: www.Rbz.co.zw.
Mugabe, Robert. 1986. "Baby Dumping." *The Herald*, May 30, 1.
——1983. Quoted in *The Herald*, September 10.
Moyo, Jeffery. 2014. "Zimbabwe: Internal Ruling Party Wrangles Stall Development." *AllAfrica.com*, 26 November. Available at: http://allafrica.com/stories/201411270116.html
Moyo, Sam, John Makumbe and Brian Raftopoulos. 2000. *NGOs, the State & Politics in Zimbabwe*. Harare: SAPES Books.
Osirim, Mary J. 2011. "Enterprising Women in Zimbabwe: Confronting Crisis in a Globalizing Era." Pp. 175–195 in *Globalization and Sustainable Development in Africa*, edited by B. House-Soremekun and T. Falola. Rochester: University of Rochester Press.
Raftopoulos, Brian. 1996. "Problems of Research in a Post-Colonial State: The Case of Zimbabwe." Working Paper No. 9, Institute of Development Studies, University of Zimbabwe.
Ramalingam, Ben. 2013. *Aid on the Edge of Chaos: Rethinking International Cooperation in a Complex World*. Oxford: Oxford University Press.
Saki, Otto and Washington Ketema. 2011. "Voices from Civil Society." Pp. 44–76 in *Zimbabwe in Transition: A View from Within*, edited by Tim Murithi and Aquilina Mawadza. Auckland Park, South Africa: Fanele.
Selwyn, Benjamin. 2014. *The Global Development Crisis*. Cambridge: Polity Press.
Shaw, Carolyn Martin. 2007. "You Had a Daughter, but I Am Becoming a Woman: Sexuality, Feminism, and Postcoloniality in Tsitsi Dangarembga's 'Nervous Conditions' and 'She No Longer Weeps'." *Research in African Literatures* 38 (4): 7–27.
——2001. "Working with Feminists in Zimbabwe: A Black American's Experience of Transnational Alliances." Pp. 250–276 in *Feminism and Antiracism: International Struggles for Justice*, edited by France Winddance Twine and Kathleen M. Blee. New York: New York University Press.United Nations. 2014. *Millennium Development Goals Indicators*. New York: United Nations Development Indicators Unit. Available at: http://mdgs.un.org/unsd/mdg/Host.aspx?Content=Indicators/OfficialList.htm

UNDP. 1998. *Human Development Report*. New York: Oxford University Press.
UNDP-Zimbabwe. 2013. *Brown Bag Dialogue Series: The Debt Issue*, no. 3. Harare: UNDP Zimbabwe. Available at: www.zw.undp.org/content/zimbabwe/en/home/library/poverty/brown-bag-dialogue-series---the-debt-issue.html
Watson, Peggy. 2003. "'Thandiwe Mhlanga,' Angela Kotler, and Hazel Hall, Arrested for Being Women." Pp. 375–377 in *Women Writing Africa: The Southern Region*, edited by Margaret J. Dyamond. New York: Feminist Press, City University of New York.
———1998. *Determined to Act: The First 15 Years of the Women's Action Group (1983 to 1998)*. Harare: Women's Action Group.
Women's Action Group (WAG). 2010. *The Marondera Experience: Traditional Leaders as Agents of Change in the HIV and AIDS Era*. WAG Project Report. Harare: Women's Action Group.
———1984. "Organizing for Social Reform in Zimbabwe: Women's Action Group Newsletter June '84, No. 1." *Journal of Canadian Woman Studies/Les Cahiers De La Femme* 7 (1&2): 47–52.
Women of Zimbabwe Arise (WOZA). 2013. "29 November is Women Human Rights Defenders Day." Available at: http://wozazimbabwe.org/?p=1504.
Women of Zimbabwe Arise (WOZA). 2007. "Maria Moyo (15 March 1950 – 6 November 2007): A Shero Remembered – A Life Celebrated." Available at: http://wozazimbabwe.org/?p=170.
World Bank. 2014. "Zimbabwe Overview." Available at: www.worldbank.org/en/country/zimbabwe/overview.
Yamamoto, Ken. 2014. "Mugabe Fighting Corruption? Forget It!" *NewZimbabwe News.com* April 9. Available at: www.newzimbabwe.com/news/news.aspx?newsID=15219.
Zimbabwe Institute. 2008. The State of Civics in Zimbabwe. Unpublished paper.
Zukas (Lueker), Lorna L. 1998. Women, War, and Social Change: The Challenge to Independence in Zimbabwe. Unpublished PhD thesis, University of California, San Diego.

10
ADVANCING WHILE LOSING

Indigenous land claims and development in Argentina

Matthias vom Hau

Introduction

In August 2013, during my most recent research trip to Tucumán, I joined a public demonstration organized by *Diaguita Calchaquí* activists, the most numerous indigenous group in this northwestern Argentine province.[1] More than 1,400 protesters walked the major avenues of San Miguel de Tucumán, paralyzing the traffic in the provincial capital for hours. Their chants and banners demanded justice for Javier Chocobar, a Diaguita leader. Chocobar was brutally murdered in a dispute over communal land claims. His suspected killers are Darío Amín, the current legal title holder and member of one of the large landowning families in the province, and Humberto Gómez y José Valdivieso, two hired guns who, as former members of the special police forces in Tucumán, were already notorious for torture during Argentina's last military dictatorship (1976–1982). More than four years after Chocobar's violent death in 2009 the three suspects still awaited trail (and are still awaiting when this chapter went to press) and move around freely – even though they themselves had recorded their deadly confrontation with Chocobar on a digital camera that was subsequently recovered by residents of Chuschagasta and handed over to the authorities.

The protestors stopped in front of the provincial government and the supreme court to voice their outrage about the province's handling of Chocobar's killing and press authorities for a speedy and impartial trial that would adhere to international standards of justice. Demonstrators drew a direct connection between the fate of Javier Chocobar, his struggle for communal land rights and the core demand of Diaguita mobilization: control over the land and territories Diaguita communities consider historically their own. Slogans such as "Valley of Tafí – Ancestral, Traditional and Present Territory of Indigenous Peoples" or "We Demand the Handing Over of Our Lands" reminded authorities that the 1994 Constitution and its redefinition of Argentina as a pluriethnic nation established the right for indigenous communities to (re)claim communal lands.

I have encountered other public demonstrations for indigenous land rights across Argentina, as well. In 2009, I witnessed similar land rights protests by the *Mbya-Guaraní*, less acculturated lowland indigenous peoples whose history and culture has little in common with those of the more acculturated Diaguitas. In Posadas, the capital of Misiones province, several hundred of them occupied the central square. In interviews with local media, Mbya-Guaraní leaders demanded that the provincial government stop issuing logging licenses for land claimed by their communities.

These vignettes are illustrative of the rise of indigenous mobilization in Argentina. Even though dominant discourses about national identity continue to depict the country as a "white nation" of European immigrants (Bastia and vom Hau 2014), Argentina has witnessed the rise of indigenous identity politics. Over the last two decades, the country has followed a larger trend of "constitutional multiculturalism" (Van Cott 2000). In 1994, the Argentine Constitution adopted a set of special rights for indigenous peoples, including the possibility to reclaim communal tenure rights for lands presently and historically used by indigenous communities (Carrasco 2000). Since then, indigenous activism has gained force across the country, something that was unthinkable even a generation ago. Indigenous activists envision the construction of a more inclusive nation that recognizes diversity. Meanwhile, they push for the implementation of the new constitutional rights to secure more territorial autonomy and control.

The recent emergence of indigenous activism in Argentina (e.g. Gordillo and Hirsch 2003), Latin America (e.g. Postero and Zamosc 2004; Sieder 2002; Yashar 2005) and across the world (e.g. de la Cadena and Starn 2007) has captured the scholarly imagination. What remains a matter of intense debate are the implications for development of these movements. Should indigenous movements be seen as transformative forces or as ultimately contributing to the persistence of the existing political and economic order? Some scholars treat indigenous mobilization, with its focus on achieving development through the recognition of diversity, as a significant step ahead compared to mid-twentieth century Latin American populism. Then the emphasis was on *mestizaje* and the dissolution of diversity into homogeneous national identities to achieve a more equitable provision of public goods (de la Peña 2005; Uquillas and Van Nieuwkoop 2003).[2] Conversely, others emphasize the limited impact indigenous movements have had (so far). Indigenous peoples remain among the most destitute citizens in Latin America (Hall and Patrinos 2005) and continue to be exposed to widespread ethnoracial discrimination (Laurie et al. 2005; Richards 2013).

At a first glance, Diaguita and Mbya-Guaraní land struggles in Argentina squarely fit the pessimistic perspective. Their activism appears to have done little to improve their situation. To date, only a fraction of Diaguita and Mbya-Guaraní communities in the Tucumán, Salta and Misiones provinces have made a successful land claim, while the foot-dragging of the courts in Tucumán with respect to Javier

Chocobar's murder sends a strong signal that violence against indigenous activists comes with impunity.

Yet, this is not the whole story. A second look at indigenous activism in Tucumán, Salta and Misiones reveals a different story, one of (at least partial) success. Equipped with analytical tools from social movement theory, this chapter focuses on multiple aspects of potential social movement impact, including not only substantive, but also procedural, cultural and structural effects. Seen in this light, some significant advances have been made, despite the fact that Diaguita and Mbya-Guaraní land struggles are far from achieving their main goal and confront a hostile political environment.

In this chapter I analyze social movement impact along three distinct dimensions. The first one concerns *power relations with other actors*. While social movements might not be able to force desired policy changes, they may nonetheless alter the balance of power between movements, their opponents and state authorities (Amenta et al. 2010). In fact, the very process of mobilization may lead to the institutional acceptance of a movement and the constituencies represented by it. This already constitutes a crucial dimension of success because it conveys external recognition by the state and/or opponents that the movement is a relevant political actor (Gamson 1990; Polletta and Jasper 2001).

This case study shows that Diaguita land rights activism in Tucumán succeeded in ending the payment of pasture rents to the current legal title holders of lands claimed by indigenous communities, a practice that was widespread until very recently. Indigenous activism in Tucumán also contributed to the completion of a survey (*relevamiento*) of indigenous land claims by the provincial government. The carrying out of the survey shows that the provincial state at a minimum recognizes indigenous land struggles as a political reality, thereby transforming the new constitutional rights from an abstract legal formula into actual political practice (see Somers 2008).

A second crucial dimension of social movement impact is *cultural change* (della Porta 1999; Melucci 1996). Social movements may transform the ways in which other actors understand and evaluate a particular issue. For example, social movements may succeed in changing how politicians, bureaucrats, other social movements and/or ordinary citizens think about the causes of war, or whether they perceive sustainable development to be an integral goal of economic policymaking (Bebbington 2007).

In this chapter, I argue that Diaguita mobilization – especially in Tucumán – contributed to a shift in how stakeholders analyze indigenous poverty. State officials, NGO activists and local academics became sympathetic to the alternative understandings proposed by indigenous activists: that indigenous well-being is closely entwined with their land rights and control over territory.

Finally, a third dimension of social movement impact involves potential effects on the *power relations among protestors*. Social movements may create new identities by transforming citizens into activists. Social movements may also foster a greater sense of political ownership and responsibility, and thereby contribute to greater participation among previously demobilized groups (Stryker 2000).

In order to explore within-movement power dynamics, this chapter focuses on the implications of indigenous land rights activism for gender relations (see McAdam 1992;Viterna 2013). I find that both Diaguita and Mbya-Guaraní women increasingly participate in protest activities and conceive of themselves as activists. A small number of Diaguita women have obtained unprecedented leadership positions in indigenous activism. Those female leaders strategically employ dominant gender norms of women as mothers and caregivers to pursue a distinctive leadership style focused on identity building and youth mobilization.

Analyzing movement impact along these three different dimensions begs the question why some indigenous movements are more likely than others to change power relations, transform public discourse, and/or instigate political participation among indigenous women. The comparison of Diaguita and Mbya-Guaraní land rights activism emphasizes group characteristics and mobilization resources, as well as the institutional contexts in which indigenous land activism unfolds.

Group characteristics and mobilization resources

Diaguita communities in Tucumán and Salta provinces are former pastoralists with a long history of interaction with the wider society, while Mbya-Guaraní communities of Misiones province are historically semi-nomadic shifting horticulturalists who did considerable hunting and gathering; they had only sparse outside contact and continue to speak Guaraní. Diaguita activists thus can draw on mobilizing resources derived from greater exposure to formal education and labor market incorporation. Accordingly, in Tucumán and Salta, Diaguita mobilizing efforts resemble an organized social movement, while in Misiones, Mbya-Guaraní mobilization is more fragmented and less organized.

Institutional contexts

At the same time, state-movement relations and the institutional legacies of past ethnic conflict are equally important to account for contemporary movement impact. Both in Salta and in Misiones, the provincial government dealt with prior rounds of indigenous protest by establishing a state organization that operates as the official representative organ of indigenous groups vis-à-vis the province. These preexisting state organizations actively pursue a "divide and rule" strategy by coopting indigenous leaders. In Tucumán, by contrast, the provincial government responded to earlier episodes of indigenous mobilization primarily by ignoring and repressing indigenous activism, and therefore did not establish a comparable mechanism of cooptation.

This chapter draws on more than 80 interviews with indigenous activists, non-activists, state officials and economic elites in the three provinces that I conducted during several research trips between November 2008 and August 2013. The interviews were complemented by frequent consultations with anthropologists and sociologists from various universities and research institutions in San Miguel de Tucumán, the city of Salta, Posadas and Buenos Aires.

The background of indigenous land struggles

Census data indicates that 31,753 individuals self-identify as Diaguitas in Argentina (INDEC 2004/5). More than half of those, around 18,000, are concentrated in the Andean valleys of Tucumán and Salta provinces. There are about 16 Diaguita communities located in Tucumán and 23 communities in Salta, and each of them includes between several hundred and 2,000 *comuneros* – members with voting rights and (potential) entitlements to communal lands. About 8,223 individuals consider themselves to belong to the Mbya-Guaraní (INDEC 2004/5). The majority of them, around 4,500, live in approximately 100 communities in Misiones province, their size varying between 50 and 450 members.

Whether Diaguita or Mbya-Guaraní, indigenous activists portray themselves as the original inhabitants who occupied the land long before the onset of Spanish colonialism. Land claims usually emphasize a continuity between precolonial and contemporary patterns of indigenous land use. As a Diaguita council member in Tucumán puts it:

> They [the current legal titleholders] wanted to kick us out with the provincial law that they have, but we do not recognize this [law], because we were the first ones here, we existed even before the arrival of Columbus, it's as simple as that, and then the nation [national government] made this law, they gave us Article 75, 17 [the article of the 1994 Argentine Constitution that recognizes indigenous communal land rights].
>
> Clara, Diaguita community council member, Tucumán[3]

To strengthen their claims to historical precedence Diaguita and Mbya-Guaraní leaders often prepare maps that document spatial memories and show the settlements, ceremonial centers and pasture, cultivation and/or hunting and gathering areas historically used by them. As one activist from Salta stresses, "we have proofs, archaeological traces, that we existed before." Other forms of evidence include legal documents, kinship trees, and academic works – especially scholarship in ethnohistory and archeology.

Diaguita and Mbya-Guaraní demands for formal titling also draw a close connection between land and territory. Land rights refer to the possession of a particular circumscribed surface, while indigenous conceptions of territory are broader and claim control over spaces used (or traditionally used) by a community and their environmental resources, including the air, subsoil, arable lands, rivers and woods. In the words of a cacique in Tucumán:

> When the state says *land*, it gives you a specific plot or maybe even the whole valley so you can plant and have your farm. Then tomorrow comes a mining company, and [the state] says 'I said land, not subsoil [rights]!', or they build a factory that contaminates the air, and the air is not yours. By contrast, with *territory* we can restrain these kinds of debaucheries.
>
> Sergio, Diaguita cacique, Tucumán

Activists thus associate "land rights" with a more fundamental struggle for the recognition of indigenous territorial rights – the rights to control the resources contained in, below and above the land they claim as traditionally theirs.

How can we account for the rise in Diaguita and Mbya-Guaraní land rights activism? First, there were changes in global and national *opportunity structures* – most prominently, the emergence of a global human rights regime and constitutional multiculturalism. The International Labor Organization (ILO) Convention 169, approved in 1989 by the Argentine government, or the United Nations Declaration on the Rights of Indigenous Peoples, approved in 1994, provided local activists with new legal frameworks and normative resources to demand the recovery of communal lands (Carrasco 2000). At the national level, the 1994 constitutional reform confirmed these new international norms by depicting Argentina as a pluriethnic nation with special rights for indigenous peoples (Van Cott 2000).

Yet, the main *motivation* for Diaguita and Mbya-Guaraní to use these new rights involves recent economic changes. Trade liberalization, in tandem with the substantial increase of export-oriented commercial agriculture (e.g. sugar, wine, soybeans) and/or dramatically expanding mining activities pose a major threat to indigenous landholding patterns (Bebbington et al. 2008; Zoomers 2000).[4] The threat is worse in the case of rural communities that do not have a formal title to the land they claim as theirs.

Historically, the economies of Tucumán and Salta were primarily oriented toward agriculture. Sugarcane dominated in the lowlands, while in the Andean valleys corn farming and cattle herding constituted the main sources of subsistence. The majority of households who today identify as Diaguita engaged in a mixture of pastoralism, small-scale farming and seasonal work in the sugarcane harvest. Over the last decades, many changes transformed these traditional subsistence strategies. In the lowlands, the large-scale mechanization of sugarcane production reduced the demand for seasonal workers. Meanwhile, in the Andean valleys where most of the Diaguitas lived – and live — the rise in tourism has led to a growing demand for summer homes and a booming hotel industry, and has intensified land sales to speculators.[5] This often resulted in the fencing of historically open pastures used by Diaguita communities. Moreover, mining activities in the neighboring province of Catamarca and in Chile have led to increased water scarcity and the decline of arable lands. In short, the Diaguita see threats to their traditional lands coming from all sides. Now, let's consider the Mbya-Guaraní of Misiones province.

For most of the twentieth century, Misiones was characterized by the expansion of small-scale horticulture and the gradual decline of the Paranaese rainforest. Non-indigenous colonists (*colonos*) cleared forest to produce *yerba mate*, a profitable plant whose leaves are used for a popular, tea-like beverage. Mbya-Guaraní households usually maintained a semi-nomadic lifestyle. They combined work as farmhands with hunting, gathering, fishing and some subsistence hoe horticulture (e.g. sweet potatoes, pumpkins). During the 1970s, the development policies of the military government – aimed at strengthening Argentina's border regions – increased land values and accelerated deforestation. Motivated by tax breaks, road building projects and the massive sale of public lands, export-oriented agribusinesses acquired major land holdings and invested in their commercial use for yerba mate, tea and soybean production (Gorosito Kramer 1982). This process also entailed the end of small-scale horticulture, and led to a greater dependence of the remaining Mbya-Guaraní communities on social assistance, small-plot gardening and the sale of handicrafts.

When being asked about their reasons to mobilize for land rights, both the Diaguita and Mbya-Guaraní activists stressed economic security. Not having a title exposes communities to the risk of possible eviction, even from lands they have lived on for generations. Land rights also provide the basis for claiming social benefits such as public housing and infrastructural investments, resources that cannot be accessed in the absence of a title. Thus, the recent expansion of export-oriented agriculture and mining is a strong incentive to mobilize to protect access to land. The next section explores whether these claims have made a difference.

The consequences of indigenous land struggles

When the focus is on land titling, the impact of indigenous mobilization has been limited. So far only a fraction of local Diaguita and Mbya-Guaraní communities in Tucumán, Salta and Misiones have made a successful communal land claim. In Tucumán, one out of 16 recognized Diaguita communities, Amaicha, managed to obtain formal titling and received around 52,000 hectares of land. This was largely because Amaicha was able to support the claim with a written legal document from the colonial period, a *Cedula Real*, which established the precise boundaries of a land title granted to the community by the Spanish Crown. In Salta, so far none of the 23 Diaguita communities has been granted a formal land title, while in Misiones around 20 out of the 100 Mbya-Guaraní communities successfully claimed titles, yet none of them has actually received these lands.

External recognition and power relations

Diaguita and Mbya-Guaraní mobilization has been more effective however, in giving indigenous communities greater access to power. One victory was the passage of a new law. Law 26,160 was adopted by the national government in 2006 to stop the expropriation of lands occupied by indigenous communities while mandating provincial states to conduct a survey (*relevamiento*) that documents communal land claims. The overwhelming majority of the Diaguita and Mbya-Guaraní leaders I interviewed see the relevamiento as a significant step towards accepting indigenous land claims as a political reality. Yet, Tucumán, Salta and Misiones – where large landowners and agribusiness wield substantial political power – varied dramatically in the implementation of the new law. As of October 2014, the land survey is almost complete in Tucumán, where the responsible team had the necessary funds and expertise. Moreover, the survey was run out of the Ombudsman Office, one of the most respected provincial state agencies. In Salta and in Misiones, by contrast, the provincial state actively sought to undermine the completion of the survey. To date, therefore, only a small number of indigenous communities have been surveyed.

In Tucumán, Diaguita activists also managed to win a direct battle against large landowners. Coordinated by the *Unión de los Pueblos de la Nación Diaguita en Tucumán* (UPNDT), the main indigenous umbrella organization in the province, almost all of the 16 Diaguita communities stopped paying pasture rents to the current legal titleholders. Ending these payments brought some modest economic improvements, yet the most important consequence was symbolic. By refusing to be charged for the use of the land they consider as traditionally theirs, Diaguita communities put their land claims into practice. A female cacica describes this experience as follows:

> We started strong, we met with the landlord and told him we were not going to pay any more pasture rents. He responded by threatening me, telling me that he was going to denounce me because I was a social agitator who broke the peace, who had stirred them up in [community name] for the wrong cause to produce a social disaster … I told him to go ahead, that I knew my rights, and that it was a gross injustice that we paid pasture rents.
>
> *Teresa, Diaguita cacica, Tucumán*

Diaguita protestors also vigorously asserted indigenous territorial control vis-à-vis the provincial state. A campaign repeatedly mentioned in interviews were the protests against the fencing of an artificial lake in the Valle del Tafí, which led the province to abandon the measure and leave the lake unfenced.

> [The provincial government] wanted to fence the entire dam [and the artificial lake created by it]. Yet we as indigenous communities told them no, that they will not close off [the lake] even though the government already had the poles ready and wanted to fence, with wire, a public resource! But we told them that we are not going to allow this. We have animals and the highway and other fences already cut routes, while the animals need to come down and drink water … We said that, as indigenous peoples of the area, we will not allow them to close the lake. But they said that it was a decision taken by law, and we said that regardless of the decision they made and all the posts they already put in, we will not let them close the lake.
>
> *Clara, Diaguita community council member, Tucumán*

Taken together, at least in Tucumán indigenous activism made a number of significant gains vis-à-vis local landowners and provincial authorities, and entailed the recognition of Diaguita land claims as a political reality that cannot be further ignored. A similar pattern can be observed when it comes to the cultural and ideological effects of indigenous mobilization in the three provinces.

Discourses about indigenous poverty and development

Gauging the impact of indigenous mobilization also requires close attention to the influence of movement framings about development and indigenous poverty on public discourse. Diaguita and Mbya-Guaraní activists emphasize that indigenous well-being is closely entwined with land rights and territorial control. Interviewees in Misiones, for example, argue against mainstream conceptualizations of income-based poverty and instead stress a strong connection between Mbya-Guaraní destitution, commercial deforestation and the expansion of soy production, which undermines possibilities for a self-sustained way of life. In their view, obtaining formal *land* titling is just an important first step towards reclaiming indigenous *territory*. As a Mbya-Guaraní leader in Misiones explains:

> Territory is life ... We occupy a cultural space with various ceremonial grounds and cemeteries ... but as indigenous peoples we are not owners of these lands, we are part of the natural system and it is us who belong here.
> *Enrique, Mbya-Guaraní cacique, Misiones*

Similarly, Diaguita leaders in Tucumán and Salta identify a close relationship between poverty and land rights.

> Our goal is to bring together development and identity. It's basically what we need to do and what we are doing therefore is [to push for the implementation of] the land survey, because we understand that a people or a community without land has difficulties to advance.
> *Roberto, Diaguita council representative, Salta*

Yet, there are significant differences between the three Argentine provinces with respect to the broader resonance of these framings. In Tucumán and Salta, NGO activists, state officials and local academics I interviewed largely support the nexus between indigenous well-being and land rights identified by Diaguita leaders. For instance, a project organizer at the National University of Tucumán described a close link between communal land claims and local development:

> A land title means that a community can take decisions that should not be taken by the government or someone else ... For instance, whether and how they want to develop tourism.
> *Sonia, project organizer, National University of Tucumán*

Another indication of the salience of Diaguita framing strategies was the defensive reaction of economic elites. In interviews, large landowners invested substantial efforts into debunking the association between communal land holdings and indigenous well-being. One interviewee talked at length to explain how collective land rights would result in "anomie," that is, more poverty and underdevelopment for local indigenous communities.

In Misiones, by contrast, the resonance of Mbya-Guaraní framing strategies is more limited. Local NGOs, state officials and academics are more skeptical about the connection between communal land rights and indigenous well-being drawn by Mbya-Guaraní leaders. For instance, a representative of a Lutheran NGO involved in supporting Mbya-Guaraní communities sees communal land rights as a problem, not a solution to poverty. If communities obtain land, "they don't know what they are doing with their land and might sell it when they are drunk." In short, there has been a more limited ideological impact of Mbya-Guaraní activism in Misiones, especially when compared to Diaguita mobilization in Tucumán.

Gender relations and women's political participation

Women were important actors in these movements. The demonstration I attended in Santiago de Tucumán included male and female protesters in almost equal numbers. An analysis of local newspapers in northwestern Argentina reveals no significant gender differences in Diaguita militancy.[6] In contrast, Mbya-Guaraní protests in Misiones are less gender-balanced. Mbya-Guaraní women participate to a much lesser extent in land rights activism than men. Yet, the fact that Mbya-Guaraní women participate in protest at all is already striking, given the far more rigid gender boundaries and the higher level of gender inequality that prevails in this indigenous group. Historically, Mbya-Guaraní women did not control their own economic resources and did not engage with public life beyond their communities (Centurión 2006; see also Blumberg 1984). By contrast, Diaguita women long have had access to their own income, from activities such as cheese making or salaried work as household helpers (vom Hau 2015).

Nevertheless, the majority of the Diaguita and Mbya-Guaraní leaders are men. This male predominance does not preclude female leadership, however, particularly in the case of the Diaguita. Since 2004 at least three of the 16 Diaguita communities in Tucumán and four of the 23 communities in Salta elected a woman as *cacica*, and many more women served as council representatives for their respective local community. Female Diaguita leaders also pursue a different leadership style. More so than their male counterparts, these women are concerned about indigenous youths and their identity commitments, worrying that the next generation of *comuneros* might not know enough or be afraid to develop a strong identification as Diaguita. In the words of a female Diaguita council member:

> I think it is a process to get to say "I am Indian." Often there is discrimination. A girl from [her community's name] told me that in secondary school they ask who is a descendant of indigenous peoples and only she raised her hand, all the others did not assume this [identity]. So it's a process. I also

analyze those who are studying outside and what they know about their roots, because at some point they will be in the majority.[7]

Clara, Diaguita community council member, Tucumán

And more than men, female activists spend significant efforts on the organization of youth-specific activities, ranging from family visits and community dances to excursions to visit Diaguita archeological sites.

The importance female leaders assign to youth participation is at least partially a result of their own distinctive recruitment into indigenous activism. Women in leadership positions are usually new to politics. Therefore, they cannot rely on previously established political networks in order to mobilize electoral support. Focusing on youths with the aim of fostering commitment and pride therefore constitutes an alternative pathway to establish a political powerbase. In fact, this strategy allows female leaders to draw on gender stereotypes about women as mothers and caregivers, predestined to engage in the socialization of the young (vom Hau 2015).

Women's land rights activism also establishes a possible pathway towards other forms of political participation. For example, one of the female Diaguita leaders, tired of the lack of female representation in the movement, founded the *Organización de Mujeres Diaguitas*, an association that seeks to provide female activists with a space to deliberate and accommodate their specific situation as women within the indigenous movement and as *indígenas* in wider society. In other words, indigenous land rights activism is clearly gendered, while also incorporating indigenous women into politics.

Taken together, the analysis of movement consequences in Tucumán, Salta and Misiones provides the following picture: Regardless of whether it is resistance against pasture rents, discourses about indigenous poverty or women's political participation, Diaguita mobilization in Tucumán appears to have a stronger transformative influence than Diaguita activism in neighboring Salta, or – and even more pronounced – than Mbya-Guaraní mobilization in Misiones. What accounts for this variation? The next section will deal with this question in detail.

Accounting for mobilization impact

Social movement theory provides important clues to help us understand under what conditions movements are likely to have an impact. Scholars emphasize that social movements are more likely to affect the implementation of desired policies or shape public discourse if they have the organizational infrastructure to sustain collective action (Andrews 2001; Cress and Snow 2000). Put differently, movements are more likely to make a difference if they have the skilled leadership and formal organization, as well as the necessary support networks, to monitor state bureaucracies, devise feasible framing strategies, name and shame opponents and/or organize sustained campaigns.

As already emphasized above, Diaguita and Mbya-Guaraní communities in Argentina exhibit contrasting histories of engaging the state and wider society.

Patterns of formal education are indicative of these dramatic differences. Around 29.4 percent of those who identify as Mbya-Guaraní are illiterate, compared to 7.8 percent for all citizens of indigenous origins in Argentina, and the national average of 2.6 percent (INDEC 2010, 2004/5). Similarly, only 31.7 percent of the Mbya-Guaraní 15 years and older completed primary school, compared to 71.6 percent of indigenous Argentineans, and a national average of 81.1 percent (INDEC 2001, 2004/5). By contrast, 2.8 percent of the Diaguita residing in northwest Argentina are illiterate, significantly less than the 7.8 percent average for all citizens of indigenous origin, and only very slightly below a national average of 2.6 percent (INDEC 2004/5). Education levels show a similar trend. Fully 84.2 percent of the Diaguita 15 years and older completed primary school, compared to 71.6 percent of indigenous Argentineans and above the national average of 81.1 percent (INDEC 2004/5). It also bears emphasis that there is relative gender equality among the Diaguita in terms of educational attainment, while among the Mbya-Guaraní differences in formal education are far more pronounced between men and women.

Taking these differences into account, it might not be surprising that the two groups vary in their land rights activism. In Tucumán and Salta, Diaguita claims for land and territory are grounded in collective action and a sense of shared mission that crosscut distinct local communities and their concerns. In each province, Diaguita communities are connected to each other through an umbrella organization, which forms an effective vehicle of interest representation. These associations also constitute important coordination mechanisms for resistance against paying pasture rents while helping to channel support from external advocacy networks and NGOs.

Diaguita activists emphasize the crucial role of formal education for both their standing within indigenous communities and their interactions with authorities and wider society. For example, a cacica in Tucumán points to a close connection between the presence of a Diaguita activist who is also a trained lawyer and protest against pasture rents:

> Diego Solar [name changed], who is a lawyer ... told them [the community assembly] that these laws do exist and that he had been to other places in the world where indigenous peoples had managed to obtain benefits at the international level, and that they should not to be afraid but have faith in themselves, and that nothing was going to happen to them. Then the families in La Honda [name changed] started to tell our "supposed" landlord that they would not pay the pasture rents anymore, and in the following year they did the same, so we are not paying anymore. Diego Solar came on various occasions and the people felt that if the police grabbed them, Diego Solar would bail them out.
>
> *Teresa, Diaguita cacica, Tucumán*

Many of the male Diaguita leaders in Tucumán and Salta also have significant experiences in political militancy, the older ones as peasant or labor activists or even as part of the guerrilla resistance against the military dictatorships of the 1970s.

By contrast, Mbya-Guaraní mobilization in Misiones is more fragmented and does not scale up into sustained collective challenges. Contentious practices and a sense of common purpose only occasionally move beyond the local level. Usually, Mbya-Guaraní mobilization is more focused on community concerns and indigenous activists do not have a coordination mechanism comparable to the UPNDT in Tucumán or its counterpart in Salta at their disposal.[8] Similarly, the Mbya-Guaraní cannot rely on comparably skilled and experienced activists.

Yet, in order to account for the distinct effects of Diaguita activism in Tucumán and Salta, the focus on group characteristics and mobilization resources needs to be complemented with close attention to the wider institutional context. Even if endowed with the right kind of organizational infrastructure and leadership, movements might confront pre-existing state structures that prevent movement impact. The basic idea here is that the likelihood of movements exerting influence on desired policies or public discourse decreases when movements confront state institutions (e.g. agencies charged with indigenous affairs) with formally defined decision-making powers to act as veto players (Tsebelis 2002). If these state institutions regard the policies or discourses embraced by the movement as a threat to their own political survival, they are likely to use their structural position to prevent policy implementation, undermine state-movement linkages and promote countervailing framings.

Seen through this analytical lens, Salta closely resembles Misiones. The two provinces dealt with prior episodes of indigenous mobilization through a strategy of controlled cooptation that led to the establishment of provincial state institutions to directly deal with indigenous affairs. In Salta, the *Instituto Provincial de Pueblo Indígenas de Salta* (IPPIS) was formed in 1986 with the explicit aim to control and contain indigenous protest that emerged in the aftermath of Argentina's transition to democracy. IPPIS constitutes the official representative organ of indigenous communities vis-à-vis the provincial state. Accordingly, it is in charge of granting indigenous communities legal status in the province, which is the basis for all subsequent claims. The IPPIS budget is primarily used for patronage-oriented spending on discretionary benefits for particular individuals or communities. Interviews both with indigenous activists and IPPIS representatives reveal that the organization sought to resist the nationally-mandated survey of indigenous land claims, largely because the organization fears that this would strengthen the national state at the expense of the province.

In Misiones, the *Dirección Asuntos Guaraníes* (DAG) acts as the primary interlocutor between communities and the provincial state. Similar to Salta, DAG's influence derives primarily from controlling the legal register of indigenous communities. DAG's relationship to indigenous communities is marked by clientelism and cooptation. Interviewees report frequent incidents of DAG officials manipulating the legally registered size of local communities, with substantial consequences for the allocation of social assistance. Moreover, in response to attempts by Mbya-Guaraní leaders to organize in a more autonomous manner, DAG created the *Consejo de Ancianos y Guías Espirituales*, an assembly of supposed spiritual leaders that is without much legitimacy among local communities, yet has formal powers to act as the official Mbya-Guaraní mouthpiece (Gorosito Kramer 2007). And again similar to Salta, DAG used its leverage to circumvent and slow down the implementation of the nationally-mandated relevamiento and the transfer of indigenous land titles.

By contrast, in Tucumán a comparable provincial organization does not exist. During the 1980s and 1990s the province employed a different strategy. It ignored and repressed incipient indigenous activism and did not build any institutional structures comparable to IPPIS or DAG. As a result, the dominant interlocutor between Diaguita activists on the one hand, and the province and the national state on the other, is the provincial office of the *Instituto Nacional de Asuntos Indígenas* (INAI), the main national state agency responsible for dealing with indigenous communities. Diaguita leaders report INAI tactics of political fragmentation. In the Valley of Tafi, for example, INAI officials encouraged the formation of several small, individual communities, apparently with the intent to prevent the formation of a larger community representing the whole valley. At the same time, though, the INAI often works together with representatives of the UPNDT to support local land struggles, for instance, by covering the legal costs of lawsuits with current titleholders. Moreover, INAI staff members also work in close coordination with other subnational state agencies to facilitate the implementation of the nationally-mandated land survey.

Conclusion

Based on a comparison of Diaguita and Mbya-Guaraní land rights activism in the Argentine provinces of Tucumán, Salta and Misiones, this chapter has explored the developmental implications of indigenous mobilization. Even though these movements are far from achieving their stated goal of control over the territories they consider historically theirs, they already have had significant consequences. Specifically, Diaguita and Mbya-Guaraní protestors have gained external recognition as a political force; they have shifted power relations with the current legal titleholders; they have shaped dominant understandings about the causes of indigenous poverty; and they have transformed gender relations, especially with respect to political participation, within indigenous communities. I have further shown that movement consequences vary sub-nationally across the three different provinces and that these differences are to an important extent driven by group characteristics and the organizational resources of indigenous movements, as well as preexisting state structures.

The chapter thus shows that, under certain conditions, such as those present in Tucumán, indigenous activism does have empowering effects that challenge the existing political and economic order. This is especially because indigenous movements enable their constituencies, as a historically disadvantaged group, to gain public visibility and extend their status as members of the political community. In doing so, indigenous movements contribute to the actual exercise of the group-specific citizenship rights granted by the 1994 multicultural Constitution.

Indigenous mobilization is also empowering because it introduces different ways of thinking and talking about development into public debate. Specifically, indigenous movements challenge the notion of indigenous poverty as an individual attribute linked to missing assets or geographical disadvantages. Instead, they associate indigenous well-being with control over territory and its resources and, consequently, conceive of poverty reduction not just as an issue of identifying the right kinds of social *policies* but as an issue of *politics*, of transforming the dominant economic model with its reliance on extractive industries. And especially in Tucumán, Diaguita activism has altered public perceptions about indigenous poverty. As such, this chapter supports recent arguments that social movements are most effective at changing how development and poverty *are understood and talked about in public discourse* (Bebbington 2007; Hickey and Bracking 2005).

At the same time, indigenous movements are constrained in their influence by the very institutions they draw on to legitimate their demands. They are also constrained by the economic and political conditions they mobilize against. While the recent multicultural constitutionalism has established new opportunities for indigenous land claims and for indigenous activism more generally, it also establishes significant barriers as to what kinds of claims it legitimizes. In Argentina, the 1994 Constitution granted *communal* land rights, thereby excluding broader *territorial* rights that would give indigenous communities a say in the management and control of environmental resources such as water or subsoil mineral rights. Moreover, the right to claim communal lands is associated with indigenous *communities*, defined as "groups of families," and thus ultimately linked to a specific location or settlement, and *not* with entire *ethnic groups*, such as the Diaguita or Mbya-Guaraní. This definition prevents land claims covering large surfaces – that might crosscut provincial (e.g. Tucumán and Salta) or even national boundaries (e.g. Argentina and Chile) (Carrasco 2000). The prevailing multicultural citizenship thus appears to accommodate "integrationist demands" more than "autonomy demands" that possibly imply a major challenge to the existing geopolitical order (Richards 2004; Hale 2002).

Similarly, the economic transformations that have motivated local protestors to embrace an indigenous identity and demand communal land rights simultaneously undercut their capacities to sustain collective action. For example, in Misiones province, the clearing of the remaining rainforest and the dramatic expansion of large-scale agriculture has undercut the livelihoods of Mbya-Guaraní communities. In Tucumán and Salta intensified land speculation has been accompanied by an ever greater sense of insecurity. To date, several Diaguita settlements have been evicted by the current legal title holders – despite a national law that prohibits the expropriation of lands claimed by indigenous communities (vom Hau and Wilde 2010).

More generally, the chapter establishes the initial building blocks of a novel analytical framework that moves beyond existing research on the consequences of social movements. The framework calls attention to a variety of causal processes by which movements might influence developmental outcomes. It also suggests that movements are more likely to affect desired policies, power relations and public discourses if (1) they have the organizational infrastructure to sustain collective action, and (2) they operate in an institutional space free of major veto players. This emerging framework illustrates why Diaguita land struggles in Tucumán had comparatively more impact than Diaguita protests in Salta and Mbya-Guaraní mobilization in Misiones. As Diaguita protests in Tucumán continue to make headway, their relative success might teach how other disadvantaged groups might obtain justice.

References

Amenta, Edwin. 2006. *When Movements Matter: The Townsend Plan and the Rise of Social Security*. Princeton, NJ: Princeton University Press.

Amenta, Edwin, Neal Caren, Elizabeth Chiarello and Yang Su. 2010. "The Political Consequences of Social Movements." *Annual Review of Sociology* 36: 287–307.

Andrews, Kenneth T. 2001. "Social Movements and Policy Implementation: The Mississippi Civil Rights Movement and the War on Poverty, 1965 to 1971." *American Sociological Review* 66: 71–95.

Bastia, Tanja and Matthias vom Hau. 2014. "Migration, Race and Nationhood in Argentina." *Journal of Ethnic and Migration Studies* 40: 475–492.

Bebbington, Anthony. 2007. "Social Movements and the Politicization of Chronic Poverty." *Development and Change* 38: 793–818.

Bebbington, Anthony, Denise Humphreys Bebbington, Jeffrey Buryc, Jeannet Lingand, Juan Pablo Muñoz and Martin Scurrah. 2008. "Mining and Social Movements: Struggles Over Livelihood and Rural Territorial Development in the Andes." *World Development* 36: 2888–2905.

Blumberg, Rae Lesser. 1984. "A General Theory of Gender Stratification." *Sociological Theory* 2: 23–101.

Burchardt, Hans-Jürgen and Kristina Dietz. 2014. "(Neo-)extractivism – A New Challenge for Development Theory from Latin America." *Third World Quarterly* 35: 468–486.

Cadena, Marisol de la and Orin Starn. 2007. *Indigenous Experience Today*. New York: Berg/Wenner-Gren Foundation.

Carrasco, Morita. 2000. *Los Derechos de los Pueblos Indigenas en Argentina*. Buenos Aires: Vinciguerra.

Centurión, Diosnel. 2006. "Posición y condición de la mujer Mbya-Guaraní de Itapúa como elementos de interacción dinámica de su supervivencia socio-cultural." *Revista Internacional de Investigación en Ciencias Sociales* 2: 27–54.

Cress, Daniel M. and David A. Snow. 2000. "The Outcomes of Homeless Mobilization: The Influence of Organization, Disruption, Political Mediation, and and Framing." *American Journal of Sociology* 105: 1063–1104.

Della Porta, Donatella. 1999. "Protest, Protesters, and Protest Policing: Public Discourses in Italy and Germany from the 1960s to the 1980s." Pp. 66–96 in *How Social Movements Matter*, edited by Dough McAdam, Marco Giugni and Charles Tilly. Minneapolis, MN: University of Minnesota Press.

Gamson, William A. 1990. *The Strategy of Social Protest*, 2nd edn. Belmont, CA: Wadsworth.

Gordillo, Gastón and Silvia Hirsch. 2003. "Indigenous Struggles and Contested Identities in Argentina Histories of Invisibilization and Reemergence." *Journal of Latin American Anthropology* 8: 4-30.

Gorosito Kramer, Ana. 2007. "Liderazgos Guaraníes. Breve revisión histórica y nuevas notas sobre la cuestión." *Avá, Revista de Antropología*, 9: 9–27.
———1982. *Encontros e desencontros. Relacoes interétnicas e representacoes em Misiones (Argentina)*. MA thesis. Programa de Pós-Graduacao em Antropologia. Universidad de Brasilia.
Hale, Charles R. 2002. "Does Multiculturalism Menace? Governance, Cultural Rights and the Politics of Identity in Guatemala." *Journal of Latin American Studies* 34: 485–524.
Hall, Gillette and Harry Anthony Patrinos. 2005. *Pueblos indígenas, pobreza y desarrollo humano en América Latina: 1994-2004*. Washington, DC: World Bank.
Hickey, Sam and Sarah Bracking. 2005. "Exploring the Politics of Chronic Poverty: From Representation to a Politics of Justice?" *World Development* 33: 851–865.
Instituto Nacional de Estadísticas y Censos de la República Argentina (INDEC). 2010. *Censo Nacional de Población, Hogares, y Viviendas*. Available at: www.censo2010.indec.gov.ar/resultadosdefinitivos_totalpais.asp
———2004/5. *Encuesta Complementaria de Pueblos Indígenas*. Available at: www.indec.mecon.ar/webcenso/ECPI/index_ecpi.asp
Itzigsohn, José and Matthias vom Hau. 2006. "Unfinished Imagined Communities: States, Social Movements, and Nationalism in Latin America." *Theory and Society* 35: 193–212.
Laurie, Nina, Robert Andolina and Sarah Radcliffe. 2005. "Ethnodevelopment: Social Movements, Creating Experts and Professionalising Indigenous Knowledge in Ecuador." *Antipode* 37: 470–496.
Leiva, Eva Cristina. 2011. "Mujeres Diaguitas en Lucha: Testimonios de Resistencia." Diploma para el Fortalecimientodel Liderazgo de las Mujeres Indígenas. San Cristóbal de las Casas, México: Centro de Investigaciones y Estudios Superiores en Antropología (CIESAS) Sureste.
McAdam, Doug. 1992. "Gender as a Mediator of the Activist Experience: The Case of Freedom Summer." *American Journal of Sociology* 97: 1211–40.
Melucci, Alberto. 1996. *Challenging Codes: Collective Action in the Information Age*. Cambridge: Cambridge University Press.
Peña, Guillermo de la. 2005. "Social and Cultural Policies toward Indigenous Peoples: Perspectives from Latin America." *Annual Review of Anthropology* 34: 717–739.
Polletta, Francesca and James M. Jasper. 2001. "Collective Identity and Social Movements." *Annual Review of Sociology* 27: 283–305.
Postero, Nancy and Leòn Zamosc. 2004. "Indigenous Movements and the Indian Question in Latin America." Pp. 1–31 in *The Struggle for Indigenous Rights in Latin America*, edited by Nancy Postero and Leòn Zamosc. Eastbourne: Sussex Academic Press.
Richards, Patricia. 2013. *Race and the Chilean Miracle: Neoliberalism, Democracy, and Indigenous Rights*. Pittsburgh: University of Pittsburgh Press.
———2004. *Pobladoras, Indígenas and the State: Conflicts over Women's Rights in Chile*. New Brunswick, NJ: Rutgers University Press.
Sieder, Rachel (ed.). 2002. *Multiculturalism in Latin America: Indigenous Rights, Diversity and Democracy*. New York: Palgrave Macmillan.
Somers, Margaret. 2008. *Genealogies of Citizenship: Markets, Statelessness, and the Right to Have Rights*. New York: Cambridge University Press.
Stryker, Sheldon. 2000. "Identity Competition: Key to Differential Social Movement Participation?" Pp. 21–40 in *Self, Identity, and Social Movements*, edited by Sheldon Stryker, Timothy J. Owens and Robert W. White. Minneapolis, MN: University of Minnesota Press.
Tsebelis, George. 2002. *Veto Players: How Political Institutions Work*. Princeton, NJ: Princeton University Press.

Uquillas, Jorge E. and Martien Van Nieuwkoop. 2003. "Social Capital as a Factor in Indigenous Peoples Development in Ecuador." World Bank Sustainable Development Working Paper 15.
Van Cott, Donna Lee. 2000. *The Friendly Liquidation of the Past: The Politics of Diversity in Latin America*. Pittsburgh: University of Pittsburgh Press.
Viterna, Jocelyn. 2013. *Women in War: The Micro-Processes of Mobilization in El Salvador*. New York: Oxford University Press.
vom Hau, Matthias. 2015. "Gendered Mobilization: Women and the Politics of Indigenous Land Claims in Argentina." Pp. 93–109 in *Shifting Grounds: Gender Impacts of Global Trends in Land Tenure Reform*, edited by Caroline Archambault and Annelies Zoomers. London: Routledge-Earthscan.
vom Hau, Matthias and Guillermo Wilde. 2010. "'We Have Always Lived Here': Indigenous Movements, Citizenship and Poverty in Argentina." *The Journal of Development Studies* 46: 1283–1303.
Yashar, Deborah. 2005. *Contesting Citizenship in Latin America: The Rise of Indigenous Movements and the Postliberal Challenge*. Cambridge: Cambridge University Press.
Zoomers, Annelies. 2000. *Current Land Policy in Latin America: Regulating Land Tenure under Neoliberalism*. Amsterdam: Royal Tropical Institute

Notes

1 This chapter builds on vom Hau and Wilde (2010) and vom Hau (2015). I would like to thank the Ministerio de Ciencia e Innovación (MICINN) in Spain for its generous funding of fieldwork leading up to this study (Grant No. CSO2011-28387, INDI-MOVE project). I also thank Sam Cohn and Rae Blumberg for excellent comments and suggestions.
2 *Mestizaje* refers to the mixing of indigenous and European populations and cultures. During the early- and mid-twentieth century, mestizaje constituted the official nation-building ideology of many, if not most Latin American states. Mestizaje was very ambivalent and often combined the celebration of the precolonial indigenous past with pressures on contemporary indigenous peoples to "modernize" and give up their cultural distinctiveness (Itzigsohn and vom Hau 2006).
3 Unless otherwise indicated, quotations are from interviews conducted by the author in Tucumán, Salta and Misiones between 2008 and 2013. Names are changed to ensure anonymity of interviewees.
4 Many scholars describe this trend as "extractivism" because the underlying economic model depends on the large-scale exportation of natural resources in order to generate government revenues (Burchardt and Dietz 2014).
5 In Salta, land speculation has been driven by a combination of tourism and the expansion of high-altitude vineyards for white-wine production.
6 The larger project on which this chapter draws combines in-depth interviews with an analysis of contentious activities and indigenous claims-making based on local newspapers.
7 This citation is taken from an interview conducted by another researcher in 2010 (Leiva 2011: 34-38).
8 Initially Diaguita activism was organized under one major umbrella association, the *Unión de los Pueblos de la Nación Diaguita*, which cut across provinces. Yet, in 2009 the organization split into the UPNDT and the *Unión de los Pueblos de la Nación Diaguita en Salta* (UPNDS).

11
WHAT WE DON'T TALK ABOUT WHEN WE TALK ABOUT THE GLOBAL IN NORTH AMERICAN HIGHER EDUCATION

Richard Handler

It has become a cliché: glance at the website of any four-year college or university in the United States and you will see the scrubbed, smiling faces of mostly white students traipsing "globally," usually doing good works but sometimes merely studying or carrying out research. "abroad." Some kind of college experience abroad is of course not new; from the "junior year abroad" that gained currency in the 1950s to today's semester-long and even shorter programs, study-abroad has been a regular feature of the American college experience for more than half a century. What's new is the coalescence of such undergraduate programs under the term *global*.

Even the term *global* is not new: "global awareness as a goal of undergraduate education" to prepare students "for a shrinking world and a changing America" was already a common theme among experts in higher education 20 years ago (Weingartner 1992: 46–47; also Barrows 1981). But 20 years ago global was an emergent term, not yet having distinguished itself among a set of terms that were used more or less interchangeably: *multicultural, international, global*. All such terms remain in play, but more and more universities are privileging the term global, at least in their public relations campaigns, and more and more in their organizational structures.

This has been the case at the University of Virginia, where I have taught since 1986. In the second half of the twentieth century, in an effort that began long before I arrived, the University of Virginia transformed itself from a provincial institution to a national research university. At the turn of the millennium, U.Va.'s leaders decreed that it should transcend its national orientation to become an "international" institution with a "global perspective."[1] Since then, the terms international and especially global have become central in the university's promotional discourses. Beyond public relations, there has been a certain amount of institutional development: the creation of an undergraduate major in "Global Development

Studies" (Handler 2013) that then morphed into a larger "Global Studies" program, money for a central space for a "global center," increased funding for interdisciplinary and inter-school global research projects. And, recently, global has appeared on our website as a primary category, featured more prominently even than the terms devoted to intercollegiate athletics.[2]

I have found, however, that such discursive centrality and website prominence go quite well with a state of affairs in which we rarely stop to think about what terms like global and international mean. International is the older term in the university context. It may or may not be ceding ground to the newer term, global, but in any case, it is this new, sexy term that I want to examine here. In particular, I want to sketch a reading of the term global that is almost always explicitly avoided in our promotional or celebratory discourses. So, to begin a sketch of "what we don't talk about when we talk about the global," I will consider what we *do* talk about when we talk about the global. My focus is local, based on my ongoing "fieldwork" at the University of Virginia. But based on what my colleagues at other institutions tell me, I think these trends are indeed national, affecting most four-year colleges and universities in the United States.

From recent public speeches of U.Va. leaders (and leaders of similar institutions), I have abstracted the following key meanings of "the global." The starting point in these visions is that we now live in an interconnected world and, in particular, in a world in which economic activity is global: it is said that it is "redundant" to talk about global business because "*all* business is global now" (Sullivan 2012: 1).[3]

From this it follows that today's students will live and work globally. Students are told that they will likely change careers several times in the course of their lives and that their success in their careers will depend on their ability to work in teams that will include members with different skills, coming from different cultures (Simon 2012: 5). In addition to teamwork, students are admonished to exercise "leadership on a global scale" and to be leaders "in our globally competitive and changing world" (Sullivan 2012: 1; Simon 2012: 3).

To produce students who can be both interdisciplinary, multicultural team players *and* global leaders, it is said that we must globalize our curriculum. Enhancing study-abroad and international travel experiences for our students is crucial in this regard. But it is also said that we should "infuse the entire curriculum with comparative and international content." "Global perspectives should be integrated" into all that we do: into teaching, research and service (Sullivan 2012: 4).

At the University of Virginia, such forward-looking discourse always runs into Mr Jefferson and tradition. Thomas Jefferson founded the university in 1819 and designed its heralded architecture as an "academical village;" it is the only university in the United States that is a UNESCO World Heritage site. His ideas are frequently invoked. "Thomas Jefferson was a global thinker," we are told, and our global "tradition of attentiveness to the world … began 200 years ago." Jefferson's travels are mentioned, and it is emphasized that his Lawn (the central, sacred space of U.Va.) is the physical manifestation of the international cultural influences that shaped him as a philosopher, architect, politician and educator (Sullivan 2012: 2–4).

Here we sometimes hear mention of the dark side of the global, slavery, also built into the brick buildings of the Lawn, constructed in part by slave laborers – although celebratory discourses do not dwell on such facts. In any case, when we begin with Jefferson as our globalizing ancestor, we must conclude by acknowledging that we have always been global, even as we also assert, as Jefferson would have wished, that now we must become even more global.

What do such assertions mean? To interpret them is to begin talking about what we don't talk about when we talk about the global at U. Va. and other North American institutions of higher learning. Let's begin with the assertion that all business is global now, an assertion that suggests that at some prior time, it was not. Yet we are also told that, two centuries ago, Jefferson was a global thinker, which suggests that global participation is nothing new. And, of course, it isn't. Human beings have traversed vast geographic and cultural distances for thousands of years. More particularly, whatever "modernity" or "the modern era" is, it's been around awhile. I choose to date modernity to the Columbian invasion of America. The modern global economy and political system has been several centuries in the making. The eighteenth-century slave trade, crucial to the emergence of modern capitalism (and to the building of U.Va. and many other US universities), was about as global a phenomenon as you could imagine, as were eighteenth- and nineteenth-century colonialisms and imperialisms, not to mention nineteenth- and twentieth-century regional and world wars. The businesses of slavery and of imperial expansion were global *then* just as their twenty-first-century versions are global *now*.

What's changed, of course, is the speed of communications and connections, but this issue figures less in U. Va. promotional discourses than one might imagine. Despite the current flirtation with MOOCs (massive open online courses) at my institution and many others, living, learning and working globally is more often discussed in terms of actual student bodies traveling than it is in terms of people connecting electronically. And traveling student bodies takes us to the question of study abroad, and more generally, the idea of infusing global perspectives into the curriculum.

With respect to study abroad, it has always seemed strange to me that, having taken enormous pains over 200 years to build a great university in Virginia, the first thing we tell students when they arrive is to go elsewhere. And while I honor the student who works hard at his or her home campus to learn another language and who wants to build on that experience by studying it in context, I also honor the student who says, as I've heard so many say, "I regret that I will never have time, in my allotted four years, to take all the great courses that are offered here." My point is that it is not particularly wise to say, without further specification, that we want all students to study abroad, or to have international experience, and it is especially not wise to couch such commands in terms of percentages (with progress, of course, depicted by increasing numbers). What counts, instead, is the quality of the educational experiences we offer. As one of my Global Development Studies students wrote me, recently, "abroad experiences are important. But they are also expensive, often unorganized, sometimes dangerous, and most of the time they lack any critical framework for thinking about what you are doing as a student or why you are doing it." Following best (but rare) practices elsewhere, our International Studies Office is working hard to create a serious "wrap-around" curriculum that will teach students how to integrate study-abroad work into their U. Va. curriculum. But we are a long way from having the will or the resources to make such a program mandatory for all study-abroad students.

So, study-abroad, yes, but not for the purpose of making U. Va. or any other institution of higher learning "more" global: like any other curricular choice, study-abroad must be justified in terms of the educational opportunities it affords. And these should be defined substantively (for example, study of a language or of a region, or study at a university famous for work in such-and-such topic), not generically and *not* extra-curricularly. I do not think it is a good thing that many, many students return from study-abroad saying that the teachers and courses weren't much good, but it was great learning to get around in another country. Learning to get around has value, but I'm not sure it's worth the sacrifice of a semester's worth of liberal arts courses, courses that students will *never* have another chance to take.

If we value the excellence of a study-abroad experience in terms of its specific academic focus, can we say that study-abroad represents a study of the global, or even that increasing numbers of study-abroad students means that our institutions are becoming more global? After all, the student who goes to India to study Hindi language and literature is not necessarily studying "the global." What exactly does the term global mean in the phrases *global education* and *global university*? In one of the celebratory speeches quoted above, bringing "global perspectives" into our work is equated with "infus[ing] the entire curriculum with comparative and international content." So let's consider at greater length the terms international and comparative in relation to the term global.

Using the term international is a way to refer to or describe the entire globe, organized as it is, in terms of the modern nation-state system. The globe depicted as an international order is the kind of globe you can buy for a child's room, marked to show nation-states divided by heavy black lines (international boundaries), with each state colored differently from its neighbors, to represent the idea that each nation has its own cultural identity. Sometimes, also, the term can be used as a kind of shorthand to refer to events or processes (including university courses) that include participants from, or considerations of, more than one nation-state.

The term *comparative* is epistemologically more complicated. One could argue that all knowledge is grounded in comparison, since in order to know some particular thing, it's necessary to know what that thing isn't as well as what it is. Thus university courses that we might think of as fairly narrow and explicitly non-comparative – for example, "Melville's Novels" – would have to be comparative – as teachers and students learn to read *Moby Dick* by comparing it to Melville's other works. But when we think of literature courses that are explicitly comparative, such as courses in "comparative literature" as opposed to those in "American literature" or "English literature," we think of courses that include materials from authors identified with more than one nation-state and, usually, more than one national language. Similarly, in the social sciences, an explicitly comparative course brings together data or case studies from different nation-states, civilizations or culture areas. Moreover, the *uses* of comparison are understood differently in different scientific or interpretive traditions. There are anthropologists who compare cases to discover sociological regularities, even "laws," and there are others who use comparison to reveal unique features of the cases analyzed together, with no presumption that comparison leads to the formulation of cross-cultural generalities. There are thus many different comparative approaches both within and between disciplines, and the term comparative itself does not specify any particular geography, whether global, international, regional or local.

In sum, in discussions of the curriculum, the terms international and comparative indicate courses that include apparently heterogeneous materials, but beyond that, they tell us little about the aims or methods of those courses. And they certainly do not tell us much about "the global."

We can make similar arguments about the term *interdisciplinary*, a term that, I find, is often conflated with the term *global*. The idea seems to be that since the globe or world is now interconnected, the study of global phenomena requires connections between the disciplines, that is, it requires interdisciplinarity (Handler 2013: 188–189). As we saw, oftentimes interdisciplinarity is imagined to make its appearance in the work world in the form of teams, each member of which contributes specialized disciplinary and cultural knowledge to a process in which a globally situated problem is to be solved. This kind of discourse depicts education as training to use knowledge instrumentally in the work world. The logic is something like this: Business is now global. Business teams will be global in the sense that they will contain people from different cultures. The problems they attack will be multifaceted and will require different "skills" for their solution. This discourse lines up the global, the interdisciplinary and the multicultural, making these terms almost synonyms. But the conflation of these terms does not really tell us much about the specific meaning of the global.

What we can begin to see is that in university promotional discourses, there is a constellation of rather standard terms, methods and programs (study-abroad, international, interdisciplinary, teamwork, comparative), the conflation of which with the term global speakers assume their audiences will understand. And those audiences *do* seem to understand these discourses; at least, they act as if they comprehend what is being said to them. And yet, when we begin to think more carefully about these terms, programs and methods as synonyms for the global, as I have just tried to do, we cannot find a way to make the older, conventional terms add up, in an analytically rigorous way, to a clear and unified understanding of the global. So I conclude that the speakers and audiences I have been describing are acting just as natives everywhere do: they are presupposing a set of ideas and values without being consciously aware either of the structure of their ideas or the range of meanings of individual terms. That is why they can act as if they understand one another as they talk about the global, without really knowing what they are talking about.

So what *are* they talking about? Why has the word global attained such discursive centrality in university promotional discourses at the turn of the twenty-first century? A simple answer can be borrowed from recent American electoral politics: "it's the economy, stupid!" The term global, I contend, has become increasingly salient because university stakeholders find themselves in a new, and increasingly treacherous, global economy in which their institutional interests and the personal and career interests of their graduates are linked ever more explicitly to global financial capital and to multinational corporations. Yes, all business *is* global now. And the increased power of capital in relation to the nation-state has led, as we all know, to a long, drawn-out struggle between market forces and the social-welfare functions of government (Streek 2011). With government apparently slowly losing that struggle, state support for institutions like U. Va. has declined, leading to ever-increasing reliance on private donors, some of whom, as we saw locally in the struggle between U.Va.'s president and board in the summer of 2012, want to remake the University to speak more squarely to the needs of global capital.[4]

A particularly dystopic vision of the brave new world of the university in thrall to global capital can be found in an essay on "the global university" by Tom Looser, an associate professor of East Asian Studies at New York University (Looser 2011). Under the controversial leadership of President John Sexton – whom one professor describes as having the "style of a maverick CEO" (Kaminer 2013) – NYU is moving aggressively to establish full degree-granting campuses in Abu Dhabi and Pudong Shanghai. According to Looser, these sites are Special Economic Zones (SEZs), spaces given over to the rule of corporate capital, lured thence by the offer of tax breaks and minimal government regulation. Construction of these new spaces has proliferated under neoliberalism, as governments have lost market share, as it were, to the markets, which have pressured national, state and local governments to reduce taxation, thereby forcing them to reduce social services and to fund themselves, increasingly, on the bond markets.

A principal tenet of neoliberalism, according to Looser, is "freedom from responsibility" to others "in favor of responsibility only to oneself" (2011: 99). SEZs are places where the social contract among citizens and between citizens and their government is abrogated in favor of the "law of corporate management" (108). An SEZ is a new kind of "territory," one "promising freedom from the state," one that is "exempted from local law" and "absolved from responsibility to [its] surroundings" (101). SEZs are often built on wasteland or on empty spaces, new from the ground up. And they are built to house the service and knowledge industries where the great new fortunes are to be made. That is why SEZs want to include world-class universities. And that is why established universities desperate to find new sources of funding are willing to consider building branches in places like Abu Dhabi and Pudong.

The culture of SEZs is a global culture. We must here understand the term global, however, to indicate a social formation that wants to be seen as global but that in fact is made up of very specific characteristics. Looser describes the sites where NYU is building in these terms:

> Each started out as a community built almost out of nothing ... All were built as islands, both literally, and because they are places of cultural, political, and economic exceptions within their own region. All were financed to some degree by global capital, and all began as tax-free economic zones. Despite their varied locales, all campuses on these islands are to be English-speaking ... The same often New York-based architects have been principal designers for much of the architecture ... Students who go to these campuses, and corporate executives who go to live in these districts, are assured that the island-like nature of the district will for the most part allow freedom from the hindrances of local custom.
>
> *Looser 2011: 100–101*

American universities that want to build campuses in such places are out to recruit students from the international elite, people who can afford to pay top tuition rates. Students who attend such campuses are looking for an education that will plug them into the global managerial and investor-owner classes. These campuses are new projects, dreamed up by administrators, not faculty, and only now inventing their curricula and recruiting their future alumni. The new curricula promise study of "world literature" and "world history," with little mention of particular languages, literatures or area studies. If "foreign" languages are to be offered on these English-language campuses, they will be Arabic and Chinese, chosen for purely instrumental purposes, as was English. To quote Looser at length again:

> In terms of curriculum, the structure of these campuses tends toward a non-area specific location, and a world that can be studied from anywhere (and therefore from nowhere in particular). There is a multiplicity of positions in this world, and campus locales, but it is multiplicity without real difference. Language fits in only at this level, too: rather than a ground and object of cultural difference, it serves more as a code – an instrument for operating within a generic world (and English and Chinese will do, really, for anywhere).
>
> *Looser 2011: 104*

NYU's Sexton envisions these global, generic, anywhere-nowhere universities as part of a system through which "faculty and students circulate," developing "habits and modes of cooperation" befitting the corporate elite (quoted in Looser 2011: 107). Make no mistake, this is an exclusive world, "with the same groups of people transiting up through life from places like Chelsea to places like Pudong Shanghai, or Abu Dabai" (ibid.). It may be global in terms of the enhanced wealth and mobility of its occupants, but it is not global in the sense of "inclusive."

U.Va. flirted with the idea of such a campus in Qatar but ultimately rejected the idea. Instead, the university adopted Semester at Sea, which is, literally, an anywhere-nowhere campus, but one that U. Va. faculty have wanted to use to develop a program in global comparative studies. Still, despite faculty efforts to enhance the curricular quality of Semester at Sea, it is hard to deny its relationship to the experience of elite cultural tourism, as I learned when I participated as a faculty member on the summer 2013 voyage. Despite faculty efforts to focus academic work within their individual courses on the various ports where we stopped, the structure of the voyage, with students invited to "sample" other worlds without having any responsibility toward them, was difficult to work against.[5]

I have had a greater degree of control to shape a curriculum with a global perspective in my work over the past five years creating (in response to student demand) an undergraduate program in Global Development Studies (GDS). Working with GDS students, I have been especially intrigued by the preconceptions they entertain as they consider and/or join the program (Handler 2013). These preconceptions fit well enough into the discourses of the global university that we have been examining. Let's start from the idea of the anywhere-nowhere university. GDS students, and more generally all or most of the many students who have done or who aspire to do global service work, start with the presumption that the world is their oyster. They wish to do good in the world. They wish to "give back," as they say. To use the phrase "give back" with no direct or indirect object is tell-tale. In the worldview suggested by this phrase, it is not necessary to know what it is that one wants to give, nor to whom one wants to give it. The only thing that matters is that the subject of the sentence desires to perform a certain kind of moral action.

Now, students *do*, of course, choose specific actions and specific persons in specific places to fulfill their desire to give back. They decide they are interested in clean water or maternal health and they decide they want to work in Haiti or Guatemala or India, or even in Charlottesville, Virginia. But what is crucial here is that the whole process starts with student desire and that this is normal and unremarkable to us.

A standard criticism of this kind of service work is that students engage in it to build their own resumés – that it is, in a word, self-serving. This is true but it is not particularly interesting, since much of what any of us does is self-serving and it may even be a good thing that such is the case. No, what's interesting is the presumption that serving others begins with self and, specifically, with a self that has no specific relationship to the other person who is to be served. Indeed, the other person to be served is an object to be chosen unilaterally by us, often on the basis of the other's culturally exotic location. This is a neoliberal conception of social relations, we might say: it is about a self that has no socially or politically grounded responsibility to anyone other than to her- or himself. The world is our oyster, to serve.

How do students choose clean water or maternal health, Haiti, Guatemala or India? Sometimes they bring these interests with them to college from their high school or family experiences. Sometimes they choose, more or less accidentally, a college course that sparks a particular interest. The curriculum of a modern liberal arts university is structured as a field for student choice. Students come from the relatively unsophisticated curricular environment of their secondary schools to the enormously richer curricular environment of the university. There, they can take courses in previously unavailable subjects such as anthropology and on dangerous topics, say, Lady Gaga (the focus of a course that recently sparked outrage at U.Va.). Our curriculum is a marketplace to spark and to slake student intellectual desire. We have structured it that way and the students understand it that way. Thus, it seems to me, this is not a socially irresponsible arena of consumer choice. The buyers and sellers are all aware of what they are doing.

But it seems to me morally perverse that we extend such a marketplace of free intellectual choice, in a kind of unthinking analogy, to the entire world. Just as our students can choose to study Hinduism and the Hindi language, they can choose to study abroad in India. If we guide them wisely, they will select an intellectually rigorous and socially grounded program in India, one that will teach them about Indian languages and cultures in a setting over which Indian educators have some control. But when we extend the analogy even further, and encourage students to choose India – an India about which they know very little – to do service work, among people who have not invited them and who have no control over their presence, then we have strayed far from our educational mission. When we allow our students to do this we are teaching them that they have the right to go anywhere, with no enduring responsibility to the people among whom they will visit.

Not only do we teach them that they can go anywhere, we teach them (usually by omission) that they come from nowhere. They believe they are motivated by universal moral imperatives that need no justification. While they understand that "culture" is something that exotic natives have, they do not think much about their own culture as both bourgeois habitus and an economically privileged sociopolitical location. "Culture" as it extends to them, they think, means they need to be "culturally sensitive" when they impose themselves through service on others. They cannot easily grasp the idea that their impulse to do service needs to be "treated" and, I think, "cured" via cultural critique.

Once I have convinced my students that they, too, have a culture, and that their motives for carrying out service cannot be assumed to be grounded in a universal morality, we can move on to consider, analytically, the features of their culture that they will try to impose (as if by magic) on the service situation – in particular, its egalitarian and technocratic ideals. They think they can will into being egalitarian social relationships between themselves and the people they go to serve. They think that cultural sensitivity and "good communications" can transcend all barriers of culture, race, class and citizenship. They do not see that their neoliberal mobility, their expectation to go anywhere and to stay only so long as it suits them, is a kind of sociality that is alien to (not to mention impossible for) the people among whom they will work. Nor do they see that their idea of teamwork – as the combining of technical skills to solve problems – almost completely overlooks the social dynamics and cultural motivations of the communities where the service is to be carried out and the problems solved. Indeed, "cultural sensitivity," which is the liberal-arts "skill" to be added to the team's toolkit, is understood to be no more than a palliative for the inevitable frictions that accompany the application of rational technocratic knowledge. This leaves no room for students to question the hegemony of such knowledge in the first place. And because in many instances of service, students do not return to the scene of the crime, as it were, they are not forced to confront the fact that the technocratic knowledge central to so many development projects almost never works.

There is a television commercial for the US Navy that aired intermittently throughout the period (2013–14) when I drafted and revised this chapter, using this slogan: "the Navy, a global force for good." In its brevity, it reminds us of the phrase, *giving back*. Both suggest an anywhere-nowhere global subject whose mobility is unlimited and whose good intentions can be asserted as unquestionable. I have suggested that similar presuppositions underpin much of the discourse of the global generated by institutions of higher education at the turn of the twenty-first century – just as they underpinned the vision of the U. Va. students who lobbied for the creation of the Global Development Studies major.

When I began working with the GDS program, I had very little idea of the discursive power of the term global, nor of the conceptions and desires of the incoming students. I had to learn how to teach them, starting from my critical-anthropological perspective, but also learning from them about the reasons for their curricular choices and their understanding of the relationship between their university education and their post-graduate careers. As these students and I, and the more than one dozen faculty members who participate on the GDS advisory board, have together developed the major, I have come to believe that the following themes should be central to an undergraduate program at a North American institution that in one way or another takes "the global" as its focus:

1. However we understand "the world system" or "global society," we have to focus on the vast differences of power and wealth that separate different actors in the contemporary international order. We cannot approach "the global" without bringing to consciousness, and then critiquing, the egalitarian fantasies of modern individualism.
2. We must replace ideas about cultural sensitivity with what I call cultural critique, a critique that starts at home. Students must be taught to see that they do not engage the global from a neutral place. At a minimum, their location in North American institutions of higher education provides them with a range of choices not available to most people in the world. They need to understand their own privilege. Equally important, they need to understand that a consumer-choice orientation to service is at best politically naïve and at worst counter-productive.
3. At a time when the international labor market is in disarray and is, literally, terrifying to students and parents, liberal arts programs such as Global Development Studies must help students consider the potential of different kinds of knowledge. Specifically, we have to analyze the relationship of liberal learning to the knowledge conveyed by the professional schools. More prosaically, we have to help students think about the term *skills*. We should encourage them to ask what kind of knowledge they want, as well as what they

want to do with it. We should help them analyze ideas of teamwork borrowed from the corporate world, where the instrumental uses of knowledge are far more valued than wide-ranging critical thinking.
4. Following from these first three points, we must teach our students that uncritical applications of the same old development concepts and skills lead not to change but to a reaffirmation of the status quo (see Cooke 2004 for examples). It is no accident that every trendy idea in the twenty-first-century development industry, from microfinance to participatory action research, has antecedents in nineteenth-century colonialism. Marx and Engels' critique of "conservative, or bourgeois, socialism" rings as true today as when it was published in the *Communist Manifesto*: "A part of the bourgeoisie is desirous of redressing social grievances, in order to secure the continued existence of bourgeois society" (Marx and Engels 1848: 242). Into this camp Marx and Engels put "economists, philanthropists, humanitarians, improvers of the condition of the working class, organizers of charity, members of societies for the prevention of cruelty to animals, temperance fanatics, hole-and-corner reformers of every imaginable kind" – a list that with only slight adjustments could include most of today's development workers and their analogues among university students doing "service."

As Marx and Engels knew, these reformers dreamed of reform without politics: "they wish for a bourgeoisie without a proletariat" (242). While very few of our students at the beginning of their work with us can imagine themselves engaging in political struggle, we can teach them that "fixing problems" without paying attention to political structures, both local and global, will never bring about the kinds of changes for a better world that they dream of. Teaching impoverished farmers to use fertilizers will do little to change their condition, absent land reform; distributing mosquito nets will do little to improve health outcomes, absent significant state resources devoted to public health infrastructure. Our students will have to get involved in the political struggles, either at home or abroad, that lead to significant resource redistributions: land for the landless, socially sustained health-care infrastructure as a human right.

As I was completing this essay, I came across an op-ed piece in the *Washington Post* on "engineering to improve the world" (Nilsson and Sastry 2014). The authors, associated with the University of California at Berkeley's Blum Center for Developing Economies, write cheerfully of an emerging field of development engineering, "dedicated to using engineering and technology to improve the lot of the world's poorest people." Castigating top-down aid programs that fail, they promote good-hearted technical innovations attuned to the opportunities of the marketplace. It is new products – not a new politics – that will solve problems: "development engineering responds to the fact that although there isn't a world governance system, there is a global marketplace."

These sorts of discourses are seductive for college students (and for editorial-page editors). Every professional school at U. Va. has its student organizations dedicated to using technical skills to engineer a better world – a better globe. It is, I suppose, only a small irony that the one small program in the curriculum dedicated to "global development" teaches its students that such organizations, and such knowledge, absent a critical politics, will never have the kind of impact of which their advocates dream.

References

Barrows, Thomas. 1981. *College Students' Knowledge and Beliefs: A Survey of Global Understanding*. New Rochelle, NY: Change Magazine Press.
Cooke, Bill. 2004. "Rules of Thumb for Participatory Change Agents." Pp. 42–55 in *Participation, from Tyranny to Transformation?*, edited by Samuel Hickey and Giles Mohan. London: Zed Books.
Handler, Richard. 2013. "Disciplinary Adaptation and Undergraduate Desire: Anthropology and Global Development Studies in the Liberal Arts Curriculum." *Cultural Anthropology* 28: 181–203.
Kaminer, Ariel. 2013. "NYU.'s Global Leader Is Tested by Faculty at Home." *New York Times*, March 9, sec. 1, 1.
Looser, Tom. 2011. "The Global University, Area Studies, and the World Citizen: Neoliberal Geography's Redistribution of the 'World.'" *Cultural Anthropology* 27: 97–117.
Marx, Karl and Friedrich Engels. [1848] 1977. *The Communist Manifesto*. Pp. 221–47 in *Karl Marx: Selected Writings*, edited by David McLellan. Oxford: Oxford University Press.
Nilsson, Lina and Shankar Sastry. 2014. "Engineering to Improve the World." *Washington Post*, October 6, sec. 1, 15.
Sexton, John. 2010. "Global University Network Reflection." New York University, Office of the President.
Simon, John. 2012. Convocation Address, University of Virginia, 26 October. University of Virginia, Office of the Provost.
Streek, Wolfgang. 2011. "The Crises of Democratic Capitalism." *New Left Review* 71: 5–29.
Sullivan, Teresa. 2012. "Mr. Jefferson's Global University." University of Virginia, Office of the President. Available at: www.virginia.edu/president/speeches/12/index.html
Weingartner, Rudolph. 1992. *Undergraduate Education: Goals and Means*. New York: Macmillan.

Notes

1   See, for example, the *Report of the 2020 Commission on International Activities*, March 2001, which opens with these broad strokes:

> International activities at the University of Virginia cultivate a global perspective in students, faculty and the community. More specifically, they position UVa within the framework of its greatest potential [sic], challenge its students and scholars to extend their horizons of growth and inquiry, and welcome international students and scholars. International programs are the ultimate expression for enriching the mind. By including different peoples and cultural traditions and framing the University's tasks in global dimensions, Thomas Jefferson's spirit of free inquiry is expanded.

The invocation of the totemic ancestor is required of all high-level visionary statements at the University of Virginia.
2 For comparative purposes, I surveyed (on September 3, 2014) the websites of all 15 of the schools in our athletic conference, the ACC (Atlantic Coast Conference). Along with Virginia, three others (Duke, Pittsburgh and the University of North Carolina) have "global" as a top-line category on their home page. Three others (Wake Forest, Notre Dame and Syracuse) have a top-line category with a different but related term, such as "international." Georgia Tech lists "Global Presence" on its home page, but at the bottom; the viewer must scroll down to find it. On the websites of the other seven universities, these categories are one click away; the surest route, I found, was to click on "academics," which brought up, among other things, study-abroad or international programs.
3 Sullivan attributed the aphorism to the dean of the undergraduate business school, the McIntire School of Commerce.
4 In an incident that garnered national attention, a faction of the Board of Visitors (trustees) was able to win a vote in June 2012 to oust U. Va.'s recently appointed president, Teresa Sullivan, on the grounds that she was not providing the institution with twenty-first-century leadership. Faculty, alumni and students rebelled, forcing the Board to back down – but as of this writing, the view from the trenches is that U.Va.'s upper administration remains locked in struggle with the Board, and that the institution as a whole continues to suffer the effects of a lack of institutional direction.
5 Before sailing, I had been told of a grotesque version of such sampling, in which Semester at Sea students staged a fake wedding in Vietnam, in order to be able to book hotels for large parties. The details are not entirely clear, but my students traveling with Semester at Sea in the spring of 2013 reported that they'd received an email from the academic dean asking them not to stage "fake weddings" in Vietnam as an excuse to "throw a party" and "play dress up." Apparently some students doing so had been proceeding under the assumption that Vietnamese weddings are not recognized by other countries (hence, aren't legally recognized elsewhere); they were also responding to the fact that Vietnamese hotels could be easily booked for lavish wedding receptions. I can think of no better example of the rejection of responsibility toward others than the staging of a sacred kinship ritual in order to throw a party.

12
LANDMINES AND SUSTAINABILITY

Remaking the world through global citizenship, activism, research and collaborative mine action

P. Preston Reynolds

I write this chapter as an activist, physician and scholar. I joined the Board of Directors of Physicians for Human Rights (PHR) in 1987 and remained active as a board member for fifteen years. I vividly remember sending a team into Cambodia in 1991, pouring over their findings, and then finalizing our recommendations published in *Land Mines in Cambodia: The Coward's War* (Asia Watch and Physicians for Human Rights 1991). We called for a universal ban on the production, use and trading of landmines. There was no other response to the data; we had to be unequivocal, uncompromising, bold. It was a Saturday in October 1992 when we joined five other organizations to form the International Campaign to Ban Landmines (ICBL). In doing so, we launched an international effort to realize these goals. The ICBL grew steadily, then rapidly, into a force of more than 1100 organizations by 1997. The ICBL included people from all walks of life committed to creating a mine-free world.

In October 1996, the PHR Board was at dinner when we received a call from one of our staff who was in Ottawa, Canada. She shared almost with astonishment that Canada's Foreign Minister Lloyd Axworthy had just issued an invitation to return in a year with a treaty. We did. It was not long after – in December 1997 – when the Convention on the Use, Stockpiling, and Transfer of Anti-Personnel Mines and on Their Destruction (Mine Ban Treaty, MBT) was signed by leaders of 122 nations. Later that month, we were awarded the 1997 Nobel Peace Prize.

The success of the ICBL and global efforts to create a mine-free world is truly stunning. In the fifteen years (1999–2014) since the Mine Ban Treaty entered into force, the world has seen (LCMM 2014):

- near universalization, with 162 governments becoming State Parties and as such, obligated to fulfill all the conditions of the MBT;

- global compliance with key provisions calling for cessation of use and trading of landmines by both States Parties and by non-States Parties;
- 88 States Parties with stockpiled Anti-Personnel Mines (APMs) have completed their stockpile destruction program. Together they destroyed more than 48 million mines, along with destruction of stockpiled landmines by states not party to the Mine Ban Treaty;
- reduction from more than 50 countries in the early 1990s to only 11 that still produce landmines or retain the right to produce them;
- 9 states not party to the MBT, among them 6 APM producers, have enacted a formal moratorium on the export of landmines; these include China, India, Russia and the United States;
- 28 states and one area reported they have cleared all landmines;
- 56 States plus four areas remain contaminated with landmines; 32 of these 56 are States Parties and thus, required by MBT provisions to clear all areas of landmines;
- tens of thousands of square kilometers of land that were dangerous or presumed dangerous because of landmines have been released for use and habitation;
- over the past 5 years alone, clearance operations have resulted in the clearance to international standards of approximately 973 km^2 of mined areas and the destruction of 1.5 million APMs, anti-vehicle mines and unexploded ordnance;
- expanding efforts to meet the MBT's provision for victim assistance through development of best practices; culturally relevant education programs; community surveys; and broader efforts to integrate these programs into national policies, plans and legal frameworks, including those related to the rights of persons with disabilities;
- sustained international funding support for demining and civilian mine education has continued, reaching almost US$446 million in 2013, with an additional $210 million contributed by affected states;
- a dramatic reduction in annual casualties from an estimated 20,000 in 1999 to less than 3,300 in 2014.

With this success, it is not surprising the ICBL issued the challenge as part of the 2014 Maputo Review Conference on a Mine-Free World for States Parties to "Commit to Complete," to ensure there are *no* annual casualties and that *all* survivors live well. The ICBL believes a mine-free world is possible to achieve within a decade if all States Parties work together with global partners. Seventy-nine countries that participated in the Maputo Review Conference signed the Maputo Declaration publicly committing to (1) complete destruction of stockpiles and land clearance by 2025 and (2) further develop programs and policies that ensure all victims, their families and communities have access to resources and are protected from discrimination.

For years, I was involved in nearly every aspect of the ICBL, which included writing, speaking, fund-raising, campaigning, reviewing drafts of documents and then sharing with others this journey of global citizenship. As a scholar, now removed from the inner workings of the ICBL, I wish to share this story.

Background

Military officials have long recognized that a maimed and crippled soldier loses his ability to fight and drains his country's medical and economic resources. Landmines were an application of this philosophy. Anti-personnel mines (also referred to as APMs or landmines) were designed to disable their victims, although they also kill. In post-conflict countries today, most landmine casualties are civilians – women and girls, boys and men – people and animals, as they walk on roads, fields and village paths.

The first large-scale deployment of anti-personnel landmines dates to World War II when German and Allied troops used them to prevent enemy soldiers from removing larger anti-tank mines. In the early 1960s, the United States introduced a sophisticated class of APMs, known as "scatterables," to stop the flow of men and military supplies from North Vietnam to South Vietnam through Laos and Cambodia. Weighing only 20 grams, less than three-quarters of an ounce, these landmines fluttered to the ground without detonating. They contained enough explosives to tear off a man's foot. With the increase in conflicts around the world beginning in the 1970s, the anti-personnel mine, like the automatic rifle, became the weapon of choice for governments and guerilla armies for the next twenty-five years (Cobey, Stover and Fine 1995: 259–260).

With an estimated 340 types of landmines in use by the early 1990s, APMs were a menace to global public health and development, particularly in poorer nations. The longevity of mines and their random dispersal from aircraft made it difficult to know the true extent of the hazard. Civilians comprised 70–80 percent of landmine victims with two-thirds of them dying in the field, due to lack of access to medical care. By the mid-1990s, experts estimated 20,000 to 26,000 persons died or were maimed annually by mine blasts (LCMM 2014: 33; Author, personal papers).

Today, in addition to injuries from traditional landmines, there are casualties from other explosive remnants of war (ERW), which refer to any ordnance left behind after a conflict. These include unexploded ordnance (UXO) and abandoned explosive ordnance (AXO). In addition, there are improvised explosive devices (IED), or homemade bombs, and cluster munitions (CM), weapons composed of a container that holds up to several hundred bomblets. Up to 40 percent of the bomblets do not explode on impact. But they can be triggered later by the slightest contact, making them very dangerous to civilians (Handicap International 2013: 1).

When the International Committee of the Red Cross (ICRC) in the late 1970s pushed governments to consider increased restrictions or elimination of such weapons, there was little support for a ban on APMs. While the 1980 Convention on Conventional Weapons (CCW) addressed the problem of landmines, it also allowed military commanders to make their own decision in the midst of battle (Hubert 2000: 3–6). By the mid-1990s, it was estimated there were 60 to 70 million mines in the ground, and 250 million mines stored in arsenals in more than 108 countries (LCMM 1999: 8–13).

When relative peace broke out with the end of the Cold War, the United Nations and other non-governmental organizations (NGOs) discovered active landmines affected every aspect of peacekeeping and nation-building. This happened twice in Cambodia, once after the fall of the Khmer Rouge in 1979 and again at the end of the 12-year civil conflict in 1991 (Asia Watch and Physicians for Human Rights 1991; Stover et al. 1994: 331–332). The UN and the ICRC were asked to rebuild the country. Once at work, these humanitarian staff found so many landmines in rice paddies that they had to cancel key programs. A particularly serious loss was the cancellation of a land-to-the-peasants program; they could not give away land that was full of landmines.

Global health and human rights advocacy: the international campaign to ban landmines

Data collection is a necessary component of many public health programs. Physicians for Human Rights (PHR) and Human Rights Watch/Asia (HRW) sent a team into Cambodia in 1991 to investigate human rights violations under the Khmer Rouge and abuses against returning refugees. The team documented the widespread impact of landmines on every aspect of Cambodian economy, life and culture, and calculated that one in every 236 Cambodians was a landmine victim (Asia Watch and Physicians for Human Rights 1991). Seeing no other alternative in an effort to uphold human rights globally, *Land Mines in Cambodia: The Coward's War* called for a global ban on the production, use and stockpiling of landmines.

Robert Muller, a Marine veteran who lost the use of his legs during the Vietnam War, also went into Cambodia and found that landmine victims were primarily civilians. Later studies conducted in post-conflict worn-torn countries on multiple continents (Africa, Asia, Europe, Asia and South America) confirmed this observation. The vast majority of victims were men, women and children, who were injured doing necessary activities of daily living. Casualties occurred in both urban and rural areas – and in every known type of ecological system.

Shortly after publication of *The Coward's War*, Muller, founder of Vietnam Veterans of America Foundation (VVAF), partnered with Medico International, a German-based organization committed to helping landmine survivors with prosthetic devices, and launched an advocacy campaign to ban landmines. Then in October 1992, six NGOs that included VVAF (USA), Medico International (Germany), Handicap International (France), Mines Advisory Group (United Kingdom), PHR and Human Rights Watch (USA) came together to form the International Campaign to Ban Landmines (ICBL). These six organizations agreed to host the first NGO conference on landmines in London in 1993. The goal initially was modest: to bring together experts in human rights, victim assistance, demining, disarmament and international law, medicine, public health and citizen advocacy to consider how a global campaign could be created to achieve a mine-free world (Hubert 2000: 7–8).

One challenge the ICBL confronted early on was reframing landmines, not as an essential military weapon, but instead, as a human rights abuse and as one of the most significant barriers to development in countries around the world. Physicians for Human Rights and Human Rights Watch conducted fact-finding investigative missions in countries on several continents and documented the indiscriminate and widespread nature of landmine injuries and their impact on civilians' ability to achieve and secure basic human rights as defined in the Universal Declaration of Human Rights and other international human rights conventions. These data, along with photographs and global advocacy by NGOs and international agencies including the International Committee of the Red Cross and the UN, were critical to changing public and government opinion on the need for landmines for military purposes. PHR and HRW published their findings in *Landmines: A Deadly Legacy* (1993), thus providing advocates with data to build a case for a global ban. Reports by the ICRC, VVAF, US Department of State and other NGOs and international agencies increasingly made clear landmines were inhumane and an unnecessary weapon of war (ibid.: 7–17).

The ICBL and others successfully re-defined landmines as a human rights issue because of their impact on the ability to secure basic rights, such as freedom of movement and the right to secure a livelihood. The ICBL and ICRC also argued that landmines were a human rights abuse because of their indiscriminate nature. A mine cannot distinguish between the footfall of a soldier or that of a civilian. The failure of accountability of armed forces to those who came after them, and the lack of maps that documented where landmines had been laid or re-laid, highlighted the need for global advocacy and action.

The ICBL emerged as a dynamic force for international peace, human rights and global health. In 1996, pro-ban government leaders came together with international agency personnel and leadership of the ICBL – which now included 1100 member organizations. Over fourteen months, individuals representing civil society and governments together drafted the Convention on the Prohibition of the Use, Stockpiling, Production, and Transfer of Antipersonnel Mines and on Their Destruction. This treaty was signed in Ottawa, Canada, in December 1997 by representatives of 122 countries. Later that month, Jody Williams, ICBL Campaign Coordinator, and the six founding organizations of the ICBL were awarded the Nobel Peace Prize (ibid.: 17–27).

At the Nobel Peace Prize ceremony, Jody Williams aptly stated that the signing ceremony for the Mine Ban Treaty:

> demonstrates that small and middle powers can work together with civil society to address humanitarian concerns with breathtaking speed .. NGOs have worked in cooperation with governments for the first time on an arms control issue, with the UN, with the ... Red Cross ... Together we have changed history.
>
> *Author, personal papers*

Mine Ban Treaty

The Convention on the Prohibition of the Use, Stockpiling, Production, and Transfer of Antipersonnel Mines and on Their Destruction requires that all parties stop producing and trading anti-personnel mines; destroy their stockpiles; clear their lands; engage in Mine Action (see later in this chapter); and participate in review activities. Intensive effort by the ICBL, ICRC, UNICEF and the governments of Canada and Norway resulted in sufficient numbers of signatories triggering an entry into force date of March 1, 1999. This remains the fastest entry into force of any major treaty in history (LCMM 1999: 3–4; LCMM 2014: 1).

The Mine Ban Treaty is a significant departure from previous disarmament and human rights conventions with the inclusion of 'Mine Action'. This obligates the parties to provide victim assistance and mine awareness education, and mandates that parties adhere to procedures that allow for transparency and accountability. We will return to these issues after first looking at landmines and the crisis in sustainable development.

Impact of landmines on sustainable development: a closer look

> After troops withdraw, landmines remain in the ground as brutal reminders that successful peace-building and development are still beyond the horizon.
> UN Secretary-General Boutros Boutros-Ghali, cited in Torres Nachon 2004: 193

> Not only do these abominable weapons lie buried in silence and in their millions, waiting to kill or maim innocent women and children; but the presence – even the fear of the presence – of a single landmine can prevent the cultivation of an entire field, rob a village of its livelihood, place yet another obstacle on a country's road to reconstruction and development.
> UN Secretary-General Kofi Annan, cited in Torres Nachon 2004: 196.

A common definition of sustainable development is "development that meets the needs of the present without compromising the ability of future generations to meet their own needs" (World Commission on Environment and Development 1987).

The concept of sustainable development has most often been separated into three constituent parts: environmental sustainability, economic sustainability and sociopolitical sustainability. Advocacy by indigenous peoples expanded these three pillars to include a fourth: cultural sustainability. Landmines undermine all four pillars, and most often impact the least developed countries around the world, rendering them unable to achieve the United Nations Millennium Development Goals and other global targets, including the conditions of the Mine Ban Treaty itself.

A closer look: social and cultural

The social and cultural impacts of landmines have been catastrophic. Not only are thousands of individuals killed every year, but those who survive suffer from disabilities their entire life, and often face discrimination in many aspects of daily living. It was estimated in 1998 there were over 300,000 landmine survivors spread over 80 countries. The cost of their rehabilitation alone was projected at that time to be over US$3 billion (LCMM 1999: 28). In Cambodia, as of 1999, one in every 236 living persons and in Afghanistan, one in every 50 persons, had sustained a landmine injury with varying degrees of disabilities (Physicians for Human Rights 2000: 3).

Mine blasts cause destruction of limbs including one or both legs, arms and hands. They also lead to blindness and deafness when the mine explodes close to the face, which occurs when a child picks up a mine when playing, or when the deminer is working close to the ground. Some mines are designed to explode high off the ground and can lead to injuries of the chest, abdomen and pelvis, with fragments penetrating deep into body cavities. In 2000, fewer than 30 percent of mine-affected countries and regions were prepared to deal with the emergency medical needs of such individuals, in part, because these injuries require a higher than usual number of blood transfusions and longer courses of antibiotics, as well as the skills of specially trained trauma surgeons (LCMM 2000: 28–29; Fak 2004: 181).

Rehabilitation from landmine injuries usually requires physical and occupational rehabilitation, and care of mental health illnesses, such as depression and post-traumatic stress disorder. Prosthetics are an essential element of post-mine rehabilitation. But the costs frequently are beyond the resources of families – especially when the victim is a child who will outgrow a prosthetic every six months just with normal development. Rehabilitation of persons left blind or deaf from blast injuries requires specially fitted aids that may simply be unavailable, as well as training in skills that are not in demand in rural or agrarian economies.

Failure to secure employment and reintegration of landmine victims back into communities contributes to higher rates of depression among survivors and a further decline in their productivity. The cycle of isolation and poverty of individuals, families and communities worsens if mine survivors lack access to rehabilitation services or do not participate in them for various reasons including anxiety, fear and cultural barriers. Children affected by blast injuries are often unable to attend school. Women are most vulnerable; first, if widowed and left to raise a family alone with the death of a spouse; or if severely disabled, they may be unable to help with food production, raising of children, maintaining a household and contributing to their community.

In some cultures, respect for wholeness, including physical wholeness, is an integral part of traditional practices. Those persons who suffer from a landmine injury may be prohibited from participating in rituals, such as entering a Buddhist monastery prior to marriage for men. The injury may make women "unmarriageable" because they also are "un-whole" or because they are perceived as being unable to contribute to their future family in terms of livelihood, child-rearing and cultural activities. Ritual dance and other physical forms of celebration may be impossible for landmine survivors if they are unable to move and sing because of loss of limb, sound or sight. Beyond the impact on individuals and their cultural traditions, the loss of an animal, such as a cow, may have larger cultural and religious significance. Most important, landmines as a weapon of social terror can destroy the fabric of entire nations as one warring group keeps another in a state of constant fear, such as what occurred within Rwanda during its internal genocide in 1994.

Sustainable and lasting peace is impossible without repair of the social fabric. This requires reinvigorating the economy; putting back into production land once unusable because of landmines; ensuring access to hospitals and schools; as well as permitting use of roads, rivers, forests, lakes and, in many parts of the world, rice paddies. Unfortunately, landmines are often placed in key geographic and population areas with close proximity to bridges, highways or rural transportation routes, water supplies and sewage plants or in the midst of centers of worship and sites of cultural and religious heritage.

A closer look: economic

Clearing lands of APMs has remained a global priority because of their devastating impact on economies. Landmines have made entire regions of countries uninhabitable. This intensifies population density in other areas. It impedes the return of refugees, thus straining the economies of neighboring countries. APMs prevent agricultural development and use of land for animal grazing. According to a report by the US State Department, "A more relevant measure of the problem is not the number of landmines per country, but the number of square kilometers of land rendered unusable by the presence or suspected presence of landmines or other unexploded ordinance"(US Department of State 1998: 5; Torres Nachon 2004: 196).

One study conducted in the mid-1990s on the social and economic costs of landmines in Afghanistan, Bosnia, Cambodia and Mozambique revealed that 25 to 87 percent of households had their daily lives impacted with the loss of a family member and/or presence of a landmine survivor who could not participate fully in what was most often an agrarian or pastoral economy. Most revealing, those households with a landmine victim were shown to have 40 percent more difficulty providing food for all members, which drove some mine blast victims into urban areas and into prostitution, drug dealing, homelessness and poverty – since access to rehabilitation services was non-existent. It was projected that without APMs, agricultural production could be increased 88 to 200 percent in Afghanistan, 11 percent in Bosnia, 135 percent in Cambodia and 3 to 6 percent in Mozambique (Anderson, da Sousa and Paredes 1995: 713–721).

Landmines have been used extensively in Africa in wars of national liberation and in internal civil conflicts, leaving this area of the world one of the most heavily contaminated. Severely affected countries include Angola, Mozambique, Somalia,

Sudan, Eritrea and Ethiopia. Other impacted countries include Zimbabwe, Rwanda, Zambia, Chad, Namibia, Burundi, Uganda, Democratic Republic of Congo, Mauritania, Sierra Leone, Liberia, Senegal, Guinea-Bissau, Malawi, Niger, South Africa and Swaziland. According to Noel Stott from the South African Campaign to Ban Landmines, an estimated 20 million mines lie buried in the soils of southern Africa, "many unmapped and unmarked"(Torres Nachon 2004: 195).

The impact of properly fitted prostheses on the health and productivity of landmine victims was recognized early as the ICRC and NGOs began to document the need for rehabilitation and socioeconomic reintegration of survivors (Stover et al. 1994: 332–335; Anderson, da Sousa and Paredes 1995; Human Rights Watch and Physicians for Human Rights 1993). This alone reinforces the need to create comprehensive victim assistance programs as a core element of sustainable development activities. Best practices show that landmine clearance has its greatest impact if coupled with initiatives focusing on economic development and Mine Action, which includes mine awareness education and victim assistance. Two examples illustrate this point.

Afghanistan

After two decades of war, Afghanistan became one of the most heavily mined countries of the world. Targeted by the United Nations in 1989, by December 1997, the UN Mine Action Programme for Afghanistan had surveyed and marked 189 km^2 of contaminated land, cleared 132 km^2 of high-priority land and 120 km^2 of former battlefield, destroyed 161,000 APMs and 549,000 UXOs. It also provided mine awareness briefings to more than 4 million people. Despite these efforts, contaminated land remained. Much of it was in the area of the capital, Kabul, which saw more than 10 landmine victims a week (Htun 2004: 71–72; Norwegian People's Aid: 2014: 15–19).

In Afghanistan, a multi-sectorial approach proved most effective. In parallel with efforts at Mine Action activities, the UN invested money in Afghanistan to eradicate poverty alongside the UN Poverty Eradication and Community Empowerment Program. The initiative was community-focused, involving Afghanis and deminers at the local level. The impact of integrating demining with economic development activities on sustainable development was significant. As noted by Nay Htun, "mine action by the UN and NGOs is cost-effective even without estimating its social benefit"(Htun: 172):

- one US dollar spent results in US$4.60 in economic returns;
- one square kilometer of land cleared yields US$2,000 for grazing;
- fifty kilometers of cleared roads provide some US$250,000 in economic benefits.

When Afghanistan's Mine Action program was reviewed by Norwegian People's Aid in preparation for 3MSP, it was rated as "good," receiving scores of 5–8 out of 10 in ten different areas related to mine clearance, mine education and land release. Some 40 percent of APM contamination remains concentrated in the Kabul area and the six other provinces that make up Afghanistan's central region. The recent decrease in funding has forced cutbacks in clearance operations. Afghanistan's clearance plan for the next 10 years foresees removal of all anti-vehicle mines and battlefield areas as well as APMs. This will only be accomplished, however, with renewed and sustained global financial contributions and global partnerships with demining NGOs and the UN (Norwegian People's Aid: 2014: 15–19).

Cambodia

Publication of *The Coward's War* in 1991 focused international attention on the landmine problem in Cambodia. The following year, the Supreme National Council of Cambodia created the Cambodian Mine Action Center. In parallel, the UNDP Cambodia Area Rehabilitation and Regeneration Program established a set of development-related activities such as microsavings and vocational education programs (Htun 2004: 173–174).

Approaching the problem of landmines in a comprehensive and integrative manner, landmine clearance again occurred alongside victim assistance programs and mine awareness education. Within a decade, the Cambodian Mine Action Center had delivered mine education programs to individuals in over 700 rural villages, with plans to expand educational activities six-fold. Equally important, it led the effort to clear over 150 minefields encompassing more than 2,500 km^2 and released 1,074 km^2 for resettlement. It also has destroyed 72,511 mines and 428,769 ERWs. NGOs and the UN invested heavily in victim assistance to ensure the integration of survivor rehabilitation in a comprehensive and culturally sensitive manner (ibid.: 172–173).

When reviewed by Norwegian People's Aid, the Cambodian Mine Action program received scores of 6–8 out of 10 and an overall rating of "good." After decades of demining work in this country, it was noted the full extent of contamination by APMs and ERW is still not known. A baseline survey of Cambodia's 124 mine-affected districts was completed in 2013; however, the survey also was continued into 2014 to capture 51 ERW-contaminated districts. After years of accelerating productivity, the pace of mine clearance appears to be leveling off. Fortunately, the amount of land made available for habitation has continued to rise, reflecting both good survey research and application of international standards for land release (Norwegian People's Aid 2014: 33–35).

A closer look: environment

Most of the research on the impact of landmines on sustainable development has focused on social, cultural and economic sectors. And yet, the environmental impacts may be just as significant.

Torres Nachon (2004) argues that APMs impact the environment directly and indirectly. The direct impact is through the destruction of natural habitats by landmine damage itself. This also includes the contamination of soil when landmines are planted near sewage plants.

Short-term or more immediate effects include destruction of vegetation and animal species from mine blasts and contamination of water supplies. Longer-term effects include leakage of heavy metals and toxic substances into the soil as landmines degrade. Long-term effects include the continued contamination of soil. Torres Nachon has written:

> there is a repetitive geographic coincidence between mine-affected zones and biodiversity hotspots ... By degrading habitats, impacting population species, altering the food chain, and placing additional pressure on biodiversity hotspots, landmines pose a considerable risk to pristine ecosystems throughout the world.
>
> *Torres Nachon 2004: 197*

In addition, some national parks are mined, including those in Africa, which are a refuge for some of the world's most endangered animal species. This places both animal and civilian lives at risk and erodes many countries' ability to generate tourism revenue.

From north to south in Africa, stories abound of mine blasts involving animals. In Libya, for example, minefields were responsible for the death of an estimated 75,000 camels, 36,250 sheep, 12,500 goats and 1,250 cattle (ibid.). In Zimbabwe, according to Martin Rupiya, "every village near Chiredzi has lost at least one animal to land mines ... In the Gonarezhou National Park, elephants and buffaloes have had to be killed after they were injured by mines" (ibid.). Anderson, da Sousa and Paredes (1995) recorded a loss of 54,554 animals from landmines in their survey of communities in Afghanistan, Bosnia, Cambodia and Mozambique, with a minimum cash value of nearly US$200 per household.

These direct effects do not exhaust all the damage done by landmines. There are important indirect effects such as those associated with the outmigration of residents; outmigration can cause the loss of land fertility as a result of a cessation of crop rotation.

As noted by numerous scholars as well as researchers for Landmines Monitor, thousands of square kilometers of land throughout the world are polluted with landmines, many of them involving protected areas, putting the biodiversity of hundreds of species of animals and plants at risk of destruction.

Creating new global priorities: post-Mine Ban Treaty implementation

The Mine Ban Treaty introduced two important features into international disarmament: accountability through post-treaty review processes and Mine Action, which includes mine clearance, victim assistance and mine awareness education.

Landmine Monitor, established by the ICBL in the summer of 1998, and published annually beginning in 1999, has become one of the major vehicles in creating a culture of accountability. Each yearly report includes an assessment of each States Party's compliance with and progress made on all of the Mine Ban Treaty conditions including destruction of stockpiles, use and selling of landmines, clearance of land and implementation of programs designed to assist victims and educate citizens about landmines. *Landmine Monitor 2014,* and all previous reports, are available at the ICBLs website (www.icbl.org).

The Mine Ban Treaty review process included a one-year post-Convention assessment of progress and then review conferences every five years. Standing Committees have been created that focus on specific aspects of the MBT. The Committees usually pair a developed country with a heavily mined developing country to ensure involvement of lower-resourced nations that shoulder the heaviest burden. These five-year review conferences and activities in the intervening years have again brought together civil society with state representatives and enabled a much more dynamic enforcement process than would otherwise be possible. The ICBL and ICRC, as well as other key organizations such as Handicap International and Landmine Survivors Network, have been critical to progress made on key issues such as victim assistance.

In addition to work by NGOs and States Parties, the Mine Action community pushed early for development of universal criteria for Mine Action, now codified into the International Mine Action Standards (IMAS). The IMAS provides a framework to ensure that Mine Action programs are safely and efficiently planned, managed and implemented. The IMAS also pushes programs to increasingly adopt best practices, particularly in areas such as clearance of contaminated lands, land release and destruction of mine stockpiles. Originally developed by the United Nations Mine Action Service in 1997, the IMAS have been expanded, revised and re-launched with support from the Geneva International Center for Humanitarian Demining (US Department of State 2013: 29).

Evolution of assistance to victims and survivors in international humanitarian law

The 1999 First Meeting of States Parties to the Anti-Personnel Mine Ban Convention (1MSP) was held in Maputo, Mozambique. It provided an opportunity to build an international strategy toward victim assistance. States Parties recognized that:

> anti-personnel mines represent a major public health threat and that assistance must be integrated into broader public health and socio-economic development strategies to ensure not simply short-term care of victims, but special attention to the serious long-term needs for social and economic reintegration.
>
> *McCallum 2011: 17*

The Standing Committee on Victim Assistance and Socio-Economic Reintegration established at the 1MSP has played a central role in advancing understanding and identifying rights and needs in relation to victim assistance. It has continued to bring together the ICBL, ICRC, national Red Cross and Red Crescent Societies and their international federation, as well as UN departments, offices and agencies, including the World Health Organization, for special meetings. These have taken place between, pre-conference and throughout major treaty review meetings. In such undramatic ways, dramatic progress has been made.

At the 10MSP held in Cartagena, Colombia in 1999, the States Parties adopted the Cartagena Action Plan. In doing so, they resolved to provide assistance to victims and survivors in accordance with applicable humanitarian and human rights law. The Cartagena Action Plan includes 14 victim assistance-related commitments. It not only reflects both substantial input by landmine survivors themselves, but also a deeper understanding that efforts to assist the victims should be integrated into broader national policies, plans and legal frameworks related to disability, health, rehabilitation, social services, employment, human rights, development and poverty reduction.

"Victim" is now defined as including not only persons directly impacted by landmines, but also families and communities. More importantly, victim assistance is conceptualized to be a holistic and integrated approach aimed at removing or reducing as far as possible the factors that limit the ability of survivors to attain and maintain the highest possible level of independence and quality of life: physically, psychologically, socially and economically. The aim should be to provide the individual with the best opportunity for full inclusion in society – for study, work and access to services – opportunities that are equal to those of other members of their community. Furthermore, it is now recognized that family members of those killed or injured often need access to programs such as psychosocial support services, education and employment or other income generation opportunities.

Although women and girls make up the minority of landmine victims, they often face greater barriers in accessing services to promote their physical, psychological and economic well-being. For cultural reasons, girls and women may not be able to obtain medical or rehabilitation services if only male practitioners are available, or they may not be able to travel to available services without a male escort who also may be injured and immobile and thus, unable to travel. Childcare responsibilities may limit the time women can be away from home to receive rehabilitative care and psychological support. Even if not directly impacted by a landmine explosion, women face additional economic burdens if a spouse is killed leaving her as a sole provider. Furthermore, in many cultures, women still have limited economic opportunities to support their families. Last, women and girls with disabilities also face greater discrimination within their immediate and larger communities (McCallum 2011).

The new framework of holistic and inclusive victim assistance programs has an emphasis on preventing discrimination against these vulnerable groups. Accordingly, children have become the focus of program development and outreach.

Beyond the Mine Ban Treaty: Convention on Conventional Weapons; Convention on Cluster Munitions; Convention on the Rights of Disabled Persons

The Mine Ban Treaty set a precedent for incorporating a legal obligation to assist survivors, no matter how tentative, into international instruments governing conventional weapons. In 2003, the High Contracting Parties to the Convention on Certain Conventional Weapons (CCW) adopted the Protocol on Explosive Remnants of War, or "Protocol V." Both Protocol V and a "Plan of Action on Victim Assistance," adopted by Parties to Protocol V in 2008, incorporate principles consistent with those in the Mine Ban Treaty. States and organizations participating in negotiations on the Convention on Cluster Munitions (CCM) also incorporated practices originating in the Mine Ban Treaty into the legal text of the CCM, adopted in 2008. The CCM entered into force in August 2010 (ibid.: 30–33).

What has emerged is consistency amongst international conventions related to conventional weapons with regard to obligations to victims for survivor assistance regardless of the weapon that resulted in disability. Added to this body of international humanitarian and disarmament law is the 2006 Convention on the Rights of Persons with Disabilities (CRPD). The CRPD is particularly relevant, as what has been known as "victim assistance" is now recognized as a fundamental human right.

United States involvement in Mine Action

While President Clinton was the first national leader to call for a universal ban on landmines, the United States has never joined the Mine Ban Treaty. Nevertheless, the US Government has been active in anti-mine activities since 1993 (US Department of State 2013). Interagency cooperation has been central to US success. This collaboration involves the US Department of State's Bureau of Political-Military Affairs (PM/WRA), Department of Defense (DOD), US Agency for International Development (USAID) and the Centers for Disease Control and Prevention (CDC). PM/WRA provides financial assistance for survey, clearance, risk education, stockpile reduction and security. USAID focuses on survival assistance by working to improve the health, integration and mobility of disabled civilian survivors. The International Emergency and Refugee Health Branch of the CDC supports programs that expand access to mine risk education and survivor assistance. The DOD contributes funds for training. Equally important, the DOD has invested billions of dollars in development of new technologies to advance demining of contaminated land. In addition, the US government has partnered with nearly 40 international organizations devoted to demining and victim assistance in distribution of billions of US federal dollars (US Department of State 2013). As such, the United States remains the world's largest donor supporting Mine Action.

In summary, over the past 20 years, the US government through these partnerships and collaborative interagency programs has operated in more than 90 countries and accomplished the following (US Department of State 2013: 7):

- donated over US$2 billion to conventional weapons destruction, most through Mine Action;
- destroyed over 1.6 million small arms and lightweight weapons and over 90,000 tons of ordnance in 38 countries;
- provided emergency assistance to support the removal or mitigation of conventional weapons, landmines and other ERW in more than 18 countries;
- provided assistive devices and other rehabilitation services to over 250,000 people in 35 countries.

At the most recent 3MSP Review Conference in Maputo, the United States announced it would move in the direction of joining the Mine Ban Treaty. This represents a welcome break from the past American tendency to avoid committing to humanitarian treaties.

Conclusion

Landmines and ERW, including cluster munitions, remain a serious impediment to global sustainable development. This becomes evident in reading ICBL country reports that detail the estimated amount of ERW that still must be cleared prior to release of contaminated lands for individual and public use. Initiatives are well established to address MBT obligations. But just as the ICBL needed money in 1997 to finish the job, present and future efforts to clear lands and provide victim assistance need billions of dollars. One strategy to prevent donor fatigue that emerged from the 3MSP Review Conference is the establishment of formal partnerships with mine-affected countries by donor organizations and governments.

As noted in the opening section of this chapter, the campaign to achieve a mine-free world is a well-organized global movement involving governments, international agencies and civil society that is on track to accomplishing this goal. There is now congruency with regard to a ban on landmines and other explosive devices, as well as international agreement on the importance of integrating victim assistance across conventions. In addition to the 162 countries that are States Parties to the Mine Ban Treaty, 112 countries have signed the Cluster Munitions Convention and 101 countries are party to Protocol V of the Convention on Convention Weapons (LCMM 2014: 7).

While the incidence of casualties has declined 60 percent since 1999, hitting its lowest level in 2013, the total number of persons affected still reached 3,308. But this is a 24 percent reduction from 2012. Progress is unmistakable. Casualties were recorded in 55 states and other areas, down from 72 states and areas in 1999. Of these casualties, 79 percent were civilians; 12 percent were women; 46 percent were children, with 16 percent of the affected children being girls. This is still believed to be an underestimate of the real tragedy, since many people who die never reach a hospital and central location. Thus, they are never recorded in country databases (ibid.: 31–34).

Since 1999, more than 3.3 million mines have been removed from the ground. In 2013 alone, some 185 km^2 of battle areas were cleared, with destruction of over 280,000 APMs and antivehicle mines. However, as of October 2014, 56 states and 4 other areas were confirmed to remain mine-affected (see Table 21.1). Five of these are considered to have massive APM contamination, defined as > 100 km^2: Afghanistan, Bosnia and Herzegovina, Cambodia, Turkey and Iraq. Five states have heavy contamination, defined as greater than 20 km^2 and less than 100 km^2: Angola, Azerbaijan, Croatia, Thailand and Zimbabwe (ibid.: 21–22).

Mine Action, which includes mine clearance, mine education and victim assistance, requires resources that are beyond the ability of developing nations to fund from their national budgets. The global community has continued its commitment to help affected countries address MBT obligations with over US$6.378 billion having been donated since 1997. The largest amount was given in 2012, US$497 million. In 2013, 31 donors contributed almost US$446 million for Mine Action

TABLE 12.1 Mine-affected states and other areas with mined areas as of October 2014

Africa	Americas	Asia-Pacific	Europe, the Caucasus and Central Asia	Middle East and North Africa
Angola	**Argentina**★	**Afghanistan**	Armenia	**Algeria**
Chad	**Chile**	**Cambodia**	Azerbaijan	**Egypt**
Democratic Republic of the Congo (DRC)	**Colombia**	China	**Bosnia and Herzegovina (BiH)**	**Jordan**
	Cuba	India		Iran
	Ecuador	Lao PDR	**Croatia**	**Iraq**
Eritrea	**Peru**	Myanmar	**Cyprus**	Israel
Ethiopia		North Korea	Georgia	Lebanon
Mauritania		Pakistan	Kyrgyzstan	Libya
Mozambique		South Korea	Russia	Morocco
Niger		Sri Lanka	**Serbia**	Palestine
Senegal		**Thailand**	**Tajikistan**	Syria
Somalia		Vietnam	**Turkey**	**Yemen**
South Sudan			**United Kingdom**★	*Western Sahara*
Sudan			Uzbekistan	
Zimbabwe			*Kosovo*	
Somaliland			*Nagorno-Karabakh*	

Notes: ★ Argentina and the UK both claim sovereignty over the Falkland Islands/Malvinas, which still contain mined areas. States Parties to the Mine Bine Treaty are indicated in bold. Areas are in italics.

Source: Landmine Monitor 2014: 22.

in 47 affected countries. The top five recipients included Afghanistan, Lao PDR, Cambodia and Bosnia and Herzegovina. In addition, affected States provided US$201 million for their own Mine Action programs and the UN General Assembly appropriated US$150 million to Mine Action as part of peacekeeping missions in 2013 – an increase of 33 percent compared to 2012 (ibid. :45–47).

Despite these contributions and collaborative Mine Action programs, in the area of victim assistance, much work still needs to be done, in part because rehabilitation and psychosocial programs must be linked to economic development initiatives. Recent surveys conducted in Cambodia, Europe and Central Asia confirm that women with disabilities continue to face greater discrimination than male counterparts. Victim assistance programs often target adults and men, leaving out children and women survivors, as well as women who become heads of households with the loss of a spouse (LCMM 2013: 53). The need to address the human rights of mine victims, including children and women, gained attention as the global community prepared for the 3MSP Review Conference. In 2013, Austria and Colombia hosted an experts' workshop on assistance to children landmine survivors that led to a guide for best practices. In April 2014, Colombia, with the support of the European Union, hosted a global conference, "Between the Worlds," with a focus on the needs of mine victims (Anti-Personnel Mine Ban Convention Implementation Support Unit 2014: 7, 13–17).

In summary, the most important recommendations emerging from over two decades of work on landmines and ERW are: (1) the global community must continue to raise money for demining and victim assistance; and (2) Mine Action must be linked with sustainable development for it to have the greatest impact on local communities and global health.

Activism alongside collaborative partnerships between civil society, international agencies and governments leads to success. Without sustained attention to the landmine crisis, our world will never heal from the wounds this weapon has inflicted upon all of us. Alternatively, continuing to work toward achieving a mine-free world will advance our collective wisdom and promote health and well-being as well as affirm global equity.

This is the first time the landmine story has been told in terms of development. Admittedly, as a scholar, it's a tale heavy with details. As an activist, it may not be as riveting as video footage of a demining team putting their lives on the line. However, this global initiative irrefutably shows we have the ability to solve a horrific and intractable crisis in development.

Afterword

As I reflect back, in the beginning we envisioned creating an international campaign that would lead to a comprehensive ban on the use, trading and production of landmines – and more, if possible. I am both deeply humbled by the humanity of all who have been involved with this campaign, and inspired, knowing we remain firmly dedicated to fundamental human rights. But we cannot rest on our laurels. There is too much at stake. We have the capacity to achieve a mine-free world. The Maputo Action Plan for victim assistance and the ICBL's "Commit to Complete" create the means and mechanisms to achieving this monumental goal. Once again, we must commit to act. And we must do so boldly and do so together – for the sake of humanity.

References

Anderson, Neil, Cesar Palha da Sousa and Sergio Paredes. 1995. "Social Cost of Landmines in Four Countries: Afghanistan, Bosnia, Cambodia and Mozambique." *British Medical Journal* (311): 718–721.

Anti-Personnel Mine Ban Convention Implementation Support Unit. 2014. Maputo Review Conference on a Mine-Free World 23-27 June. Available at: http://maputoreviewconference.org

Asia Watch and Physicians for Human Rights. 1991. *Land Mines in Cambodia: The Coward's War.* New York: Human Rights Watch.

Cobey, James C., Eric Stover and Jonathan Fine. 1995. "Civilian Casualties due to War Mines." *Techniques in Orthopedics* (10): 259–264.

Fak, Glenna L. 2004. "The Victim Assistance Provision of the Mine Ban Treaty." Pp. 179–190 in *Landmines and Human Security: International Politics and War's Hidden Legacy*, edited by Richard A. Matthew, Bryan McDonald and Kenneth R. Rutherford. Albany, NY: State University of New York.

Handicap International. 2013. "Cluster Bombs: An Immediate and Ongoing Threat to Civilians: Cluster Bombs Violate the Rules of International Humanitarian Law." Available at: http://reliefweb.int/sites/reliefweb.int/files/resources/Sept_2013_Cluster_Munitions_Factsheet.pdf

Htun, Nay. 2004. "Landmines Prolong Conflicts and Impede Socioeconomic Development." Pp. 169–177 in *Landmines and Human Security: International Politics and War's Hidden Legacy*, edited by Richard A. Matthew, Bryan McDonald and Kenneth R. Rutherford. Albany, NY: State University of New York.

Hubert, Donald. 2000. *The Landmine Ban: A Case Study in Humanitarian Advocacy*. Occasional Paper no. 42. Providence, RI: The Thomas J. Watson Jr. Institute for International Studies.

Human Rights Watch and Physicians for Human Rights. 1993. *Landmines: Deadly Legacy*. New York: Human Rights Watch.

Landmine and Cluster Munition Monitor (LCMM). 2014. *Landmine Monitor 2014*. Geneva: Landmine and Cluster Munition Monitor. Available at: http://the-monitor.org/index.php/LM/Our-Research-Products/LMM14

——2013. *Landmine Monitor 2013*. Geneva: Landmine and Cluster Munition Monitor. Available at: www.the-monitor.org/index.php/publications/display?url=lm/2013/

——2002. *Landmine Monitor 2002*. Geneva: Landmine and Cluster Munition Monitor. Available at: www.the-monitor.org/index.php/publications/display?url=lm/2002/

——2000. *Landmine Monitor 2000*. Geneva: Landmine and Cluster Munition Monitor.

——1999. *Landmines Monitor Report: Executive Summary*. Geneva: Landmine and Cluster Munition Monitor. Available at: www.the-monitor.org/index.php/publications/display?url=lm/1999/english/exec/

——n.d. "Fact Sheet: Banning Antipersonnel Mines: A 15-Year Overview of Major Findings, 1999-2014." Available at: http://the-monitor.org/index.php/LM/Our-Research-Products/Maputo-3rd-Review-Conference

Matthew, Richard A., Bryan McDonald and Kenneth R. Rutherford. 2004. *Landmines and Human Security: International Politics and War's Hidden Legacy*. Albany, NY: State University of New York.

McCallum, Ron. 2011. *Assisting Landmine and other ERW Survivors in the Context of Disarmament, Disability and Development*. Geneva: Anti-Personnel Mine Ban Convention Implementation Support Unit. Available at: www.gichd.org/fileadmin/GICHD-resources/rec-documents/Brochure-Assisting-Survivors-June2011.pdf

Norwegian People's Aid. 2014. *Clearing the Mines*. Oslo. Available at: www.npaid.org

Physicians for Human Rights. 2000. *Measuring Landmine Incidents & Injuries and the Capacity to Provide Care*. Boston: Physicians for Human Rights.

Stover, Eric, Allen S. Keller, James Cobey and Sam Sopheap. 1994. "The Medical and Social Consequences of Land Mines in Cambodia." *Journal of the American Medical Association* (272): 331–336.

Torres Nachon, Claudio. 2004. "The Environmental Impacts of Landmines." Pp. 191–207 in *Landmines and Human Security: International Politics and War's Hidden Legacy*, edited by Richard A. Matthew, Bryan McDonald and Kenneth R. Rutherford. Albany, NY: State University of New York.

United States Department of State. 1998. *Hidden Killers: the Global Demining Crisis*. Washington, DC: United States Department of State.

United States Department of State. 2013. *To Walk the Earth in Safety*. Washington, DC: United States Department of State. Available at: Available at: www.state.gov/documents/organization/214358.pdf

World Commission on Environment and Development. 1987. *Our Common Future*. Oxford: Oxford University Press.

INDEX

3-D printing 84–100

Abiu Lopez, Ezequiel 36
Abramitzky, Ran 107
age structure and growth 85, 91–2, 97
Afghanistan 17–18, 22, 23, 115–133, 211, 212–213, 214, 219
Africa, North 21, 100, 102, 103, 140
Africa, sub-Saharan 3–4, 35, 59, 66, 67, 76, 77, 100, 103
agricultural policy 157
agriculture 93, 94, 95–97
Ahmed-Ghosh, Huma 136
airports and development 7–8
Albania 55, 100
Alesina, Alberto 102, 103
Algeria 22, 140, 219
Altbach, Philip 8
Amenta, Edward 175
Amin, Samir 35, 87
Amsden, Alice 91
ancient civilizations 69–73
Anderson, C. Arnold 8
Anderson, Neil 211
Anderson, Siwan 105
Andorra 138
Angola 219
Anderson, Siwan 101, 102, 103
Andrews, Kenneth 183
Antonini, Blanca 36

apartheid 156
Argentina 96, 115, 125–126, 173–190, 219
Armenia 100, 219
Arnold, Fred 102, 104
Arnold, Jens 60
Arokiasami, Perianayagam 105
Asia 14, 21, 59, 66–83, 85, 86, 97, 100–114
Asia, Southeast 66–83
Atlanta 7
Australia 90, 96
authoritarianism 66
automobile industry 10–11
Azerbaijan 100, 219

Babones, Salvatore 61
Bahri, Javed 148
Baldwin, Richard 89
Balibar, Étienne 37
Bangladesh 92, 128, 105, 139–140
Baran, Paul 35
barber/beauty shops 57–58
Barber, Nigel 108
Barro, Robert 52
Barrows, Thomas 191
Barry, Joyce 127
Bartlett, Bruce 52
Bastia, Tanja 174
Bebbington, Anthony 187
Beck, Frank 1, 2
Beder, Sharon 117

Bell, Lis 36
Bell, Shannon 127
Beebe, James 137
Bernard, Ted 116
Berry, Brian 10
Bhat, Mati 106
Blau, Judith 108
Blaydes, Lisa 122
Bolivia 138
Bongaarts, John 100, 104, 105
Boserup, Ester 22, 102, 103
Bosnia 211, 214, 219
Boston 8–9
Boston College 8–9
Boston University 8–9
Bowman, Mary Jane 8
Bracking, Sarah 187
Brandeis University 8–9
Brazil 15, 56–58, 67, 90–91, 96, 97, 118
Brown, Judith 138
Brown, Lester 121
Buckingham, Susan 127
Budig, Michelle 106
Bureaucracy, Weberian 67
bureaucratic authoritarianism *see* authoritarianism, developmentalist state
Burma *see* Myanmar
Bush tax cuts 55–56

Cai, Fang 56
Caldwell, J. C. 107
Caldwell, Pat 107
Calves, Anne 103, 141–142
Cambodia 67, 69–70, 74–75, 76, 78, 79, 80, 207, 211, 213, 214, 219
Campanhole, Adriano 57
Campanhole, Hilton 57
Canada 96
capital 86
capital flight 88
Caprioli, Mary 17, 21–22, 140
Carrasco, Morita 174, 187
Carroll, Lee 108
Catalano, R. T. 104
Cernansky, Rachel 126
Chad 212, 219
Chanda, Ateendam 69
Chase-Dunn, Christopher 11
Chen, Lincoln 105
Cheung, Min Lee 72

Chibber, Vivek 66, 67
Chikowore, Godfrey 157
Chile 219
China 3, 19, 56, 69, 70, 71, 72, 76, 77, 80, 92–93, 97, 100, 105, 106–107, 108, 205, 219
Cho, Lee–Jay 103
Chogugudra, Patricia 161
Chung, Woojin 100, 103, 104
Christ, Katelyn 52
citizenship 35–36, 37
Clark, Brett 122
Cobey, James 206
Cole Jonathan 8–9
Collier, Paul 43, 66, 72, 76
Collins, Randall 22, 134, 143
Colombia 96, 219
commodity exports 95–97
Congo, Democratic Republic of 212, 219
consumption 86, 87, 88, 89, 91, 93
Cooke, Bill 201
Cooney, Mark 22
Copeland, Curtis 139
corruption 18, 34, 56–57, 67, 69, 80, 139, 140, 144, 155, 157, 158, 159, 168
Coto, Canica 36
Cress, Daniel 183
crisis tendencies in development 1–32
Croatia 219
crime 108
Cronin, Brenda 13
Crony capitalism 14–15, 16, 155–172
Cuba 45, 219
Currie, Janet 53
Cyprus 219

Daley-Harris, Sam 14
Dankleman, Irene 128
Das Gupta, Monica 20, 100, 104, 105, 107, 139
Da Sousa, Cesar Palha 211
DaVanzo, Julie 105
Dawon, Martin 157
debt 4, 156, 158
decade of women 161
deindustrialization 94
democracy and development 66
de la Cadena, Marisol 174
de la Pena, Guillermo 174
DeLavande, Adeline 107

Della Porta, Donatella 175
De Mooij, Ruud 60
Denmark 16, 55
Denton, Fatma 128
dependency theory 33–50, 84
de Soto, Hernando 56–57
development and human welfare 1–5
development, pros and cons 1–5
developmentalist state 66–83
de Vries, Jan 87
digital technology 94
disaster relief 33–50
discourse analysis 33–50, 181–182, 191–203
DiVanzo, Julie 100
Dollar, David 21, 24
Dominican Republic 36
Donaldson, Mata 103
Doner, Richard 66
Dorman, Sara 162, 164
dos Santos, Anselmo 57
Doubleday, Veronica 136
D'Souza, Stan 105
Dube, Leela 103
Dubois, Laurent 34
Duffield, Mark 35
Dupuy, Alex 37, 38, 44
Durand, Jose 58
Durlauf, Stephen 8, 60, 61–2

ccofeminism 115–133
ecology and development 2, 93, 115–133, 139, 178–179, 180, 213–214
econometrics, limits of *see* quantitative methods, limits of
Ecuador 219
Eder, Anja 76
Ederveen, Sjef 60
Edlund, Lena 100, 101, 105, 108
Edmonds, Kevin 39
education 5–9, 18, 20–21, 23, 93, 97, 139, 141, 144, 157, 160, 184
Edwards, Andres 116
Egypt 219
Eisenstadt, Shmuel 72
Eisler, Riane 142
Elendour–Enyegyeh, Parfait 103, 141–142
Elgin, Ceyhun 55
elite blockage of development 66, 70–71
Elizondo, Gabriel 45

El Salvador 55
embedded autonomy 67, 68
empowerment 134–155, 173–190
energy 85, 92, 93, 97, 99
Engelman, Robert 20
Engels, Friedrich 201
England, Paula 106
entrepreneurship 13–24
Eritrea 212, 219
Essof, Stephen 161
ethnic divisions 69, 76–78, 155, 173–190
Ethiopia 116, 212, 219
Europe, Eastern 15, 104
Europe, Western 15, 55
Evans, Gareth 46
Evans, Peter 66, 67, 68, 69
exploitation 2
export–oriented development 14, 84–5

Fanon, Franz 35
Farmer, Paul 34, 44
Fazio, Christine 56
Ferguson, James 35
fertility 18, 19–20, 20–21, 93, 100–114, 139, 140, 144
Fichtner, Jason 52
Fine, Jonathan 206
Firebaugh, Glenn 1, 2
flexible production 84, 93, 94–5
foreign aid 33–50, 148, 157
France 93
Frank, Andre Gunder 35
Freed, Ruth 104
Freed, Stanley 14
free trade *see* protectionism
Frentz, Nathaniel 64

Gamson, William 175
Gardner, Abby 34, 44
Gardner, Gary 121
garment production 88–90, 96
Gaskill, Luann 58
Gatti, Roberta 21, 24
GDP, long term trends in 2–4
Geadeh, Yolanda 116
Geffrard, Robertson 39
Gemmell, Norman 60
gender and development 1–2, 17–24, 100–172
gender and ecological preservation 139

gender and political participation 138, 155–172, 182–183
gender and social movements 155–190
gender and war 21–22, 134–172, 216
gender inequality 1–2, 5, 134–172
Georges, Josiane 42
Georgia 100, 219
Germany 12, 55, 90, 92
Ghana 118
Gibbs, Lois 2010
Giulani, Paola 102, 103
"global", conceptualizations of 191–203
globalization 55–56, 85, 89, 92, 95–97, 196–198
global Universities 196–198
Golden, Reid 108
Goldin, Claudia 19
Gordon, Cameron 6
Gorski, Philip 87
Gottesman, Evan 79
Grameen Bank 140
Graves, Lucia 126
Great Britain see United Kingdom
Griggs, David 116, 125
Guilmoto, Christophe 100, 103, 104, 106, 107
Guinea 43
Guinea–Bissau 212

Haiti 33–50, 55
Hale, Charles 187
Hall, Gillette 174
Haller, Max 76
Halli, Shiva 106
Halwell, Brian 121
Harrison, Ann 53
Harvard University 8–9
Harvey, David 33
health 139, 140, 144, 204–222
Hesketh, Thomas 107, 108
Hess, Peter 20, 139
Hickey, Sam 187
Higham, Charles 75
higher education 8–9, 12, 90, 191–203
higher education, state support of 8–9, 12, 196
Hill, Kenneth 105
Hill, M. Anne 8
HIV/AIDS 139, 164–165, 167
Hobson, John 46

Holian, Laura 23
Htun, Nay 213
Huang, Chye–Ching 60
Hudson, Valerie 140
human capital 5–9, 20–21, 85, 86, 87, 90, 91, 93, 139, 140, 141, 157
human rights 2, 35–36, 163
hunger see nutrition
Huq, Emadul 105
Huntingdon, Samuel 37
hyperinflation 156–157

ideologies elite responsibility 71–73
IMF 4, 73–74
import substitution 14, 15–16, 96, 99
India 3, 8, 19, 20, 67, 69, 72, 92, 105, 107, 205, 219
indigenous rights 173–191
indigenous social movements see social movements
Indonesia 107
industrial revolution 9–10
inequality, class 1, 5, 13–16, 34, 155–190
inequality and development 13–16
inequality, gender see gender inequality
infanticide 100–114, 160
inflation see hyperinflation
informal economy 54–55
infrastructure 5–9, 85, 86–87, 88, 89, 90, 136
Inglehart, Ronald 122
inheritance systems 141–142
institutional capacity 69
interdisciplinarity 195
internally displaced persons see refugees
international campaign to ban landmines 204–222
Iran 22, 140, 219
Iraq 22, 140, 219
Ireland 55
Ireson, Carol 17
Irwin, Michael 8
Isele, Elizabeth 13
Israel 219
Italy 92

Jackson, James 55
Jackson, Pamela 108
Jacques, Martin 72
Jahdav, Apoorva 106

Japan 53, 67, 69, 72, 78, 90
Jasper, James 175
Jerven, Morten 3
Johnson, Jake 39, 44
Jochelson, Karen 107
Johnson, Merrill 89
Jones, Tom 156
Jordan 22, 140, 219
Jorgenson, Andrew 122

Kachingwe, Sarah 157, 161
Kaminer, Ariel 196
Kapuscinksi, Rystard 35
Karki, Yagya 104
Kasarda, John 8
Katz, Claudio 60
Katz, Jonathan 39
K-Cycles 5, 9–12
Keay, John 72, 77, 78
Kelsall, Tim 157
Kentor, Jeffrey 122
Kenya 115, 126
Ketema, Washington 161
Kieschnick, Michael 58–59
Kim, Hee-Kang 107
Kim, Jim Yong 21
King, Elizabeth 8, 20–21, 24, 139
Kishor, Sunita 104
Khan, Ahmed 141
Klasen, Stephan 100, 105
Kleinhaus, Karine 104
Kohli, Atul 66, 67
Kondratieff Cycles *see* K-Cycles
Koo, Hagen 14
Koolwal, Gayatri 102
Korea, North 219
Korea, South 14, 67, 69, 72, 80, 90, 100, 103, 219
Kosovo 219
Kristof, Nicholas 126
Krugman, Paul 85, 88–89, 92
Kuwait 23
Kyrgyzstan 219

labor costs 89, 92, 97
labor militancy 89
labor violations 34
Lahiri, Sijal 102
Landes, David 12
landmines 204–222

land rights 138, 168, 173–190
Lange, Matthew 68, 71
Laos 17–18, 70, 73–74, 77, 81, 219
Lapchick, Richard 160
Latin America 15–16, 59, 69
Laurie, Nina 174
Leach, Melissa 117
Lebanon 219
Lee, Chulhee 100, 105
Lee, June 107
Lei, Xiaoyan 106
Leite, Antonio 57
Lenski, Gerhard 20, 22, 139
Lewis, Arthur W. 96
Li, Zhou 56
Liberia 212
Libya 214, 219
Lin, Justin Yifu 56
Linzer, Drew 122
literacy and development 8, 12
Littig, Beate 117
Liu, Lan 107
Liu, Lige 106
location theory 85
Long, Cate 6
Looser, Tom 196, 197
Lundahl, Mats 39, 40, 41

Maddison, Angus 2–4
Made, Patricia 159
Maes, Jan 14
MacGregor, Sherilyn 128
Makumbe, John 157
Malawi 212
Mali 100
Mankiw, Gregory 54
manufacture 84–99
markets 14, 85
Marx, Karl 201
marriage squeeze 106–108
Martins, Marcelo 57
Mason, Andrew 8, 20–21, 24, 139
Massachusetts Institute of Technology *see* MIT
Massachusetts, University of at Boston 8–9
Mauritania 212, 219
Mayer, Paul 104
McAdam, Douglas 176
McBride, William 52, 60
McCallum, Ron 215, 216

medical care *see* mortality
Melucci, Alberto 175
Mencher, Joan 20
Mendoza, Martha 39
Menon, Saraswathi 129
Merchant, Carolyn 117, 127
Mesina, Rita 117
Messner, Stephen 101, 108
Mexico 20, 78, 96, 99
Meyerson, Harold 11
Michel, Carlin 39
microcredit 14, 139–140
microenterprise 13–24, 56–58
microfinance *see* microcredit
Middle East 21, 100, 102, 103, 104, 140
Mies, Maria 116
migration 36, 92
Milazzo, Annamaria 101, 105
millennium development goals 161
Mills, Cheryl 39
MIT 8–9, 12
Mitchell, Daniel 52
modernization theory 87
Moffat, Linda 116
Moghadam, Valentine 136, 144, 148
monetary flows 87–88
Montenegro 100
Moore, Niamh 117
Moraes, Andrea 117, 118
Morales Pablo 34
Morgan, Clara 142
Morocco 53–54, 219
Morris, Ian 72
mortality 1, 2, 18, 21, 100–114, 140, 144, 204–222 *see also* infanticide
Motlagh, Jason 140
Moyo, Sam 157
Mozambique 211, 214, 219
Mpofu, Nomasomi 159
Mueller, Hans-Peter 69
Mugabe, Robert 155–172
Muhsam, H.V. 106
multinationals 73–74, 159
Murdock, George 141–142
Musgrave, Richard 54
Musil, Robert 127
Myanmar 61, 69, 219
Myrdal, Gunnar 71

Nagorno-Karabakh 219

Nam-Hoon, Cho 104
Namibia 212
narcotraffic 18, 144
neoliberalism 33–50, 73–74, 156, 168, 197
Nepal 104
Newell, Peter 117
New Orleans 7–8
NGOs *see* non–governmental organizations
Niger 100, 212, 219
Nigeria 67, 87, 100
Nilson, Lina 201
Nixon, Rob 117, 122, 127
Nolan, Patrick 20, 22, 139
non–governmental organizations (NGOs) 33–50, 87, 135–6, 145, 148, 157, 158–159, 161–162, 163–165, 167, 169, 204–222
Norris, Pippa 122
Northeastern University 8–9
Norway 16
Nunn, Nathan 102, 103
nutrition 1, 2, 18, 139, 140

Olivier, Djems 44
Oppenheimer, Valerie Kincaide 11
Osirim, Mary 159
Oztunali, Ogur 55

Pakistan 100, 148, 219
Palestine 219
Paredes, Sergio 211
Park, Chai Hin 104
Park, Imook Han 103
Parks, Bradley 117
Pastore, Jose 57
Patel, Archana 104
patriarchy 17–22, 100–114, 134–154, 156, 165–167
patriliny 22, 103, 141–142
patrilocality 142
Patrinos, Harry Anthony 184
Pebley, Anne 105
Perkins, Patricia 117, 118
Peru 219
Philippines 67, 92, 107
physicians for human rights 204–222
Political Violence 138, 173
Polleta, Francesca 175
pollution 92, 93
population and development 93, 100–114

population growth 106
Portes, Alejandro 55
post-developmentalist critique 1–5
Postero, Nancy 174
post-scarcity 84–99: defined 91
predatory states 67
production-on-demand 84 see flexible production
protectionism 16, 95–6, 99
Psachropoulos, George 21
Putterman, Louis 69

quantitative methods, limits of 59–62
Qian, Nancy 102

Rabke, Kulcur 127
Rabushka, Alvin 52
racial ideology 174
Rahman, Mizamur 101
railways 10
Raftopoulos, Brian 157, 158
Rahman, Mizamur 105
Ramachandran, Vijaya 39
Ramalingam, Ben 159
Rapiya, Martin 214
Rauch, James 67, 69
Ray, Debraj 101
Reddy, P. H. 106
Redlick, C. J. 52
Reed, Larry 14
refugees 136, 138, 145–146, 156
regional underdevelopment 88, 89
remittances 92
repression 163, 167–168, 173
research, role in development 6, 12
re-shoring 86, 92, 97
resource curse 148
restaurants 57–58
Richards, Patricia 174, 187
Rivas, Maria Fernanda 24
Roberts, J. Timmons 117
Roberts, Maryse 117
Robinson, Joan 84
Rodriguez, Leonicio 58
Rodrik, Dani 84, 85
Roldan, Marta 20
Ross, Michael 122, 148
Roy, T. K. 104
Russia 205, 219 see also Soviet Union
Russo, Christina 126

Rwanda 138, 211, 212

Said, Edward 35
Saito Katrine 141–142
Saki, Otto 161
Salazar–Paredes, Andres Wilfredo 2
Sampson, Robert 101, 108
Saudi Arabia 22, 23, 140
Scandinavia 16
Schuller, Mark 34, 39
Schultz, Paul T. 8
Schuyler, Daniel 52
Self, Sharmantha 102
Sen, Amartya 106
Senegal 212, 219
Senghaas, Dieter 16
Serbia 219
service economy 85, 92, 97
service learning 198–200
sex preference 100–114
Shah, Anup 34
Shankar, Satry 201
Sharma, Anjali 117
Shaw, Carolyn Martin 163, 164
Shiva, Vandana 116
Shuzhuo, Li 104
Sieder, Rachel 174
Sierra Leone 212
Simon, John 192
Sineath, Sherry Aldrich 104
slavery and development 15
Snow, David 183
social movements, effectiveness of 173–191
social movements, gender and see gender and social movements
Somalia 211, 43
Somalialand 219
South Africa 8, 212
Scott, South 108
South, U.S. 15, 89–90
Southeast Asia see Asia, Southeast
sovereignty 34–50
Soviet Union (former) 87 see also Russia
Spain 16
Sri Lanka 219
Standing, Guy 4
Stanford University 12
Starn, Orin 174
state autonomy 69
state capacity 5–9, 33–50

state, role of in development 5–9, 12
state shrinkage *see* state capacity
statistical methods, limits of *see* quantitative methods, limits of
steel industry 10
Stewart, Rieky 116
Stiglitz, Joseph 54
Stover, Eric 206, 207
Strachan, Janet 117
Streeck, Wolfgang 196
Strell, Ethan 56
study abroad, inadequacies 193–194
Sudan 212
Sudan, South 43, 219
Sudan, Western 219
Sullivan, Teresa 192
sustainability *see* ecology and development
Swarmy, Anand 24
Swaziland 212
sweatshops 2
Sweden 55
Sydee, Jasmin 117
Syria 22, 140, 219
Sze, Julie 127
Szirmai, Adam 5

Taiwan 90
Tajikistan 219
tariffs *see* protectionism
taxation 51–65
tax evasion 54–55
teaching international issues 191–203
tea party 5–9, 51–65
technology and development 6, 12, 16, 19, 84–99
Terry, Geraldine 117, 128
textiles, machine 9–10
Thailand 67, 69, 71, 73–74, 77, 78, 219
Thomas, Duncan 103, 127
Timor 115
Tinker, Irene 116
Tomljanovich, Marc 60
Torche, Florencia 114
Torres Nachon, Claudio 209, 211, 213–214
Tortella, Gabriel 16
transnational mobilization 163
transportation costs 85–86, 88, 89, 92–93, 97
Trapper, Nancy 136
treaties, international 204–222

Trouillot, Michel-Rolph 47
Trussell, James 105
Tsebelis, George 185
Tufts University 8–9
Turkey 219

Uganda 23–24, 115–133, 212
United Arab Emirates 23
United Kingdom 9–10, 12, 76, 90, 93, 219
United States 7–8, 12, 15, 16, 19, 36, 51–65, 67, 78, 88, 89, 90, 91–2, 93, 205, 217–218, 219
universities, global *see* global universities
Upchurch, Dawn 105
Urdang, Stephanie 160
Uquillas, Jorge 174
Uzbekistan 219

Van Cott, Donna 174
Van der Hoof Holstein, Cassia 34, 44
Van Nieuwkoop, Martien 174
Vasconcellos, Luis 107
Vazquez Garcia, Veronica 117
Venables, Anthony 85, 88–89, 92
Venezuela 45
Vietnam 69, 70–71, 72, 76–77, 78, 79, 80, 90, 100, 103, 219
violence, political 173
Viterna, Jocelyn 176
Vroman, Wayne 53–54

Walker, Andrew 73, 74
Walker, Barbara 118
Wallerstein, Immanuel 33, 35, 37
Walz, Julie 39
war and development 21, 75, 76, 134–155, 204–222
Wartenberg, Julia 2
Wasylenko, Michael 60
water 145–146
Watson, Peggy 163, 164
Weber, Max 67, 87
Weidemann, Jean 141–142
Weingartner, Rudolph 191
Weisbrot, Mark 44
welfare states 88
Weller, Robert 20, 139
Welzell, Christian 122
West Bank/Gaza 22
Wilde, Guillermo 174, 187

Williamson, Jeffrey 15–16
Wink, Claudia 100
women's economic activities 13–16, 17–24, 134–155
women and development *see* gender and development
women and inequality *see* gender inequality
women and microenterprise 13–16, 17–24, 134–155
women and social movements *see* gender and social movements
women, legal status 142
women, political participation of *see* gender and political participation
women, religious status of 142
women and war *see* gender and war
world bank 87
world systems theory 33, 34–35

WuDunn, Sheryl 122
Wyatt, David 73

Xing, Zhu Wei 107, 108

Yamaguchi, Kazuo 104
Yamamoto, Ken 158
Yashar, Deborah 174
Yemen 219
Yount, Kathryn 104, 105
Yugoslavia 77

Zambia 212
Zamosc, Leon 174
Zhan, Heying 101
Zhao, Gracie 107
Ziltener, Patrick 69
Zimbabwe 155–172, 212, 214, 219
Zurich Dataset 69, 76

eBooks
from Taylor & Francis
Helping you to choose the right eBooks for your Library

Add to your library's digital collection today with Taylor & Francis eBooks. We have over 50,000 eBooks in the Humanities, Social Sciences, Behavioural Sciences, Built Environment and Law, from leading imprints, including Routledge, Focal Press and Psychology Press.

Choose from a range of subject packages or create your own!

Benefits for you
- Free MARC records
- COUNTER-compliant usage statistics
- Flexible purchase and pricing options
- All titles DRM-free.

Benefits for your user
- Off-site, anytime access via Athens or referring URL
- Print or copy pages or chapters
- Full content search
- Bookmark, highlight and annotate text
- Access to thousands of pages of quality research at the click of a button.

Free Trials Available
We offer free trials to qualifying academic, corporate and government customers.

eCollections
Choose from over 30 subject eCollections, including:

Archaeology	Language Learning
Architecture	Law
Asian Studies	Literature
Business & Management	Media & Communication
Classical Studies	Middle East Studies
Construction	Music
Creative & Media Arts	Philosophy
Criminology & Criminal Justice	Planning
Economics	Politics
Education	Psychology & Mental Health
Energy	Religion
Engineering	Security
English Language & Linguistics	Social Work
Environment & Sustainability	Sociology
Geography	Sport
Health Studies	Theatre & Performance
History	Tourism, Hospitality & Events

For more information, pricing enquiries or to order a free trial, please contact your local sales team:
www.tandfebooks.com/page/sales

www.tandfebooks.com